Improving Comprehension with Questioning the Author

A Fresh and Expanded View of a Powerful Approach

Isabel L. Beck • Margaret G. McKeown

◪SCHOLASTIC

New York • Toronto • London • Auckland • Sydney
Mexico City • New Delhi • Hong Kong • Buenos Aires

Praise for *Improving Comprehension with Questioning the Author*

"Beck and McKeown have outdone themselves! This book is a powerful resource for teachers who want to improve their students' comprehension through lively and cognitively engaging discussion. The book is research-based, classroom friendly, and especially easy for teachers to follow. It's a book for all times, all teachers, and all students."

—JUDITH A. LANGER, Distinguished Professor,
Director, Center on English Learning & Achievement

"Absolutely wonderful! We need more books like it, ones that help teachers put the significant findings from reading research into classroom practice. There is ample talk about improving students' engagement with texts, but it's not always clear to teachers how to achieve this goal. With this book, it all becomes crystal clear."

—TIM RASINSKI, author of *The Fluent Reader*, Professor
of Education, Kent State University

"Beck and McKeown have used their unparalleled expertise to develop an approach that teachers will appreciate for its power and elegant simplicity. Questioning the Author can help students effectively integrate information in the text with their own background knowledge and—over time—become more competent readers on their own. Novice teachers who use QtA will breathe a sigh of relief. Veteran teachers will conclude: 'I wish I had this twenty years ago!'"

—KATHLEEN J. BROWN, Director
University of Utah Reading Clinic

"Proficient readers need to read deeply—to make inferences, ask good questions, monitor the coherence of the text, be aware that text is an act of communication by an author, and critically evaluate the information presented to them. Questioning the Author is the only method that directly scaffolds all of these cognitive and social mechanisms. With this book, teachers have access to an approach that is firmly grounded in both science and classroom practice. Bravo."

—ART GRAESSER, professor, University of Memphis,
coeditor of *Handbook of Discourse Processes*

"This book really is a feast. It demonstrates once again why Isabel Beck and Margaret McKeown are leaders in our field. Teachers will want to read and study this book with colleagues, systematically try out the wonderful ideas it offers up, then share with each other their adventures in improving reading comprehension."

—CLAUDE GOLDENBERG, California State University, Long Beach, author of *Successful School Change: Creating Settings to Improve Teaching and Learning*

"When I use QtA with my students, they tell me they make connections to previous sections of text that they never did before. My eighth graders tell me that they now pose queries when they read independently. 'QtA is in my head,' one student said, 'and I'm thinking and connecting all the time.' With this book, which is written with such clarity and conviction, teachers have the power to break the cycle of having students merely recite information. QtA helps young readers learn to interpret a text and to discover the big ideas behind the facts an author has chosen."

—LAURA ROBB, teacher, consultant, and author of *Teaching Reading in Social Studies, Science, and Math*

"Compelling and comprehensive! This book reads more like a novel than a teaching manual. Beck and McKeown provide clear, step-by-step instructions, accompanied by classroom examples, on how to plan and manage classroom discussions of text, and how to keep the dialogue on track in almost every conceivable situation.

Teachers who believe that wide-ranging classroom discussions are not productive or are intimidated by them should read this book. While Beck and McKeown have developed their approach to improve comprehension of texts, they have also invented a general paradigm for learning. I expect that data will show that teachers who embrace this approach find themselves engaged in classroom discussions often, with benefits to all involved."

—RON COLE, Director, Center for Spoken Language Research, Boulder, CO

"I love this book. Many teachers wrestle with how to teach comprehension. They can read about theory, they can learn different strategies, but they are still left wondering, 'What do I do?' This book has the answers. I have rarely read such a powerful and teacher-friendly book that brings the classroom to life. Reading the book is like having a professional developer right there with you, coaching you and guiding you through this powerful method of teaching comprehension. I recommend this book to all teachers who want to know, 'How do I *teach* comprehension?'"

—JANICE A. DOLE, Associate Professor of Teaching and Learning, University of Utah

"There are a hundred reasons to admire Questioning the Author. Here are my top three:

1. It reframes the learning and reading we already pursue in school into meaning-constructive pursuits that highlight students comprehension activity.

2. It mirrors the process of inquiry pursued by expert readers and in every discipline.

3. It helps students think about the author and see that all authors are out to get us to believe, know, or do something. Beck and McKeown's simple, powerful Queries—*What is the author up to here?*—remind us to evaluate a text's ideas.

These three considerations are important to reading, learning and democratic thinking, but are rarely addressed in school. QtA addresses them all."

—JEFFREY D. WILHELM, Professor of Literacy, Boise State
University, and author of *Reading Is Seeing*

"Beck and McKeown have created the text for teachers looking for new ways to help students comprehend narrative and expository texts. QtA is especially critical for teachers whose students think that their lack of understanding is due to their own limitations as readers. Imagine their excitement and positive responses when they are helped to see that their struggles with comprehension may be due to the author's writing style or word choice."

—LAURA ROEHLER, Professor Emeritus, College of
Education, Michigan State University

"This book makes clear how important it is for teachers to know their students, analyze the potential problems texts can pose for them, and then seed discussions with questions that help students overcome these challenges. It's through these "persistent and consistent" routines that teachers and students are able to soar into rich, purposeful discussions of texts of all kinds. Beck and McKeown remind us that young readers can only reach these high altitudes of understanding when their ideas are properly tethered to the meanings of a text. With this new volume on Questioning the Author, teachers have a full set of tools at their disposal for maximizing students' responses to texts and for helping them learn from one another."

—DONNA OGLE, Professor of Reading and Language,
National-Louis University

"What Beck and McKeown have done for vocabulary and beginning reading they have now done for comprehension. That is, they have provided a theory- and research-based approach to teaching comprehension that is practical to implement and proven successful. This is a must-have volume for anyone who cares about teaching students to comprehend what they read."

—GALE M. SINATRA, Professor of Educational Psychology,
University of Nevada, Las Vegas

Acknowledgments

Our work with Questioning the Author has involved teachers, students, and colleagues who have contributed in an assortment of ways. We wish to acknowledge them with much gratitude. We have had the privilege of working with hundreds of teachers and thousands of students who have brought Questioning the Author to life in classrooms. Many of these teachers and students are from across the country, and we have not met them personally.

Closer to home, we are grateful to an array of individuals with whom we have worked throughout many stages of developing Questioning the Author: the teachers who initially tried the approach with their students—Chris Cortinovis, Lisa Donovan, Linda Perhacs, Kelly Sweeney, and Don Weisz—and the teachers who contributed to the second phase in which we developed the cases—Karen Connelly, Gail Friedman, Margaret MacDonald, Lori McDowell, Ruthann McQuillan, and Karen Wiley. These teachers opened their classrooms to us, put forth great effort in implementing Questioning the Author, and shared their reactions in ways that strengthened it.

We are indebted to colleagues and graduate students who participated from the inception of the idea of Questioning the Author and helped it become a viable approach: Cheryl Sandora, Kathleen Shoop, Jo Worthy, Rebecca Hamilton, and Linda Kucan.

Additionally, we especially want to acknowledge Rebecca Hamilton and Linda Kucan, who helped us author the first versions of two books about the approach.

The development of the material in this book was partially supported by funds from the Office of Educational Research and Improvement (OERI) of the United States Department of Education, with additional funds from the Spencer Foundation. We acknowledge their support with appreciation.

Cover and interior design by Maria Lilja

ISBN-13: 978-0-439-81730-1 • ISBN-10: 0-439-81730-7
Copyright © 2006 by Isabel L. Beck and Margaret G. McKeown
All rights reserved. Published by Scholastic Inc.
Printed in the USA.

2 3 4 5 6 7 8 9 10   23   12 11 10 09 08 07 06

Contents

Questioning the Author: Helping Students Engage Deeply with Text

Our approach to comprehension instruction, Questioning the Author, focuses on the importance of students' active efforts to build meaning from what they read and the need for students to grapple with ideas in a text.

The work we have done in comprehension, as well as that in decoding and vocabulary, has kept us close to schools. We have visited classrooms, worked with teachers, and interacted with students. One of the rewards of being close to classrooms is that we have heard students say so many precious things. Many of them can be classified as "Out of the mouths of babes. . . ." Our favorite comes from a fifth grader, but first, some context:

Al Shanker, late president of the American Federation of Teachers, used to describe passive students by suggesting that if folks from Mars visited our planet, they would report to their superiors that among the peculiar Earth behaviors they observed was that five days out of seven adults help children get ready to go to a building where they sit and watch adults work.

Now let's imagine those Martians were hovering in their spaceship outside Gail Friedman's fifth-grade class, which had been implementing Questioning the Author during the year. Ms. Friedman had just asked the class to jot down what they liked and didn't like about QtA. One student wrote:

> What I like about QtA is that people let other people know
> what they're thinking. What I dislike is that it makes us work
> too hard! When we're done, it makes us feels like we're dead!

On reading that, those Martians at least would have been compelled to add a footnote to their report, for clearly, the students had done the work of building meaning from text. Ms. Friedman had become expert at helping her students to take on the responsibility of figuring out what they were reading.

Some History of QtA

The findings from our initial implementations of QtA, which took place in the classrooms of five teachers with about 120 fourth- and fifth-grade students in two different school districts, pointed to dramatic changes in classroom discourse. They came from comparing reading and social studies lessons that were taught by our collaborating teachers before and after they implemented Questioning the Author. (For a full discussion of these results see Beck, McKeown, Sandora, Kucan, & Worthy, 1996; McKeown, Beck, & Sandora, 1996.) The changes in discourse included the following:

- Teachers asked questions that focused on considering and extending meaning rather than retrieving information.

- Teachers responded to students in ways that extended the conversation rather than in ways that merely evaluated or repeated the responses.

- Students did about twice as much talking during QtA discussions than they did in traditional lessons.

- Students frequently initiated their own questions and comments, in contrast to rarely doing so in traditional lessons.

- Students responded by talking about the meaning of what they read and by integrating ideas rather than by retrieving text information.

- Student-to-student interactions during discussions developed.

A later study found that QtA was also effective with older students, and in contrast to another discussion technique. In a study that compared QtA with Junior Great Books, an approach in which discussion occurs after the reading of whole-text selections, sixth- and seventh-grade students in the QtA classroom both recalled more from the selections they read and were better able to provide high-quality responses to interpretation questions after reading (Sandora, Beck, & McKeown, 1999).

We have spent close to 15 years developing, reflecting on, and revising QtA. This book marks the second generation of our work with QtA, following two earlier books: *Questioning the Author: An Approach for Enhancing Student Engagement with Text*, which was published by the International Reading Association in 1997, and *Questioning the Author: Accessibles*, published by the Wright Group in 1999. Since their publication, we have continued to implement QtA in classrooms. At the time of the writing of this book, we had been involved in the training— either personally or once removed—of about 2,000 teachers.

In our work with QtA, we have talked extensively with teachers and students about their experiences. We learned that as teachers began implementation of QtA, they were often concerned about the impact it would have on control and classroom management. As the year progressed, they found that not only was it possible to, as one teacher said, "share control of the discussion with students and not lose acceptable classroom decorum in the process," but that the involvement of students in ideas became an exciting and extremely satisfying aspect of classroom lessons. Teachers eventually found that classroom management was actually less of a concern during QtA lessons, because the students became so involved in the discussion.

The teachers also told us that their expectations of their students changed as they observed them dealing with ideas and expressing themselves in QtA discussions. One teacher commented that she now expected her students to "think and learn and explain rather than memorize, dictate, and forget."

We learned that students' views about reading and learning were affected. We saw evidence of these changes in responses students gave when we interviewed them at the end of the school year about their reading and social studies classes. One student talked about the need for the kind of thinking and questioning that the class did:

> Sometimes when the author is not being real clear, it's kind of
> hard because then in the way back of the story is a sentence that

> you need to figure out and put the clues together, but you don't
> have all the clues.

She then described what happened as a result of working to figure out the ideas:

> So we understand what the author's really telling us instead
> of just reading the story and saying we're done.

Another student described her view of reading in QtA as follows:

> It's more creative than just asking regular questions or just plain
> reading, you know, like if you don't think about what you're reading
> and you just read, that's not reading. You're just looking at scribbles
> on a piece of paper.

Our continued work with QtA allows us to expand on what we have written about the approach. Our history with QtA has also provided us with innumerable new examples of students' and teachers' interactions with text. Thus, we have replaced all the examples from the earlier book and provided an assortment of new ones that reflect our updated thinking.

The book is divided into two sections. Section 1 includes the topics that were covered in the original *Questioning the Author* book: theoretical and empirical background; Queries; planning; discussion; and implementation. In Chapter 1, we have augmented the discussion of the theoretical background by focusing on the contributions of the concepts of coherence and attention to current thinking on comprehension. We also provide a more extensive discussion of the three decades of our work that underlie this book. In Chapters 2 through 5, in addition to expanding and updating our discussion of the topics and providing new examples, we have added "frequently asked questions" and our responses.

Section 2 is derived from our *Accessibles* book, which can be viewed as a collection of 25 cases based on our observations in teachers' classrooms. The cases include classroom examples of issues that arose as teachers implemented QtA, ways that teachers handled the issues, and our commentary on the issues and solutions.

From our decade and a half's worth of experiences with QtA, we have gained an enhanced understanding of what it takes to support teachers and students as they learn to make the process of building understanding a habit of reading. In writing this book, we have incorporated what we have learned in ways that we hope will bring about an enriched perspective of QtA for our readers.

CHAPTER 1

Texts and the Way Students Understand Them

Texts can get tricky for young students, even in places where we may not expect it, as shown in the excerpt below from a fourth-grade class discussion of a text about the "great mix of people" who populated the Hawaiian Islands, including Chinese, Filipinos, and Puerto Ricans. Here is the sentence that tripped up students: "About one seventh of the people are the offspring of Polynesians—the first people of the islands."

MS. S:	So, what is this all about? What do you think, Antoine?
ANTOINE:	I think that when the first people came, they're Polynesian and they just kept on having children and they stayed there.
MS. S:	Okay, so they kept having children. Is that what the author meant by offspring?

HEATHER:	I think offspring is the people from different countries that came to the Hawaiian Islands.
MS. S:	We all agree that people from all these countries live in the Hawaiian Islands. Offspring of these people are their children. And their children's children. And their children's children's children.
DARLA:	I wanted to say, my cousin's grandma, she's Filipino and she has a son, and my dad, my dad's father's brother, married her and I think they had offspring children.
MS. S:	Okay, I think maybe we're a little bit confused about what this word *offspring* means. Antoine, tell Darla who she's an offspring of.
ANTOINE:	She's an offspring of a Polynesian.
MS. S:	No! Oh, my goodness! Wait a minute! Alex. Alex, tell Darla whom she's an offspring of.
ALEX:	You're an offspring of your mom and dad. And your dad is an offspring of his mom and dad.
MS. S:	Everybody in this room is an offspring. That's a tricky word. How many of you think the author could have picked another word?
ALEX:	Not me. I think it was a perfect word.
CHARLENE:	Oh, sure, now you say that, after we all figured it out.

As this example shows, a single word can impede comprehension. Texts are of course made up of hundreds of words, and thus, there are hundreds of opportunities for readers to become confused. As writing instructors often say: Readers are like sheep that an author is trying to herd in a particular direction. If there is a hole in a fence, the sheep are sure to find it and go astray. In a sense, all our research—and the QtA approach we developed in response to our findings— is dedicated to preventing our student readers from going through those holes. A little later in the book we'll elaborate on the value of helping students see that it is indeed often the text, and not the student, that is "at fault" when comprehension wanders. But for now, we want to share the research that led to this insight.

Our Research on Texts and Comprehension

Helping students deal effectively with text arose as a focus for us some decades ago. In our attempts to understand how students comprehend text and to develop ways to support students' comprehension, we considered and studied three sources: the textbooks that students read, the text-based lessons intended to guide students' reading, and the students themselves. All these sources were investigated against a backdrop of theory of and research on reading.

Our eventual purpose was to develop effective comprehension instruction; however, we reasoned that we should begin by understanding current instruction and analyzing its potential effectiveness. Our foray into text-based comprehension research started in the early 1980s with an analysis of the suggested comprehension questions from the teachers' editions of basal readers (Beck & McKeown, 1981). The prevalent instructional practice in the basals was to design questions that represented levels of comprehension from simple to complex based on taxonomies of comprehension. As an example, Barrett's (1967) taxonomy, probably the most frequently referenced taxonomy in the reading instruction literature, contained the following major categories: 1. literal comprehension, 2. reorganization, 3. inferential comprehension, 4. evaluation, 5. appreciation.

A number of studies have used taxonomies of comprehension such as Barrett's to assess questions that appear in basal readers and classroom reading activities. Most often the studies conclude that comprehension would be enhanced if more attention were given to higher levels of comprehension through questions that elicit inferences, evaluation, and appreciation. (See, for example, Bartolome, 1968; Cooke, 1970; Guszak, 1967; Rosecky, 1976.) Although that intuitively makes sense, it also points to a limitation of a taxonomic approach to developing questions. Questions developed from taxonomies do not take into account that information within a text is not always "ripe for the picking"; a question that *seems* to prompt students to pluck information from a higher branch on the taxonomic tree may in fact require lower-level thinking to answer and vice versa.

Consider two hypothetical questions for the story "The Three Little Pigs": "What did the third little pig use to build his house?" and "How many bricks did the third little pig use?" The two questions would be equal in terms of taxonomy, since both query literal information from the story. Yet the question of the number of bricks is trivial while the question of the building material used is of central importance to the story. Similarly, posing questions from higher taxonomic levels does not necessarily lead to greater comprehension. For example, less processing of ideas from the text would be required to answer an appreciation-level question such as "How would you have felt if you had been the wolf?" than to give a summary or synthesis of story events. Yet appreciation is on a higher level in the taxonomy than synthesis or reorganization.

Another problem with a taxonomic approach to developing questions is that taxonomies are not intended to address the relationship *among* the questions for a particular text. And yet for effective teaching that promotes comprehension, that relationship is critical. The questions need to be carefully sequenced to help students consider the overall concept of the story. Questions developed and sequenced according to their taxonomic levels will likely only tap isolated pieces of information without following the logic of story events, which doesn't help readers build a coherent representation of the story. In fact, a taxonomic sequence of questions may disrupt the flow of story ideas rather than facilitate it.

The Story Map

Faced with these issues, we developed the notion of a "Story Map" (Beck & McKeown, 1981). A Story Map is a unified representation of a story based on a logical organization of events and ideas of central importance to the story and their interrelationships. To create one, a teacher begins by determining the story's major events and ideas and then develops a series of questions that elicit students' understandings of their progression. Creating even the most basic Story Map requires students to make inferences and recall explicit events.

We conducted a study to test our ideas of how well questions that were based on a Story Map versus those based on a taxonomy contributed to students' comprehension. We compared two third-grade basal story lessons whose question sequences were taxonomic to lessons for the same stories that we had revised using Story Map questions (Beck, Omanson, & McKeown, 1982). Children who received the revised lessons recalled more of the stories and correctly answered more questions than children receiving the original basal lesson. We also revised the background knowledge that children in the Story Map group received before the lesson. Thus, we cannot tell the extent to which each of the components—activation of background knowledge and Story Map questions—contributed to the superior outcome for the experimental group.

Examining the During-Reading Experience

Later we developed a processing description of the way in which components of the basal and revised lessons had influenced the children's comprehension (Omanson, Beck, Voss, & McKeown, 1984). The processing description suggested that both providing students with background knowledge and presenting them with a logical sequence of questions contributed to enhanced comprehension. Our conclusion from this work was that an account of what children do *during* a reading lesson gave us more insight into how to design reading lessons than a description of what children do *after* the lesson. Such insight gained from the processes in which readers engage in the course of reading has been a major influence on our thinking.

We also studied the role of providing background knowledge before reading with fifth-grade students reading passages on the American Revolution (McKeown, Beck, Sinatra, & Loxterman, 1992). We found that providing background knowledge enhanced comprehension if the text to be read was itself coherent (that is, the information was clear and logically organized, and the ideas were connected). In that study, all students were provided with a carefully developed background-knowledge module that dealt with issues and events that paved the colonists' route to revolution. Then they read one of two versions of four short textbook passages about events leading to the American Revolution. One version of the four passages was taken directly from a social studies textbook. The other version was one that we had revised to make the passages more coherent.

We had previously studied more and less coherent passages (Beck, McKeown, Sinatra, and Loxterman, 1991) to determine the extent to which more-coherent text enhanced comprehension. There was a strong finding that it did. But a particularly interesting finding here was that those students who read the coherent text were able to use what they had learned from the background-knowledge module to focus on and remember the most important information from the text. The students who read the unrevised textbook version, although they received the same background information, were less able to exploit the advantage provided by that information (McKeown et al., 1992).

The studies that we have discussed here, as well as other studies we participated in (see, for example, Loxterman, Beck, & McKeown, 1994; Sinatra, Beck, & McKeown, 1993) show that students' comprehension can be improved through carefully crafted lessons and text that takes into account what we know about influences on comprehension. That is, lesson features such as the following have a positive influence on comprehension:

- **coherent texts** (because readers need to build coherence for understanding to take place)

- **relevant background knowledge** (because such knowledge is needed to fuel comprehension)

- **a logical sequence of questions** (because comprehension requires an organizing framework)

It is important, however, to keep in mind that although students who received the upgraded texts or lessons did better than students who did not, these students rarely approached optimal or ideal comprehension. In general, we observed that although some students developed coherent representations of what they had read, many developed only a superficial understanding by simply gathering words from the text, and a disheartening number did not seem to approach even a cursory understanding of what they had read. In the material that follows we provide examples that illustrate the kinds of responses we got when we asked students to tell us about what they had read.

In all our studies, we engaged with students on a one-to-one basis. We asked them to read a given text and then tell us about what they had read. All the sessions were tape-recorded and later transcribed. Following is a short social studies text that students responded to in several of our studies.

BOSTON TEA PARTY

George III, the king of England, said that there had to be a tax on something to prove that the British had the right to tax. So there was still a small tax on tea. The colonists remained firm. They would not pay any tax passed by Parliament. Colonial women refused to buy or serve tea.

British merchants were not selling much tea. So Parliament passed a law that greatly lowered its price. Boatloads of tea were sent to America. Since it was cheaper than ever, the British thought that surely the colonists would buy tea now!

They were wrong. Tea was burned. Tea was left to rot. Ships loaded with it were not allowed in ports. In Boston the Sons of Liberty dressed up as Indians. Late at night they went to Boston Harbor and threw more than 300 chests of tea into the water. This action was called the Boston Tea Party.

(Silver Burdett, 1984)

The two "recalls" below are quintessential examples of students "reading" a text and simply not getting it. It should be noted that both students were considered average readers.

Tina's Recall:

It's about the Boston Tea Party, and it's about a whole bunch of, like, they were bringing loads over and it was rotten, and all that, so they went back and got more loads and dumped all the tea into the water.

Darryl's Recall:

The Boston Tea Party, um, they threw more than three hundred bags of tea and some of it was left to rot and, um, some threw it in the water, and, um, the action, what they were doing, was called the Boston Tea Party, 'cause nobody was buying their tea so they just threw it away and let it rot.

It's clear from their responses that Tina and Darryl simply did not understand what they had read. They neither knew what was important nor did they connect ideas to develop a coherent representation of the events and ideas. Tina seemed to have retrieved the label for the major event, "Boston Tea Party." Beyond that she simply relayed some detached snippets of other events, such as that loads of tea were brought over, but she did not seem to know from or to where, or by whom. She knew that they were left to rot—but again, she didn't understand by whom or why. She did not even communicate any sense of understanding that a conflict between two parties was being described. Darryl gave more information about what the tea party was—throwing tea into the water. But he, like Tina, did not seem to understand that it was a conflict between two parties. It seems instead he thought that the tea sellers were disgruntled and were throwing out their own tea. This kind of confused recall was more typical of students' responses to social studies texts, whereas superficial recall was more typical of narrative text. Consider the following excerpt from *Ralph S. Mouse* by Beverly Cleary, and two students' recalls of the text.

RALPH S. MOUSE

Ralph thought of the old hotel with its shabby lobby warmed by a crackling fire. He missed the reassuring tick of the rasping old clock. He even missed—sort of—his brothers, sisters, and cousins. He wondered what they would say if he went home with Ryan without his motorcycle. . . .

The scoffing of his relatives was something Ralph could not face. Never. And as he walked slowly back to the book bag in the library, he heard a dog bark in the distance and was reminded of the coyotes that howled in the night in the song about the lonely man trying to hitch a ride on the highway. What a sad world he lived in.   (Cleary, 1983)

Adam's Recall:

> Ralph was thinking about the hotel where he lived. He misses the tick
> of the clock, and he even sort of misses his relatives. He's sad about
> the world he lives in. He didn't go home with Ryan without
> his motorcycle.

Adam's recall suggests that he identified some major points: Ralph missed his home and maybe even his relatives and that he is without his motorcycle. But Adam doesn't put those points together in a way that indicates he understands *why* Ralph doesn't want to go home without his motorcycle. Below we provide Brittany's recall of the same excerpt. She was one of the few students who provided a coherent representation of the important aspects of the text.

Brittany's Recall:

> Ralph misses his home at the hotel, but he can't go home because he's
> afraid his relatives will tease him because he lost his motorcycle. He
> keeps getting sadder, like when a dog barks, he thinks about coyotes in
> a sad song he heard about a lonely guy.

Note that Brittany selected the same story points as Adam, but she presented them in a way that indicates understanding: "He can't go home because he's afraid his relatives will tease him because he lost his motorcycle."

Theoretical Orientation: Attention and Coherence

Brittany's recall demonstrates that her attention was focused on what was important in the text and that she was able to connect those ideas in a coherent manner.

The concepts of attention and coherence gained currency among comprehension researchers in the early 1980s, when we were beginning our work in the area. This theoretical orientation is a cognitive-processing perspective that views comprehension as an active process of attending to information in text, making decisions about what is important, holding that information in memory as other information is encountered, and making connections to new relevant information—all toward building a coherent representation of what a text is trying to communicate. Kintsch and van Dijk (1978) were the most prominent among the many researchers explicating aspects of this perspective and its implications.

(See, for example, Fletcher, van den Broek, & Arthur, 1996; Graesser, Singer, & Trabasso, 1994; van den Broek, 1994; van den Broek, Young, Tzeng, & Linderholm, 1998.)

The cognitive-processing perspective highlighted aspects of reading that had not been emphasized in earlier theory—namely, that reading is an active mental process, not a passive one of simply receiving information. Readers must engage with ideas and make sense of information. Further, text itself is not a perfectly created, complete message but a source of information designed to be interacted with by the reader. Thus, for comprehension to occur, the reader must connect and integrate information as she or he proceeds through a text. During reading, a reader attempts to make sense of information contained in the sentence being read. Making sense requires the reader to select relevant information to attend to and then connect it to one of two possible sources—either information from preceding sentences or relevant background knowledge. The reader can connect two pieces of information, such as an idea in the sentence being read and information from a prior sentence, only if she or he attends to both of them at the same time. Yet human capacity for attention is limited; one can hold only so many ideas at a time. Successful comprehension depends on *choosing* the most relevant pieces of information to attend to, which the reader can then carry over in memory to the next sentence to be read. Skilled readers are better able to choose information that is likely to be relevant to subsequent information.

Connecting information throughout the course of reading enables the reader to build a coherent representation. Thus, another key to successful comprehension is being able to recognize or construct logical relationships among ideas. Good readers are better at putting together text information and background knowledge to draw inferences that keep the flow of the text ideas building smoothly. Poor and novice readers are more likely to fail to generate needed inferences and are also more likely to jump to conclusions beyond those justified by the text.

Taking Theory Into Practice

Given the kind of text recalls we were seeing in our studies and the text-processing perspective on comprehension that prevailed, we began to formulate what was needed to assist students' understanding of text. Clearly, the answer lay in helping students in the course of reading the text. That is, we needed to intervene in what they were doing when they were casting their eyes on text and require them to consider—attend to, focus on—what the text offered, and use that to make sense for themselves. In our first attempts to intervene in students' processing, we used a Think Aloud procedure to figure out what students were thinking as they went through a text. We gave students a text to read and stopped them after each sentence to ask them to talk about what they had read. As we proceeded, we began to alter the questions we asked to see if we could get more language and more thoughtful articulations. It was in that round of exploration that we discovered that when we asked open questions, especially those that referenced the author (i.e., "What do you think the author is trying to say?") we were more likely to get useful information or to get the students to take a further look at the text content.

How Revising Text Gave Us a Young Reader's Perspective

As we developed our approach to comprehension instruction, we also drew on the research we'd done on revising texts to make them more comprehensible for students (Beck, McKeown, Sinatra, & Loxterman, 1991). Our major question in these studies was: To what extent can students' comprehension be improved by having them read texts that have been revised to be more coherent?

To develop coherent text passages, we read passages from textbooks, trying to understand what the author's goal was for the passage and what each idea was supposed to contribute to the goal. We then formed our understandings into coherent, clear text statements. As we worked through texts in this way, we realized that our efforts to make connections and grapple with ideas were exactly the efforts we would want young readers to make as they constructed meaning from their texts. So it occurred to us that we might encourage an orientation toward building coherence in their reading by giving students a "reviser's eye." It is a reviser's task to make text understandable, and what we wanted students to do was to make text understandable to themselves. If they could be shown that reading is a roll-up-your-sleeves-and-dig-in kind of task, it might promote the kind of active engagement with text that is needed for learning to take place.

Taking Active Engagement Into Instruction

Active engagement in reading has received much attention in recent years from reading researchers and educators. This attention has been reflected in the development of several instructional approaches. One encourages students to respond actively to what they read through collaborative discussion. A number of different methods of fostering collaborative discussion have been developed, such as the Reflective Thinking Project (Anderson et al., 1992), the Book Club Project (McMahon, Raphael, Goately, Boyd, & Pardo, 1992), the Conversational Discussion Groups Project (O'Flahavan & Stein, 1992), Instructional Conversations (Goldenberg, 1992), and the Junior Great Books reading and discussion program (Denis & Moldof, 1983).

A related body of work on discussion-based approaches to comprehension comes from the field of English-language-arts education (for example, Langer, 1986, 1990; Nystrand, 1997). The foundation of this work involves the examination of social processes in classrooms and the context they create for the development of cognitive and linguistic tools for comprehension (Applebee, Langer, Nystrand, & Gamoran, 2003).

A major difference between QtA and the approaches cited, from both the fields of reading and English-language arts, is that with the latter, discussions take place after reading, and the ongoing process of building meaning that takes place during reading is not addressed.

A second approach toward encouraging readers to assume more active roles has focused on the teaching, modeling, and practicing of strategies that mature readers use as they read, such as predicting, inferring, and summarizing. A number of different strategies as well as a number of different teaching methods have been proposed, such as Reciprocal Teaching (Palincsar & Brown, 1984), Informed Strategies for Learning (Paris, Cross, & Lipson, 1984), Direct Explanation (Duffy et al., 1987), Transactional Strategies Instruction (Pressley et al., 1992), and Cognitive Process Instruction (Gaskins, Anderson, Pressley, Cunicelli, & Satlow,

1993). Promoting the use of reading strategies attempts to focus on the ongoing process of reading. A potential drawback of strategy-based instruction, however, is that both teachers' and students' attention may be drawn too easily to the surface features of the strategies themselves rather than to the meaning of what is being read. In fact, some researchers have questioned the necessity of emphasizing specific strategies if the goal of reading as an active search for meaning was upmost in a reader's mind (see, for example, Carver, 1987; Dole, Duffy, Roehler, & Pearson, 1991; Pearson & Fielding, 1991).

A third approach to activating readers' engagement is based on promoting an active search for meaning. Students are directed to explain the information presented in their textbooks to themselves as they read. Chi and her colleagues have found that self-explanations can be elicited from students, and that when they are, students are better able to learn the material (Chi, Bassok, Lewis, Reimann, & Glaser, 1989; Chi, de Leeuw, Chiu, & LaVancher, 1994).

QtA shares features with these other approaches. However, it's unique in that it combines teacher-student collaboration with during-reading explanatory responses and emphasizes the fallibility of the author, a notion that we will consider shortly.

Defining QtA

As illustrated in Figure 1.1, Questioning the Author is an approach for text-based instruction that was designed to facilitate building understanding of text ideas. The goal of building understanding is supported through the use of Queries and Discussion. Before we consider the specific aspects of Questioning the Author, we first provide a snapshot of this approach in action.

In the discussion, from a fourth-grade class (see page 26), we can see the kinds of reactions students had to the text, how the teacher posed Queries and used student responses to keep the discussion flowing productively, and how the students worked together to build understanding of some key ideas.

In the story, *Sound of Sunshine—Sound of Rain*, by Florence Parry Heide, a brother and sister respond to the world very differently. As the plot unfolds, we learn that the children are African American and are living in a racially prejudiced community. The girl has responded to her environment with anger and wariness.

FIGURE 1.1

Building Understanding

TEXT ←——————— **QUERIES** ————————→ **DISCUSSION**

- Fallibility of the author
- Construction of meaning: segmenting text for interspersed reading

- Collaboration
- Construction of meaning: responding to students

Her brother, who is blind and younger, is unaware of the racial environment. The climax of the story occurs when a shopkeeper refers to the sister as "this colored lady" needing to "go back where she belongs."

In the discussion segment, the students, most of whom are African American, have just read this climactic scene. Notice that some of the children are immediately confused by what's meant by "this colored lady," seeing it as an anachronistic term, but they do reach the understanding that racial prejudice is involved.

MS. W:	What did the author tell us in that section? Charlene, you have a really confused look on your face. What's going on?
CHARLENE:	What she mean by *colored lady*? It says, "Better wait on this here colored lady..."
MS. W:	"Better wait on this here colored lady first." What does that mean?
CARLOS:	(*Pointing to and rubbing his skin*) This part.
LAMONT:	She means wait on a black person.
MS. W:	What do you think about that? Kristen?
KARA:	Um, I have a question. How long ago was this?
DENICE:	I think it was back then.
MS. W:	What do you mean how long ago was this?
DENICE:	Because the terms they're using.
KARA:	Because you know how it says, "Better wait on this here colored lady first." I thought they only said that early—1800s, 1900s—calling all black, ah, African Americans colored people.
MS. W:	What do you think, Wilmer?
WILMER:	Well, I think this lady's talking about racism. This lady's being racist.
ROSETTA:	To a child.
MS. W:	Yes. Lamont said the same thing. Let's see what happens and maybe we'll figure more things out.

In the next segment, as the sister and brother leave the store, the sister expresses anger and her brother brings up a remark from a conversation about the colors of balloons with Abram, a man he knew, saying, "Abram says color don't mean a thing." The text segment ends with the sister declaring, "I wish everyone in the whole world was blind."

MS. W:	Oh, my! I want to start with that very last sentence: "I wish everyone in the whole world was blind." What's that all about?
BRENDA:	It's so nobody's talking about what color you are.
DANISHA:	They won't know because they won't be able to see you.
MONTY:	And they won't be complaining.
WILMER:	Color wouldn't matter?
MS. W:	Did we hear that before? That color doesn't really matter.
MARYANNE:	Yeah, we heard it from Abram.
SHIKARA:	When Abram was describing color, it sounded like he was describing people.
MS. W:	What do you mean it sounded like he was describing people?

Notice in this next section that Shikara refers to Abram's initial description of the features of colors (e.g., some colors are soft, some loud, some tender).

SHIKARA:	'Cause people are loud sometimes and sometimes their voice is soft and some are big, some are little, and some are short, like, real tall, and some are tender, like a little bit chubby or something like that.
CARLOS:	He said [colors were] covers for things
MS. W:	He said it was covers for things.
DANISHA:	Because everyone is the same in the inside. Because, like you said, like, the colors is just a cover, like, everyone is the same inside, but they might be like they have a different color, or complexion, or something outside.
MS. W:	Oh, so you've connected it back to Abram and his discussion about the color of the balloons.

With the transcript of the classroom discussion as a backdrop, let's briefly consider each aspect of Questioning the Author as illustrated in Figure 1.1. We begin with the more global aspects that appear on or above the arrowed line.

Building Understanding

Building understanding, the goal of QtA, is what a reader needs to do to read successfully. As indicated earlier, building understanding is not the same as extracting information from the page, which was an older view of reading. Rather, building understanding involves actively figuring out what information we need to pay attention to and connecting that to other information (see, for example, Anderson, 1977; Beck, 1989; Beck & Carpenter, 1986; Kieras, 1985; Palincsar & Brown, 1989; Rumelhart, 1980; Schank & Abelson, 1977; van Dijk & Kintsch, 1983). In the classroom snapshot (pp. 26-27), we saw the way in which students paid attention to Abram's view of color and inferred from it his attitude toward people.

This current view of reading has significant implications for teaching, of course. A student can't learn by simply "getting" information from a source, nor can a teacher simply deliver it to a student. A more expert reader must reveal to a young reader how to crack open a text's meaning by engaging with it until it makes sense. QtA is an approach that gives teachers the tools to do this.

Text

QtA has been successfully used with both expository and narrative texts. This includes social studies textbooks, science textbooks, basal reading selections of both fiction and nonfiction, novels, narrative nonfiction, informational books, short stories, and poems. When students read a text in a QtA lesson, they are taught to address text ideas immediately, while they are reading. That is, they are taught to consider meaning, to grapple with the ideas on the page that are right at the end of their noses. This is different from asking students to answer questions about a text after they have finished reading it.

Discussion

The teacher and students build meaning as they read through discussion. (Although QtA was designed as a whole-class approach, it is also effective in small groups and other configurations, as we discuss in Chapter 5.) Classroom discussion is certainly not a new idea. But the purpose of discussion in QtA, and the kind of interactions students engage in during a QtA discussion, depart from many of the conventions of classroom discussions. For example, classroom discussions are typically characterized by students sharing ideas *after* they have already read a text and formulated their own thoughts and opinions about what the text says and means. The goal of a QtA discussion is to assist students with the process of developing meaning. Therefore, the discussion takes place *in the course of reading the text for the first time* so students can share in the experience of learning how to build meaning from a text.

Although discussion is a key aspect of a QtA lesson, it's not the focus. Rather, it's a means toward achieving a goal, and that goal is always the same: to understand the text. Discussions that survey students' ideas about a text or have them argue their opinions serve a different purpose; QtA discussion looks at text through a tighter lens, as a means to ensure that students are indeed comprehending what they read.

Perhaps one of the best ways to understand the distinction is to remember that unlike many kinds of discussions, in a QtA discussion, the teacher is actively involved. The teacher is right in there the whole time, as a facilitator, guide, initiator, and responder.

Queries

In a QtA lesson, students are prompted to interact with the text and converse about it through Queries. These general probes are phrased in such a way that they encourage young readers to take notice of a text—to consider meaning and develop ideas, not just passively receive and then retrieve information. Queries tend to be open-ended, and they place the responsibility for building meaning on students. Some examples of Queries are "So, what is the author trying to tell us?" or "Why is the author telling us that now?" We will talk a great deal more about Queries in the next chapter, but for now it is important to know that Queries are a key instructional tool in QtA discussions.

Let's consider for a moment how QtA plays out in a classroom. As a class reads a text, the teacher intervenes at selected points and poses Queries to prompt students to consider information. "What's the author telling us in that last paragraph?" the teacher may say. Students respond by contributing ideas: "I think the family is suspecting that someone was in their house when they were away." Students' responses may then be built upon, refined, or challenged by other students, or the teacher may prompt the student to elaborate. For example: "They suspect someone has been in their house." "What makes you say that?" Students and the teacher work collaboratively, interacting to grapple with ideas and build understanding. "Because the box wasn't where they left it." "The box was their secret." "Now they are afraid someone has figured out their secret."

Given the importance of building meaning as one reads, how do you get students to do it? How do you get students to become actively involved as they read, to dive into even difficult information and exert real mental energy to make sense of it? To answer this, let's look again at the diagram in Figure 1.1 on page 25. We already described QtA as an approach that is designed to assist students with building understanding of the ideas in a text through the use of Queries and Discussion. The features below the arrowed line in the diagram begin to explain how QtA prompts students to react to the text in a different way.

Fallibility of the Author

Four-color covers, elegant typefaces, hundred-plus pages of words—whether a dog-eared paperback novel or a hefty social studies textbook, any published work carries authority in a reader's eyes. To young readers, the unimpeachable authority of an author is not always a positive thing. We believe it can negatively influence the way students attend to and deal with information in the text.

Textbooks may carry the greatest authority, and thus be the most problematic, by virtue of their central role in the curriculum. They are often viewed as above criticism by both students and teachers. So when students have difficulty understanding what is in their textbooks, they tend to attribute the problem to their own inadequacies as readers. To avoid blaming themselves, they may disengage from the reading process—merely skim over what they read, apply the least effort possible—because not to try is not to fail.

An important mechanism for helping students engage with text in QtA is to "depose" the authority of the text. As a starting point, a teacher lets students know that what's in a book is simply someone's ideas written down, and that this person may not have always said things in the clearest or easiest way for us to understand. This can be big news for students, and it often has a positive, liberating effect on them as readers. Texts become less impersonal, less authoritative, and more comprehensible.

In our research, we have found that over time students see that sometimes it's an author's failure to communicate ideas clearly that is a problem rather than their lack of ability to comprehend the ideas. As a result of this shift, students tend to feel more confident in working at understanding text and more willing to wrestle with ideas as they read. So QtA, by deliberately placing responsibility on students for wrestling with meaning, aims to teach students that they can become skilled at thinking through what an author might have meant to say at various points in the text.

Interspersed Reading

We teach students that readers should "take on" a text little by little, idea by idea, and try to understand, while they are reading, what ideas are there and how they might connect or relate those ideas to one another. We do this to simulate what a competent reader does in the course of reading. The competent reader is continually expending effort as she reads to make sense as she goes along, even though it may seem like one smooth, seamless process. She does not withhold understanding from herself until a section of text is completed.

Now let's consider what teachers often do when they teach from a text. It is fairly typical practice to assign students material to be read and then to pose questions to evaluate their comprehension. This is basically an "after-the-fact" procedure—students are left on their own until reading is complete. This may not lead to productive reading for several reasons. First, students may have questions in their minds as they read, or they may finish a text knowing only that they are lost but not sure why. Moreover, there is no way for teachers to know whether some students have constructed misconceptions about the passage but think they have understood. Second, even though students hear "right" answers in after-reading questioning, they may never understand what makes them right. In QtA the goal is to help students understand what a portion of text is about as they read it for the first time. The emphasis is on articulating a clear understanding of "just" that portion before tackling the next portion, to tease out what an author is intending to say right there. This orientation disciplines both teachers and students to build their understandings in small doses. No one gets lost in a vast sea of text. Or put another way, the local understanding gets settled sufficiently so that global understandings are founded on solid ground.

Building meaning in the course of reading means going back and forth between reading relatively small segments of text and discussing the ideas encountered. This back-and-forth process requires decisions about where to stop reading and begin discussion. It is the task of a QtA teacher to analyze and identify the important concepts of a text ahead of the students and make decisions about how much of the text needs to be read at once and why. Later, when we address planning, we will discuss in greater detail how to make decisions about where to segment a text and how to introduce the concept of author fallibility to students. For now, we are introducing these concepts to provide a sense of the "big picture" of QtA.

Collaboration

Remember that the point of QtA is to get students to consider an author's ideas and, if necessary, to challenge an author's words or organization of ideas in an effort to deduce the intended meaning. To accomplish this, we teachers have to shift some responsibility from ourselves to our students; too often, we do the thinking and the talking. We need to hear student voices, encourage their contributions, and urge them to be unafraid to test their ideas in front of others. We need to model for them how to collaborate with their peers and us to construct meaning.

Considering text as a group gives students a powerful opportunity to hear from one another and to consider alternative possibilities, but it can be intimidating for them at first. The beauty of QtA discussion is that it puts the author in the hot seat—everyone understands that the author, not the teacher, has presented the class with this challenge. Students and teacher are suddenly on the same team. Everyone is in play, grappling, running with ideas—everyone is engaged in this fun, rigorous game of working out a text's meaning. The chance for misconceptions to accumulate diminishes, and the opportunity for authentic, meaningful discussion about important ideas increases.

QtA creates an extremely interactive role for the teacher. The teacher has the important task of responding to student responses in ways that highlight those aspects that contribute to meaning making. That helps students both recognize and build on those aspects. To accomplish this, teachers need to be particularly attentive to what students say and then consider how to use their contributions to move the discussion productively.

Ending Notes

Here are a few key points to keep in mind as we wrap up our discussion of texts and how students understand them:

- Studies of students reading school texts show that they often do not adequately comprehend what they read.

- Although comprehension can be improved by designing lessons that include a logical sequence of questions, provide relevant background knowledge, and offer more coherent text, students' comprehension is still often sparse.

- Successful comprehension is an active process in which readers attend to information as they encounter it in text, hold relevant pieces in memory, and then connect those pieces to subsequent text information with the goal of building an overall representation of the ideas presented in the text.

- Questioning the Author is an instructional approach based on supporting students' engagement with text by mimicking the way competent readers build meaning from text.

- Questioning the Author operates by having a teacher pose Queries, open-ended prompts to consider text context, during the initial reading. As students respond, the teacher follows up in ways that encourage students to elaborate, connect, and collaborate toward building meaning from what they are reading.

CHAPTER 2

Queries

Jerome is a new student in a sixth-grade class, and the teacher, a QtA veteran, has asked a classmate, Ryan, to tell him what reading class is like. Ryan tells Jerome that the class reads all together and then Ms. O'Connor asks things like "What's the author trying to say?"

Jerome looks puzzled. "What!?" he exclaims. "How're you supposed to know that? I'm no mind reader!"

Ryan sets him straight: "In here we learn that that's what you're supposed to do when you read. You go and figure out what the author's trying to tell you. Or else you're never gonna understand when you read."

"You go and figure it out." Wow, does that capture the take-charge attitude and ownership we want students to have about their reading process. We found that responses such as Ryan's where characteristic of students in QtA classrooms when we interviewed them and compared their responses with those of students in the same school who had not experienced QtA (McKeown & Beck, 1998). In particular, QtA students expressed the purpose of reading in terms of understanding. Asked about what they did as they read, the QtA students described "figuring things out, thinking about what an author was saying" (McKeown & Beck, 1999, p. 124). Students' responses suggest that they had internalized QtA Queries as the way to approach text.

In this chapter, we'll look closely at the nature of Queries. We'll also explore how they differ from traditional questions and why we think they serve students better in building understanding than do traditional questions. We'll share transcripts of lessons to show what Initiating Queries and Follow-Up Queries are and how they are used in classroom discussions. Finally, we will talk about some additional considerations for narrative texts.

How Queries Differ From Traditional Questions

The major points of comparison between Queries and traditional questions are summarized in Figure 2.1.

Queries are designed to assist students in dealing with, and grasping, text ideas as they encounter them. In comparison, traditional questions follow a fairly typical pattern of instruction, in which students read a passage, the teacher initiates a series of questions, students respond, and the teacher evaluates their responses to text. This pattern, which has been documented as being a very prevalent teaching practice, is referred to as the IRE pattern of instruction: I, initiate; R, respond; and E, evaluate (Dillon, 1988; Mehan, 1979). At its best,

FIGURE 2.1	A Comparison of Some Traditional Questions and Queries
QUESTIONS	**QUERIES**
• assess student comprehension of text information after the fact	• assist students with developing the meaning of text ideas in the course of reading
• focus on teacher-to-student interactions, which generate individual students' responses that the teacher can evaluate	• facilitate group discussion about an author's ideas and encourage student-to-student and student-to-teacher interactions
• used before or after reading	• used during initial reading

the IRE pattern assesses comprehension; it does not assist with the *process* of comprehending. Moreover, the IRE pattern is after the fact and tends to rely on questions that ask students to recall what they have read rather than help students to build an understanding of a text.

You might say that IRE is kind of an exit strategy, whereas Queries help students gain entrance to a text. Queries focus students' attention on the text and hone their ability to assess the quality and depth of a text's ideas as they construct meaning. This focus is far different from that of traditional questions designed to assess only the accuracy of student responses.

The second important distinction between questions and Queries is that the teacher often asks traditional questions in order to evaluate individual students' understandings. In contrast, Queries aim to facilitate group discussion about an author's ideas. To be sure, questions are useful for giving teachers a quick idea of which students are getting it and which aren't. Generally, however, a question is directed to the entire class but only one student provides the answer. This individual student assumes all the responsibility while releasing the other students from any share in it. The action takes place between the teacher and one student, and the classroom dynamic can take on the character of a quiz show. Students compete for the chance to announce the right answer, and the teacher lets contestant-students know when their answers are good enough to win the prize of approval.

Queries, on the other hand, are designed to change the role of the teacher from quiz-show host to discussion facilitator. A teacher who uses Queries focuses less on evaluating student responses and more on encouraging students to consider an author's ideas and to respond to one another's interpretations of those ideas. As a result, student-to-student and student-to-teacher interactions tend to increase, transforming the context for learning from a competitive one to a classroom of spirited learners grappling with an author's text and working together to understand it.

The last distinction we want to emphasize is that questions are typically used before or after reading, whereas Queries are used in the course of an initial reading. They're not before the fact or after the fact—they're right on time! After all, comprehension doesn't falter after reading but during reading, and so Queries are designed to aid comprehension at a student's true point of need.

Let's consider further the effects of timing. When teachers ask questions after reading, students may get some messages that teachers may not intend. Students may assume that questioning is a different and perhaps unrelated exercise from reading. Right and wrong tends to move to the center of attention for both teacher as evaluator and student as the one being evaluated. Is this the message we want to convey to students? Isn't it a more accurate message that readers are always questioning as they read? Questioning and reading are symbiotically related to each other; one enhances the other in mutually beneficial ways.

Comparing the Effects of Questions and Queries: Two Lessons on the Middle Ages

To get a better sense of the nature of Queries—what they are, what they accomplish, and how they differ from some traditional questions—we will consider several examples. The first is based on an excerpt from a social studies textbook used in a sixth-grade class about manor life during the Middle Ages. We will look at a transcript of a portion of the lesson as it unfolded, with the teacher's traditional questions driving the discussion. Following that, we will show how the same text excerpt was handled by a teacher who was using QtA and how Queries can be used to direct the discussion. Then we will consider the difference between what students seemed to understand as a result of a Query-driven lesson and a question-driven lesson. Below is the excerpt.

Question-Driven Lesson

Around A.D. 800 a system called feudalism was put to use. This system mandated that people behave in particular ways. Manors were so large that many people never had to leave them their entire lives. The manors were made up of villages which were inhabited by people who provided everything they needed to live right on the manor. Because of this there was no need for money.

MS. K: What's the name of the system that was in place in the Middle Ages?

STUDENTS: Feudalism.

MS. K:	Yes. Feudalism. We read before that lords owned manors and that their serfs lived on the manors, too. So did the people ever get off the manors?
STUDENTS:	No.
RUTHIE:	They lived there their whole life?
MS. K:	Why didn't they have to go any other place?
DAVID:	They had everything they needed.
MS. K:	The manors had villages where they could get anything they needed, so they didn't have to have any_____?
STUDENTS:	Money.

Notice what the teacher did. She went through the text almost sentence by sentence and asked questions that could be answered by retrieving information from the text, and indeed most of the students did exactly that. The teacher never checked to see whether understanding lay behind that retrieval, and she was the only one who provided any explanations. Most important, the teacher made no attempt to connect this piece to prior readings about the changing economy of the Middle Ages. Thus, there was no opportunity for students to explore their understandings of the consequences of the insularity of life on the manors. This lack of opportunity is a good example of a crucial issue in teaching comprehension: the teacher's establishing in her own mind, prior to the lesson, the understanding she wants students to gain from the text. We'll look at this issue in more detail in the next chapter. For now, take a moment to reflect on how the lesson might have been more effective if the teacher had planned what she wanted students to gain from the text. In the next lesson, we'll witness a teacher who planned more effectively.

Query-Driven Lesson

Now let's look at how the same text excerpt was handled by a teacher who had been engaged with Questioning the Author. The transcript, which is also from a sixth-grade discussion, illustrates a teacher's active role in encouraging students to develop meaning.

MS. L:	Okay, so what has the author told us about these manors?
ANNA:	That you never really had to leave them in your whole life because everything was there for you. But I just want to say that before [earlier in the text] they said that the economy was decreasing. So was that maybe because they didn't, like, have any money?

As shown, the teacher began with an open-ended Query designed to elicit a characterization of manors. Notice that Anna not only portrays an important feature of manors, but also proposes a connection to prior text. This illustrates that students in this classroom were quite accustomed to producing thoughtful responses to Queries. They were adept at making connections to earlier readings and portions of text, as they had been engaged with QtA for some time. Let's continue:

MS. L:	Did everybody hear Anna?
KATHY:	Can you say that again, Anna?

[*Anna repeats her comment*]

MS. L:	Okay, did they say the economy decreased?
STUDENT:	It was altered.
MS. L:	Altered, which means what?
STUDENTS:	Change.
MS. L:	But what do you think about Anna's question that not having money might be connected with that economy change?

The teacher has quickly cleared up a confusion between *decreased* and *altered* and then moves right back to the important concept that Anna has raised.

LAUREN:	I agree with her because you wouldn't have trade if you didn't use money.

Lauren is referring to discussion of earlier text that explains that trade as a source of power declined in the Middle Ages. Notice now how the teacher poses Queries that encourage students to elaborate on Lauren's line of discussion about trade.

MS. L:	So now there's not this trade? So what happens when you don't trade goods?
NICK:	You don't trade ideas or goods or anything.
MS. L:	So what happens when you don't trade ideas?

The teacher pounces on Nick's wonderful insight that ideas wouldn't be traded either. Nick provided the teacher with an opening for a major idea she wanted the students to reach—the insularity of the manors and its effects.

LEAH:	Well, people will kinda stay stupid because they wouldn't have any other different ideas.
MS. L:	We don't want to stay stupid. So how does that connect to what Nick said?
TYLER:	I think they're kind of connected because they're all like the same thing. People just don't really have smart new ideas.

Leah's and Tyler's responses indicate that students are extending the notion of insularity to its effects on the spread of ideas in a society.

MS. L:	Smart new ideas. Hmm . . . Nick?
NICK:	I think intelligence equals power.
MS. L:	Intelligence equals power. Okay, keep that thought in mind as we read on about life in the Middle Ages.

The students have come to recognize the bigger picture, having integrated features of life on the manor with the broader economic situation they had read about earlier. These understandings will serve them well as they read further about the social and political developments of the period in history. Compare it with the first lesson and the differences are striking, as we'll discuss now.

Three Major Differences

What do these transcripts tell us? We think they illuminate three major differences between the two approaches to prompting students. First, traditional questions tend to restrict thinking. By seeking specific answers, these questions ask students to retrieve information, not analyze or think about it. We want more than that from students, and the Queries seem to do the job, which is our second point.

Instead of limiting the thinking students do about the ideas in the text, it's almost as if the Queries lift the lid off the text, exposing ideas so students can discover them for themselves. And third, the kinds of questions we ask students can either contribute to engagement with ideas or erode engagement. That is, what we ask and what we expect of students influence their understanding and engagement. (Think about it: Would *you* be inspired and engaged by a question that begins "What was the name of the system that … ?" It's kind of an intellectual dead end.)

To capture some of the important differences between the two approaches, a summary of some characteristics of the question-driven and the Query-driven discussions is presented in Figure 2.2.

In the question-driven discussion, students' responses mirrored the language of the text, while in the Query-driven discussion, students' answers reflected more original thought and analysis expressed in their own language. Also, there were differences in the dynamics of the two lessons. Questions tended to promote few opportunities for students to respond to one another or consider peers' ideas. The question-driven discussion was product oriented, and the product was what students remembered or what they could find in the text. In contrast, the Query-

---

FIGURE 2.2

A Comparison of Question-Driven and Query-Driven Discussions

QUESTION-DRIVEN	QUERY-DRIVEN
STUDENT RESPONSES	
• brief answers	• longer, more elaborate answers
• in author's language	• in student's language
DISCUSSION DYNAMICS	
• student responses are characterized by unrelated bits of information	• student responses are part of ongoing connected discussion
• little student engagement	• high student engagement
• product oriented	• process oriented
• all questions teacher-initiated	• some questions student-initiated

driven discussion was characterized by student-to-student interactions as well as student-to-teacher exchanges, a more natural context for considering ideas. The goal was not to get the right answer, but to get involved in the text and think about it. The Queries engaged the students, and the discussion came to life.

To sum up, we believe that there are distinct advantages to Query-driven discussions. In Query-driven discussions, students do the work. As we saw in the transcripts, Queries put the responsibility for figuring out what an author is trying to say on students. It's up to them to consider how information connects to build meaning. The discussion allows them to formulate complete thoughts, react to one another's ideas, and consider new notions. Students learn to take an idea and turn it upside down, look at its underside, consider it from different angles. They acquire a deeper understanding of major text ideas, and just as important, they can begin to acquire an appreciation of the power of reading and thinking and expressing ideas in a collaborative discussion.

Types of Queries

Now let's discuss two types of Queries, and how they accomplish the goal of QtA. We refer to Queries as either Initiating or Follow-Up. Initiating Queries launch discussion, and awaken students to the notion that an author is putting forth ideas—it's up to them to identify them. Follow-Up Queries keep discussion moving along the most productive lines and help students elaborate and integrate those ideas.

Initiating Queries: Opening the Discussion

We will first consider the content or wording of Initiating Queries, and then we will look at lesson transcripts to get an idea of how they work in a classroom discussion. Four examples of Initiating Queries follow:

- What is the author trying to say here?

- What do you think the author wants us to know?

- What is the author talking about?

- What's the important message in this section?

These are just examples. There's nothing magical about the way they are worded. The important thing is to understand the purpose. In fact, relying on a specific wording for Queries can be counter-productive. A friend we know rarely cooks anything. She enters a kitchen with great caution and little confidence. One day, she asked how to marinate and grill chicken. We started to explain: "Put a little Italian dressing and water in a pan; add some brown sugar and spices, and. . . ." While we were trying to give her a general idea of what to do, our friend was writing down every word and kept interrupting to get precise measurements of how much water to use, how many teaspoons of this and of that. She wanted to know how to place the chicken on the grill, how often to turn it, and how to know when enough was enough. To this day, she uses the ingredients and procedures exactly as she first learned them. She was interested to learn that we vary our portions and ingredients almost every time we use them.

The point of the story is that, especially when we are new at something or do not have a deep understanding of the larger concepts involved in a task, we tend to want and need recipes. Beginners love formulas. They feel secure knowing there are reliable and specific steps to follow. Our friend does not have a deep understanding of cooking or of "how food works." Therefore, she doesn't experiment or take risks. Our friend cannot be flexible in the kitchen, nor can she have much fun or confidence there. We caution against using specific Queries in this way, as formulas or recipes.

Think about it this way: If you were planning a cross-country road trip one summer vacation, which would be more conducive to a rich exploration of our country, a TripTik provided by the automobile club or road maps and state maps? The TripTik provides a specific route, one possibility for getting to a destination. But it's not necessarily the best route—and it's not the only route. Queries are more like road maps; they provide guidance, perspective, and several possible routes to the destination of understanding. They help you and students navigate, but they aren't meant to navigate for you.

A Query's goal is more important than the way it is worded. And the major goals of Initiating Queries are to make public the messages or ideas presented by an author. They draw attention to the important text ideas and remind students that those ideas were written by an author. Seeing Queries in action should clarify what we mean.

Initiating Queries in Action: Fourth Graders Discuss a Story

The lesson transcript we will look at next is from a fourth-grade discussion of the story "Game of Catch" by Richard Wilbur. The students have already discussed the beginning of the story and established that Monk and Glennie are two boys who are playing catch in a very accomplished way. They then read a section of text that introduces a new character, Scho. The author provides some subtle clues that Scho is not so accomplished. He's dawdles nearby as the boys play, and Glennie asks him if he has his glove, which he "obviously hadn't." Scho's posture and the interchange with Glennie suggest that Scho doesn't have the familiarity and comfortable fit that Monk and Glennie have with each other. Here is the text segment that was discussed:

> **They were going on and on like that, in a kind of slow, mannered, luxurious dance in the sun, their faces perfectly blank and entranced, when Glennie noticed Scho dawdling along the other side of the street and called hello to him. Scho crossed over and stood at the front edge of the lawn, near an apple tree, watching. "Got your glove?" asked Glennie after a time. Scho obviously hadn't. "You could give me some easy grounders," said Scho. "But don't burn 'em."**

Notice that the teacher sets the discussion in motion with a basic, open Query, and Luis provides a spare response that is not quite on target. The next exchange, with Lauren, turns the discussion to Scho.

MS. M:	So what's happening now? Luis?
LUIS:	They are asking each other, like, where is your mitt at?
MS. M:	Okay, they are asking, where is your mitt? What's that all about? Lauren?
LAUREN:	They are asking, asking Scho if he wants to play with them.

Next the teacher pursues the significance of Scho, and Julianna is able to provide the key to that—he is not as able a player as the other boys.

MS. M:	Okay, they are asking Scho if he wants to play with them? So what's this, what's this about Scho? Julianna?

JULIANNA:	Um, he is not as good as them because he doesn't want them to throw it as hard as they throw to each other.

The teacher pursues this hypothesis to make sure that other students have grasped it and prompts them to find the evidence from the text that supports it. Neil makes an attempt to prove it, and then Arvin articulates it well.

MS. M:	Oh, okay. So he is not as good. Anybody pick up on that also?
STUDENTS:	Yeah.
MS. M:	Neil, did you pick up on that also? He is not as good as them? How does the author let you know that?
NEIL:	He doesn't want to, um, use his glove because he thinks he won't catch the ball.
MS. M:	What? How does the author, how does the author let you know that, that he is not going to be able to catch the ball? He doesn't think he can catch the ball.
ARVIN:	He, um, he tells them that he doesn't have his glove and he says when, um, you could give easy grounders to him but don't burn 'em.
MS. M:	Don't burn 'em? What's that mean? Don't burn 'em? Shane?

Below Shane and Tannen combine to provide a good explanation of "don't burn 'em."

SHANE:	It means that when they throw him the grounders don't, like, burn his hands.
MS. M:	Don't burn his hands. Don't burn his hands.
TANNEN:	Don't throw them fast and hard.

Finally, the teacher recaps what the students have provided.

MS. M:	Okay, don't throw them fast and hard. Don't throw fast and hard to him. Okay, so Scho fits in a little differently here than the guys we are already talking about.

The Initiating Query, "What's happening now?", set in motion a discussion in which students were building an understanding of text ideas rather than retrieving text information. Gradually, as the contributions of Julianna, Arvin, Shane, and Tannen were combined with the teacher's responding and probing, they arrived at an understanding that Scho has been invited to play catch with Monk and Glennie, but that he is not as good as they are, and that Scho is aware of this, because he asks for easy grounders. We believe that those understandings, which will take on an important role as the story progresses, would have been less likely to be constructed without the Initiating Query that got it all started.

To sum up, we saw three specific effects of the Initiating Query. First, students did the work; the teacher asked students to do the thinking. The teacher started a discussion and set things in motion with a clear goal in mind. She guided the students to a realization about the text, but she did not tell them what the realization was.

Second, and consequently, students discovered the difference between knowing what an author says and inferring what an author means. The Queries helped them see that an author carefully selects words that in turn create details that—by inference—create a portrait of people, or ideas, and so on. In the process, students helped one another get the job done; they needed to hear and respond to one another's ideas to enhance the meaning. Notice, though, that they had to be prompted and encouraged to keep digging. Finally, the tone of the interactions was positive; there was evidence of engagement and personal investment in ideas and thought.

Follow-Up Queries: Guiding Students Along Productive Lines of Thought

As we move to Follow-Up Queries, we want to reemphasize that these examples are not recipes, but rather suggestions for accomplishing specific goals. We talked about the goals of Follow-Up Queries a little earlier: to help focus the content and direction of a discussion and to assist students in integrating and connecting ideas to build meaning. Now let's consider six examples of Follow-Up Queries.

First we present two related Follow-Up Queries that encourage students to consider the ideas behind an author's words—that is, to go for what the text means rather than what the text says:

- So what does the author mean right here?

- That's what the author said, but what did the author mean?

Next are two Follow-Up Queries that help students connect ideas that have been learned or read previously. These Queries are particularly useful for supporting students' efforts to build a coherent representation. They guide students to relate information from different parts of a text and to see that a connection or linking piece of information may be missing from the text:

- Does that make sense with what the author told us before?

- How does that fit in with what the author told us?

The final two examples of Follow-Up Queries help students figure out an author's possible reasons for including certain information:

- Does the author tell us why?

- Why do you think the author tells us that now?

Follow-Up Queries in Action: Sixth Graders Discuss Nonfiction

Let's consider an example of how meaning is built in a discussion, noting in particular the role of Follow-Up Queries. The example is from a sixth-grade social studies lesson on Egypt.

THE LIFE OF A SCRIBE

Pharaohs depended on written records to keep their government in order. A number of writers called scribes traveled through Egypt to keep records of details great and small. They went out into the fields with local leaders to record how much grain farmers harvested. Scribes also determined how much farmers owed to the government. Scribes drafted letters and marriage contracts for townspeople. Because writing was taught to only a few, scribes were highly respected in Egyptian culture. It was a great honor to become a scribe.   (Macmillan/McGraw-Hill, 1997)

MS. C: So what's the big idea? What do you think the author wants you to know?

SHAQ:	Scribes kept records, like of how much grain grew and stuff.
DARNELL:	That scribes were highly respected and honored.
MS. C:	Just because they wrote down numbers? How does that fit in with what else the author told us?

Notice that Shaq and Darnell have simply pulled information from the text. The teacher then challenges them to fit together these two details, to determine why writing is significant and would give the scribes respect. Notice that she says, "How does that fit in?" This is good language for signaling to students that you want them to connect to previous ideas and text. In the next response, Jake makes the connection that fits Shaq's and Darnell's comments together meaningfully.

JAKE:	That scribes are some of the only people who knew how to read and write. They knew something most people didn't.

After Jake's response, the teacher presses further, asking for a higher level of meaning. Olivia is able to supply an appropriate interpretation.

MS. C:	Ah! So what does that mean about being a scribe?
OLIVIA:	It was a really big deal. You, like, had power.

The lesson continues with the following text segment:

After the boys mastered a simple type of hieroglyphics used for record keeping, they graduated to writing on papyrus. Papyrus is a reed plant that grows along the Nile.

Ancient Egyptians used these reeds to make a kind of paper, also called papyrus. Papyrus paper was not very different from the paper we use today. Did you notice how similar the words papyrus and paper are? Our modern word comes from the ancient one!

Scribes used sharpened reeds as pens. They dipped the reeds into small disks of red or black ink. Then the scribes carefully wrote the information they needed to record on their rolls of papyrus paper. Scribes had to have good penmanship. They also needed to be good at math. After

> all, they had to keep correct records of the pharaoh's many goods. Scribes also figured out the number of workers and the amount of materials needed to complete building projects.
>
> (Macmillan/McGraw-Hill, 1997)

MS. C:	So after all that, what do you think the author wants us to know about scribes?
STACY:	That papyrus was used a lot, that they had good penmanship and had to be good at math.

As we saw in the previous segment, the student's initial response merely repeats information from the text. The teacher adeptly follows up by posing a Query that nudges students to pursue the *meaning* of that information.

MS. C:	That's what the author said, but what does the author mean?

The next two students offer responses that address the meaning of the scribes' skills.

TABATHA:	They had to keep good information, be correct and all.
CIERRA:	Because if they messed up, they might displease the Pharaoh.

The teacher probes again, asking students to fit the idea developed into information they had read in an earlier section, and Pete is able to do that.

MS. C:	How does that make sense with what the author told us before?
PETE:	Their life could be in danger, if the Pharaoh was angry about how they did their job.

Let's summarize the specific effects of the Follow-Up Queries in "The Life of a Scribe" transcript. First, we can see that with the teacher's guidance, the students were able to link earlier text information with new information. Second, students' comments built on previous comments to connect ideas and make sense of the text. Finally, meanings and explanations emerged from several sources, not from the students alone, not from the teacher alone, not from the text alone, but from a collaboration that involved all three.

Considerations for Narrative Text

Although all of the Queries we have discussed work for both expository and narrative texts, we have developed some additional Queries especially targeted at narrative texts. We've done so because of the differences between narrative and expository texts, particularly the kinds of exposition found in school textbooks. These additional Queries take into account the special characteristics of narrative texts in terms of authorship, purpose, and structure.

Authorship

Let's first consider differences in authorship. Authors of expository textbooks are frequently made up of teams of content experts who are well-versed in their specific fields but who may not be professional writers. They may not be as concerned with presentation, coherence, and eloquence of language as they are with accuracy and coverage of information. Authors of narrative text, whether they write fiction or nonfiction, are generally writers by craft. They are professional writers whose prose is considered good enough to publish. Nevertheless, their writing can be difficult to understand. Narrative texts exhibit the same kinds of problems as expository texts, such as difficult language, unfamiliar content, confusing organization, and density of content.

Purpose

Expository text and narrative text are written for different purposes. Expository text is intended to present information and not necessarily adhere to a chronology. The goal is to be explicit and abundantly clear. (Even though expository writers don't always succeed with this clarity, that's their intent.)

The purpose of a narrative text is to tell a story. But even within this frame of chronological storytelling, the author's purpose is to convey ideas implicitly, to show, not tell. Thus, there can be plenty of literary devices in a text to impede a reader's understanding. For example, a story line may not be straightforward. An author may employ flashback, shifting narrators, dialects, hyperbole, and other techniques that make the narrative harder to comprehend. Authors of narrative text may also embed (or bury!) foreshadowing, themes, metaphors, symbols, and other significant details throughout their stories. Their purpose? To deliberately *suggest* meaning rather than *state* it.

Structure

Finally, the structures of expository and narrative texts differ. Expository texts have unique elements such as headings, sidebars, and graphs, and various text structures such as compare and contrast. They don't necessarily follow a chronology. In narrative texts, authors may structure their work in ways that challenge readers. They make myriad decisions about plot structure, taking into account character motivation, conflict, character change, and resolution. The unique elements of narrative texts are not the domain of fiction writers alone; for example, a biographer will take his cues about how to structure his book based on the arc of his subject's life, the richness of certain settings, the dramatic potential of particular relationships, and so on.

Queries for Narrative Text

We will consider six Queries that have been particularly useful in addressing the unique aspects of narrative text. The first two Queries help students think about character motivation and consider the "big picture" of where a character is and how he got there.

- How do things look for this character now?
- Given what the author has already told us about this character, what do you think he's up to?

Just as the author constructed a character and a set of circumstances in which that character acts in believable and consistent ways, the reader must also understand the character well enough to construct his or her own representation of the character.

Three other Queries can effectively focus students' thinking on the author's crafting of the plot and characters:

- How has the author let you know that something has changed?
- How has the author worked that out for us?
- How is the author making you feel right now about these characters?

These Queries can enhance students' awareness of the author and remind them that plots are created by authors who plan complications and resolutions.

The use of dialogue to provide information or move the plot is a common device that authors employ in narrative texts. A useful Query to draw attention to the idea that the author is revealing something beyond the words of the conversation is:

- What is the author telling us with this conversation?

Narrative Queries in Action: Sixth Graders Read Fiction

Let's see how some of these Queries for narrative play out in an actual lesson. We'll look at a series of brief exchanges taken from the transcript of a sixth-grade class reading a section of *Tuck Everlasting* (Babbit, 1986). The novel is about a family that has found eternal life by drinking from a secret spring. A girl, Winnie, has discovered their secret, and thus the family—Mae, Tuck, and their teenage son, Jesse—has taken her with them to keep their secret safe.

Tuck Everlasting: Discussion Snapshot 1

"I'm sorry about everything," said Mae. "I just didn't know no other way but to bring you back with us. I know it ain't very happy for you here, but ... well ... anyway, you have a good talk with Tuck?"

"I guess so," said Winnie.

"That's good. Well. I'm going back to bed. Get a good sleep."

"All right," said Winnie.

But still Mae lingered. "We been alone so long," she said at last, "I guess we don't know how to do with visitors. But still and all, it's a good feeling, you being here with us. I wish you was ... ours." She put out an awkward hand then and touched Winnie's hair. "Well," she said, "good night."

"Good night," said Winnie.

MS. C:	Okay, so what is the author telling us with this conversation between Winnie and Mae? Ashley?
ASHLEY:	How Mae really likes her, and she wanted her to stay a while.
MS. C:	So Mae likes Winnie. What's behind that?
ROBERT:	Mae, like they never see hardly any other people, or have friends or people visit or anything. So they're lonely, and it's like she doesn't even know how to act with visitors.
MS. C:	And Winnie is not exactly an ordinary visitor. What do you think, Anna?
ANNA:	Well, she's also trying to, like, apologize for the way they treated her—taking her with them and all, like Winnie said, kidnapping her, because she found out they had this secret, living forever.

Notice here how the teacher gets the students to go beyond the words in the conversation to the message the author is providing about the characters. Ashley picks up on Mae's affection for Winnie. Then Robert, prompted by the teacher's next probe, elaborates on that idea to explain why having Winnie at her house might mean so much to Mae.

Tuck Everlasting: Discussion Snapshot 2

Tuck came, too, a little later, to peer down at her anxiously. He was wearing a long white nightshirt and his hair was rumpled. "Oh!" he said. "You still awake? Everything all right?"

"Yes," said Winnie.

"I didn't mean to go disturbing you," he said. "But I been laying in there thinking I ought to be setting out here with you till you went to sleep."

"You don't have to do that," said Winnie, surprised and touched. "I'm alright"

MS. C:	Do you see a change here? How does the author let you know that something has changed? Caroline?
CAROLINE:	Winnie says she's touched, like "you don't have to do that." She was sort of happy, um, that he actually cared.
MS. C:	So she was surprised and touched by it? Okay, go ahead, Rich.
RICH:	Before, she was all angry at the Tucks, thinking they were criminals who just kidnapped her.
CINDY:	Outraged.
RICH:	Yeah, outraged that she was in that place, their house. And now she really softened up her feelings.

In asking about what has changed, the teacher is drawing attention to the beginnings of Winnie's shift in attitude about the Tucks, which is subtle but instrumental to the plot. Note that the Query launches students on a discussion of the important change in Winnie's feelings.

Tuck Everlasting: Discussion Snapshot 3

> **Winnie lay with her eyes wide. She felt cared for and— confused. And all at once she wondered what would happen to the Tucks when her father came. What would he do to them? She would never be able to explain how they had been with her, how they made her feel. She remembered guiltily that at supper she had decided they were criminals. Well, but they were. And yet . . .**

MS. C:	All right, we've been talking about how Winnie's feelings have changed. But let me ask you: How is the author making you feel right now about the Tucks?
KASEY:	Before I was feeling kind of upset that Winnie was feeling like that she was kidnapped, and so I was feeling like I didn't like the Tucks. And then Mae and Tuck come down and they do this, and it makes me feel different.

SHATIRA:	The author's making it seem, kind of showing how the Tucks really are good people. They have good hearts.
MS. C.:	Nakia, you wanted to jump in here?
NAKIA:	That they just want her to be comfortable. What they did wasn't to be mean, or they didn't mean to scare her, but they just took her with them 'cause they had to.

A hallmark of good literature is the way authors get hold of readers' feelings. Note that the teacher asks how the author is making them feel as readers. In doing so, the teacher is exploring that, as the character Winnie changes her feelings, the author also manages to shift the readers' feelings.

In the text that leads up to the following excerpt, Mae and Tuck's teenage son, Jesse, has just suggested to Winnie that she, too, drink from the spring and join the Tucks, so that the two of them could spend their lives together.

Tuck Everlasting: Discussion Snapshot 4

> All she could do was stare at him.
>
> "You think on it, Winnie Foster," Jesse whispered earnestly. "Think on it some and see if it don't sound good. Anyway, I'll see you in the morning. All right?"
>
> "All right," she managed to whisper in return. He slipped away then, back up the creaking steps, but Winnie sat upright, wide awake, her cheeks burning. She could not deal with this remarkable suggestion, she could not "think on it." For she didn't know what to believe about anything. She lay down again, finally, and stared into the moonlight for another half an hour before she fell asleep.

MS. C:	So how do things look for this character now? How do things look for Winnie right now?
SHATIRA:	Now she's more confused than she was before.
EZRA:	First she was mad, then she got happier about the Tucks, and now she's feeling like practically in love with Jesse!

The Query, which asks students to think about how things look for Winnie, goes far beyond a simple predictive question such as "What's going to happen?" It prompts young readers to take the character's perspective. It invites them to reflect not only on what might occur but on how the character is being affected by an ongoing or changing situation.

Ending Notes

We wrap up our discussion of Queries with the following points:

- Queries differ from traditional questions in that Queries are more process oriented—intended to assist students in the process of comprehending.

- In contrast to Queries, traditional questions are more product oriented because they are used to assess comprehension.

- Initiating Queries work to make an author's ideas public text and launch discussion.

- Follow-Up Queries encourage students to keep the discussion focused and integrate ideas to construct meaning.

- Narrative texts require additional Queries because of their authors' use of literary techniques that can pose special challenges to readers.

Figure 2.3 on page 57 presents examples of the different kinds of Queries that we have discussed.

FIGURE 2.3

Examples of Queries:
Initiating, Follow-Up, and Narrative

Initiating Queries

- What is the author trying to say here?

- What do you think the author wants us to know?

- What is the author talking about?

Follow-Up Queries

- So what does the author mean right here?

- That's what the author said, but what did the author mean?

- Does that make sense with what the author told us before?

- How does that fit in with what the author has told us?

- But does the author tell us why?

- Why do you think the author tells us that now?

Narrative Queries

- How do things look for this character now?

- How does the author let you know that something has changed?

- How has the author worked that out for us?

- Given what the author has already told us about this character, what do you think he's up to?

- How is the author making you feel right now about these characters?

- What is the author telling us with this conversation?

Perhaps the most important message of all is that Queries drive the process of constructing meaning. In the next chapter, we will address the kinds of decisions made in planning for a QtA lesson.

Frequently Asked Questions

1. Does every Query have to have the word *author* in it?

No, but it's useful to mention the author frequently to remind students that someone wrote the text in their books and that they are engaged in figuring out what that person is trying to tell them. Students need to be reminded that they are trying to understand an author's ideas.

However, just inserting the word *author* in a question won't change a traditional question into a Query. For example, "What temperature did the author tell us it was?" is still a question that asks students to retrieve information from the text rather than build an understanding of the ideas in a text.

2. What is the difference between an Initiating Query and a Follow-Up Query?

Initiating and Follow-Up Queries are both intended to support students in building an understanding of major text ideas. We have made the distinction only because they are applied differently in a discussion. Initiating Queries are used to set a discussion in motion. For example, "So, what has the author told us here?" or "What is the author trying to tell us about the Arctic tundra?"

Follow-Up Queries are used to respond to students' comments, encourage them to grapple with ideas, and move the discussion along. For example, "So, what did the author mean when he said the colonists didn't like the new law? What's that all about?" or "How does that connect to something the author said earlier?"

3. How do I know if I have asked the right Queries?

There are no right and wrong Queries—only effective and less effective ones. The response a Query elicits is the best measure of its effectiveness. If students respond by attempting to construct meaning—by connecting ideas, using the text as a resource, questioning, and solving problems—then you have evidence that you have asked an effective Query.

If a Query falls flat and students merely parrot back an author's words or repeat already stated information, then you have evidence that your Query has been less effective.

4. Can I ask some traditional questions?

Yes. Asking a traditional question now and then is fine as long as it supports meaning building. The key is to avoid questions that shift the focus of a discussion from developing ideas to retrieving text information. Sometimes you'll find you need to ask a traditional question to ensure your students are clear about the basics of what's happening. For example, "Who's telling this story?" or "Where are our characters now?"

5. How can I come up with effective Follow-Up Queries during a lesson?

Follow-Up Queries pose difficulties because they must be developed during a lesson, in response to the discussion as it unfolds. Several devices have been shown to help, especially in the early weeks of implementing Questioning the Author. First, as you plan the lesson, try to anticipate how students may respond to the text and jot down some potential Follow-Up Queries.

Second, during discussion, try to use part of a student's response, or include some of the specific terms or sentences of the text to develop Follow-Up Queries. For example, "Doris said that the colonists didn't follow some laws. What's she getting at when she talks about these laws?" or "The author says that the settlers wanted to 'worship God in their own way.' What do you think the author means by that?"

Student comments and the texts themselves can provide a kind of jump-start for developing a Follow-Up Query in the midst of discussion.

6. What can I do to get students to respond to Queries in thoughtful ways and not just repeat text information?

Students are probably used to retrieving information from a text rather than building an understanding of text ideas. They may not understand that construction of meaning is what you want them to engage in. Students need to be reminded that the goal is to figure out what an author means—not just what she says. Try being just that explicit when you respond to a student. For example, "You have told me what the author said, but can you tell me what the author means by that?" or "Why do you think the author would tell us that?"

CHAPTER 3

Planning

As a new QtA teacher, Ms. K wrote in her journal about planning a text-based lesson about the attack on Pearl Harbor:

> I was frustrated about the vast amount of prior knowledge that the author had assumed the students possessed. I was such a wreck about my own lack of prior knowledge on the subject that I spent the whole lunch period prior to teaching this text discussing Pearl Harbor with the other teachers (specifically the social studies teacher). I couldn't help thinking that I had taught this same lesson [before] without [doing] any research. Amazing!

In this brief journal entry, we see the power of QtA to change a teacher's perspective on lesson planning, classroom texts, and her own role. Notice that she takes the author to task for assuming too much prior knowledge, a critical stance she may not have adopted without experience with QtA. Then she reels at the thought that she has used the text before in previous lessons without her, let alone her students, having the requisite background.

Although she seems flustered in the above excerpt, she came to relish the changes in her class—and in herself—as a result of QtA. In a journal entry not much later, she writes that her students are demanding more not only from the text, but from themselves, their classmates, and their teacher, [which] "forced me to acquire a deeper understanding about the ideas presented in the text."

In this chapter, we describe the process of planning in Questioning the Author and show how it may transform the teacher's thinking about text. In QtA, the approach to lesson planning and decision making differs in several respects from more traditional ways of lesson planning. To plan a lesson, some teachers rely on their teacher's manuals for the kinds of questions and activities to use. An unfortunate consequence is that the teachers themselves rarely scrutinize the material. The work has already been done, and many teachers trust that it has been done well. Other teachers plan by looking over the text and making their own decisions about what to focus on. They tend to view the text as basically comprehensible and authors as more or less infallible, and they look to the text mainly to find the ideas students will be held accountable for recalling. They don't interact with it significantly themselves, and so they can't possibly know what a young reader's experience of it might be as he tries to make sense of it.

Though it may seem reasonable to view teacher manuals as reliable resources for content and instructional expertise, in many cases we have found that the suggested questions fail to tap real understanding (Beck & McKeown, 1981). Furthermore, the texts students are expected to read can be very dense and difficult for young learners to understand (Beck, McKeown & Gromoll, 1989). Yet teachers often overlook or underestimate the hard work it may take on the part of young readers to comprehend those texts. QtA addresses these issues by encouraging teachers to adopt a new way of thinking about lesson planning, a way that involves teachers in trying to anticipate the kinds of comprehension roadblocks students may encounter when reading a text and the kinds of support they can offer to help students. The relationship between planning and teaching is different in QtA than in traditional teaching. Let us elaborate.

Think about putting on a stage production of a play. In rehearsals, directors do more than have the actors rehearse their lines for the performance. They block out scenes, determine what specific moves are most dramatic, and practice orchestrating the simultaneous demands of onstage movements, picking up cues, timing costume changes, and so on. A director's job is to anticipate audience response and reaction, decide what will enhance the production's overall success, and prepare for potential problems. They sit in an audience seat to view the play from the perspective of a theater-goer.

Planning and teaching a QtA lesson is not all that different from producing a play. However, in a QtA lesson, the teacher is both the director and an actor. As the director, the teacher blocks out the lesson in terms of what will be discussed and tries to anticipate how the lesson may develop. And the teacher must imagine the lesson from another's point of view—the student's. As an actor, the teacher must be ready to improvise as the lesson develops in ways he or she may not have anticipated.

Thus, preparing a QtA lesson calls for a special approach to planning. A key first move for the teacher is to read the text that will be discussed ahead of time and try to tune in to the words, ideas, transitions, and other elements that may be daunting for a young, less skilled reader. We have found that taking the role of the student helps teachers perform in their roles as facilitators. With this orientation in mind, let's consider the three QtA goals of planning.

Goals of Planning

1. **Determine the major understandings** students should develop from a text and anticipate problems that they may encounter.

2. **Segment the text** by deciding where to stop reading and initiate discussion.

3. **Articulate Initiating Queries and potential Follow-Up Queries** that will help students develop understandings of the text ideas.

We will discuss each goal in turn, demonstrating how it works using sample texts.

Determine the Major Understandings

Let's consider the first goal: to read the text closely in order to determine the major understandings. At first, the difference between familiarizing oneself with a text and determining major understandings may not seem obvious, but there is an important distinction. When preparing for a traditional lesson, teachers usually do not take into account an author's overall intent for the entire work or for a particular section. Most of the time, the author is in the background of our aware-ness, while the content of the text is in the foreground. The text is considered to be a source of fixed information or, in the case of narrative, a story with a fixed outcome. Teachers tend to think of text as a finished product, something past tense in nature, a place to find meaning that has been wholly determined.

In QtA, we deliberately put the author at center stage as a way of signaling to students that the text is neither fixed nor perfect, and that we as teachers don't have all the answers to questions of meaning. (In traditional lessons, it's as though teachers hold "right" answers tightly against their chests like a hand of cards.) In QtA, we let it be known to young readers that the author—not the teacher—is a more interesting source of answers. The author will help us unearth a text's major understandings during class discussions, if we Query him about his intent, right down to his crafting of particular sentences and word choices. We've found that students readily embrace this notion. Why? Because when the author is a *participant* in the discussion, reading becomes an interactive experience, more like a conversation, in which points are argued, participants can interrupt to have something clarified, and meaning is enhanced *in the course of* the exchange.

We ask that teachers take this conversational stance from the get-go when planning a lesson. That is, read the text as a reader having a conversation with an author. The purpose of the conversation is to determine the major points the author is making and which of those are most important for students to under-stand. For example, while reading *The Adventures of Huckleberry Finn*, a teacher may come upon a particularly significant passage and develop a Query along the lines of "What does Mark Twain seem to be saying about slavery here?" Or while reading Russell Freeman's *In Defense of Liberty: The Story of America's Bill of Rights*, a teacher may say, "What does the author want us to understand about free speech here?"

Reading to Anticipate Challenges to Comprehension

We also ask that teachers read to anticipate problems the text may pose to young and less experienced readers. As skilled readers, we don't usually have trouble comprehending a text, even when it is poorly written. We are good at making inferences about ideas not explicitly stated and making connections to previously read or known information. We do these things automatically, which makes it all the harder for us to predict the places in a text that students may find confusing. Yet, in order to anticipate and plan for problematic portions of a text, we need to learn to identify them.

To find these trouble spots, we need to be aware of the kinds of things that are potentially difficult, such as a preponderance of abstract language, unfamiliar content, and transitions between paragraphs that are not particularly effective. One way to develop that awareness is to consciously monitor your comprehension process as you read the text. Notice when you're doing extra work. That could include having to reread a portion of text to understand it, or stopping to think about how one idea follows from another. Teachers who find themselves going off "automatic pilot" when they read, doing extra work, can be reasonably sure that their students will also encounter difficulties and may not be able to resolve them.

In the sections that follow, we present two examples of planning, one for a narrative text and the other for an expository one. In each case we discuss decisions for major understandings, segment points, and Queries.

Planning a Narrative Text

The first text we'll look at is "The Raven and the Whale," an Inuit folk tale retold by Lawrence Millman (1987). As you read the story, which appears on page 66 (see Figure 3.1), consider the kinds of understandings that you would want students to construct. Then, we'll see what kinds of decisions a QtA teacher made when she planned for this lesson. The numbers inserted in the story indicate text segments, which we will explain subsequently.

Determining the Major Understandings

The QtA teacher who planned a lesson using this text decided that the major understanding for students to construct is the following: The raven is a character of extravagant self-interest. He has a habit of trying to make things grander for himself, through deceit and with no concern for others. But his character catches up with him. In fact, the cleverest of his tricks, the ability to change from animal to human form, leads to his dying twice!

The author provides information in key text phrases that allow readers to build understanding of the raven's character. These key phrases include:

- The woman was very pleasant company. Likewise she did all the work.

- "Is there anything you would like?" the woman would ask him.

- "Yes. . . I would like to touch the lamp."

- "You must never, never touch the lamp," she told him. But this made the raven all the more curious. . . . he walked up and pecked at it. . . . and the woman fell down dead."

- "[The whale] was dead. . . . they were floating toward a human village, so he turned himself into a man. . . . "I've just killed this enormous bowheaded whale without even using a harpoon. . . ."
No one believed him. Perhaps he could show off his hunting prowess once again? "Whenever you wish," he declared.

Phrases that provide information from which readers can build a representation of the raven's demise include:

- [A] herd of narwhals was sighted . . .

- He got into a kayak and paddled it toward the herd.

- [T]he kayak was knocked over and he was pierced by a narwhal's horn.

- But as he died, he turned back into a raven, and was eaten by one of the narwhals.

- Thus did the mighty hunter die. [Key here is the author's single point of irony.]

Now let's think about problems young students may have in developing the understanding, the nature of the raven's character. The major problem is that the nature of the raven's character is never discussed explicitly, nor are any evaluations made of his actions. Readers need to build these ideas for themselves. For example, the woman and the whale both die from the raven's actions, yet the events are only reported, and the focus is on the raven's subsequent actions rather than the consequences ("He walked up and pecked at it. Instantly the lamp went out and the woman fell down dead. Now the raven stumbled around in the dark.

FIGURE 3.1 **Planning a Narrative Text**

The Raven and the Whale

There was once a raven who by accident flew into the mouth of a big bowheaded whale. He flew right down the throat and ended up in the belly. There he saw a little house built of ribs and soft hides; a shabby little house, just like a human dwelling. ❶ Inside this house was a young woman minding a blubber lamp. "You may stay here as long as you like," she told him, "but you must never touch this lamp." For the lamp was the whale's heart. ❷

The raven decided to stay there for quite awhile. The woman was very pleasant company. Likewise she did all the work. "Eat," she'd say, and offer him some fish, mussels, or crabs which the whale had swallowed. There would be more mataq than he could eat in a dozen lifetimes. ❸

"Is there anything you would like?" the woman would ask him.

"Yes," said the raven. "I would like to touch the lamp."

"You must never, never touch the lamp," she told him. ❹

But this made the raven all the more curious. More than anything else, he wanted to touch that lamp. He gazed at it for long hours. ❺ And once, while the woman's back was turned, he walked up and pecked at it. Instantly the lamp went out and the woman fell down dead.

Now the raven stumbled around in the dark. At last he found the throat-passage and crawled through it. Then he climbed on top of the whale, which was dead. ❻ He saw that they were floating toward a human village, so he turned himself into a man. "Behold!" he exclaimed, "I've just killed this enormous bowheaded whale without even using a harpoon...." ❼

No one believed him. Perhaps he could show off his hunting prowess once again? "Whenever you wish," he declared. And he went to live in that village, waiting for the opportunity to show off his ability. ❽ Then one day a herd of narwhals was sighted in the harbour. "Leave this to me," he said. He got into a kayak and paddled it toward the herd. ❾ Almost at once the kayak was knocked over and he was pierced by a narwhal's horn. Thus did the mighty hunter die. But as he died, he turned back into a raven, and was eaten by one of the narwhals. ❿

. . . He climbed on top of the whale, which was dead"). Then the raven unabash-
edly turns his misdeed into a brave deed, but again, the action is simply reported
("Behold!" he exclaimed, "I've just killed this enormous bowheaded whale
without even using a harpoon. . .").

The events of his dying are simply reported as well, with no comment made
on the fact that he dies twice. Moreover there is little in the text that supports
the irony of his second death, which occurs while he's trying to make one of
his cunning transformations. Readers must infer that from the reporting of
the events.

Segmenting the Text

After reading "The Raven and the Whale," determining the major understanding
we want students to build, and making some decisions about anticipated areas of
difficulty, we are ready to think about segmenting the text. By segmenting, we
mean determining where to stop reading to initiate and develop discussion toward
building meaning.

It is the major understandings that drive decisions about segmenting, not
paragraph breaks in a text or where the text ends on a page. Sometimes a single
sentence needs attention because the information it presents is key to constructing
meaning. In other cases, a series of paragraphs can be dealt with all at once because
there's not much of importance or because they are all about the same idea.

Let's look now at how one teacher thought through "The Raven and the
Whale" and segmented it, which is shown on page 68 (see Figure 3.2). Her
discussions would seem to support students in building a coherent representation,
although it is certainly not the only way one could have set about developing the
lesson. What is most valuable is the close reading in which the teacher engaged,
developing a focus for the story—the raven's character—anticipating text statements that could be confusing to her class, and keeping those issues in mind while
determining where to stop reading and start discussion. We move now to the
Queries the teacher developed for each segment.

FIGURE 3.2 **How One Teacher Segmented the Text**

1 The teacher determined that the first segment should include the material up to "just like a human dwelling," which provides the story's odd setting—inside a whale.

2 The second segment provides two key pieces of information, that there is a woman living inside the whale and that the lamp that she tends is the whale's heart.

3 The third segment describes the amenities that the raven is enjoying inside the body of the whale. As the story progresses, it will be important for students to remember the raven's luxurious living situation so it can be connected to an upcoming idea, that he wants more.

4 The fourth segment reveals that the raven wants to touch the lamp, planting the seeds of a problem.

5 In the fifth segment, the seeds grow into a clear conflict, giving students the opportunity to express the turn that plots customarily take at such a point—he's going to touch the lamp.

6 The sixth segment reveals that the raven has touched the lamp, which has resulted in the death of both the woman and the whale. Notice that the decision was made not to stop at the end of the paragraph, after "the woman fell down dead," but to include the full extent of the consequences—that the whale died as well—in one segment.

7 The seventh segment reveals important aspects of the raven's character—he's an opportunist. Not only has he caused the death of two creatures, he is attempting to turn the events to his own benefit.

8 The eighth segment seems to have both settled things and left things hanging. He has settled into a peaceful existence in a new village, but he has been challenged to prove himself in the future.

9 The ninth segment provides the situation in which the raven is going to have to prove his prowess.

10 The tenth and final segment provides a fitting end for this character, in which he dies twice.

Developing Queries

Now let's consider how the QtA teacher developed Queries for "The Raven and the Whale." Recall that in planning Queries for a text, a teacher develops Initiating Queries to launch discussion, anticipates how students may respond, and develops potential Follow-Up Queries to help focus and move the discussion forward.

1 As noted, the first text segment established that the setting was inside a whale. The Initiating Query that the teacher decided on is: ***"How has the author started things off for us?"*** Consider if the teacher had instead asked, "What's the setting?" A question such as this would have elicited one-dimensional answers, such as "In a whale." In contrast, the more open Query of ***"How has the author started things off for us?"*** prompts students to put together the information in the segment as the setting. And in a sense, the Query leaves room for a student to say something insightful beyond stating the setting.

2 The Initiating Query for the second segment is designed to bring forth the very important information that the lamp was the whale's heart and should never be touched: ***"What has the author told us now?"*** In case students failed to mention that the lamp was the whale's heart, the teacher anticipated asking the Follow-Up Query: ***"What about this lamp?"*** Again notice that the question requires bringing ideas together, rather than simply retrieving information, as would a traditional question such as: "What is the lamp?"

3 The Query for the third segment is about the raven's life, ***"So, how do things look for the raven?"*** The Query is meant to establish the amenities that the raven is enjoying in the body of the whale. However, the teacher anticipated that students might respond by simply repeating text words, so she planned the Follow-Up Query: ***"What kind of life is he having?"***

4 The intention of the Query for the fourth segment, ***"What's this all about?"*** is that students see that the seeds of a problem have been planted. If students do not recognize that this portends an important conflict in the story, the teacher planned to follow up with: ***"What's the author doing here by giving us this little scene?"***

5 The purpose of the fifth Query is to dramatize that the plot thickens. The teacher planned to ask, ***"What do you see going on here?"***

6 In the sixth segment, the Query *"Now what has happened?"* is intended to spark discussion that the raven's desire to touch the lamp has had dramatic consequences—both the woman and the whale have died. If students don't connect this to the woman's warning, the teacher's Follow-Up Query would be *"How does this fit in with what the woman had told the raven?"* Additionally, to extend students' thinking about the raven's character, she developed the Follow-Up Queries *"Why do you think he'd do that?"* and *"What does that tell you about the raven?"*

7 To establish the deceitful situation the raven creates in the seventh segment, that he hunted a whale, the teacher developed the Query *"What's this raven up to now?"* To connect the situation to aspects of the raven's character, she developed the Follow-Up Query *"How does this fit in with what we already know about this raven character?"* Additionally, the teacher wanted to make sure that students notice that the raven has also transformed himself into a man, so she planned as a follow-up *"What's happened to the raven just now?"*

8 For the eighth segment, the Query *"What's happened now?"* allows students to establish ideas about the raven's life in the village as he waits to prove his prowess.

9 For the ninth segment, the teacher wanted students to see that the time has come for the raven to prove his prowess. So her Query was *"How does this connect?"*

10 In the final segment, the raven dies twice! The teacher wanted to open up discussion and give students a chance to talk about what they see in the story, so she decided to begin with the Query *"What do you think about the way the author has finished up this story?"* She also planned Follow-Up Queries to help students consider how the raven deserved his fate: *"How do you think this ending fits in with the events in the story?"* *"What was it that happened to him at the end?"* *"Why do you suppose the author chose to kill him twice?"*

The most important concept we want you to take away from this example is that a Query should be developed to help students grapple with text toward building a coherent representation of the major ideas, not to extract a specific answer or to prompt recall of pieces of information.

Planning an Expository Text

In this section we will describe how a teacher planned a lesson for a fifth-grade social studies text excerpt about aspects of the colonial route to revolution. Again, the numbers in the excerpt, which is shown on page 72 (Figure 3.3), indicate text segments. One teacher's segmenting decisions are shown on page 73 (Figure 3.4).

Determining the Major Understandings

The major understanding that the teacher wanted students to develop was that events surrounding Britain's passage of the Stamp Act represent a turning point in relations between Britain and the colonies because the colonists didn't think the British parliament had a right to tax them. The rift between Britain and the colonists widened and grew deeper while the bond among the colonies became stronger, and colonists across colonies worked together in a unified protest. Britain's reaction showed the realization that something in the relationship had changed.

So what are the key phrases that pertain to the major understanding? Phrases that communicate the colonists' reaction to the taxes—that relate to their organization of a boycott of British goods and of holding a meeting of delegates—are as follows: "The colonists began to act against the tax." "They organized a boycott of British goods." "The colonists also held a meeting to protest the tax." "Each of the colonies sent delegates to the meeting." "Delegates pledged that the citizens of their colony would not buy from Britain." Much of the reason for the colonists' strong reaction to the new tax stems from the principle behind the phrase "no taxation without representation."

Key phrases that present Britain's view of the colonists' actions include: "[The British] found it very worrisome." "Colonists had protested British laws before, but this was something new." "Never had colonists come together to decide and agree on a course of action."

Problems may arise for students in trying to build an understanding of the ideas noted above because the significance of the issues in the text may not be readily apparent from descriptions of the actions themselves. Much of the historical significance rests on the abstract concept of representation in a government body. For example, when the text states, "The colonists began to act against the tax . . . . They organized a boycott of British goods," the students may have trouble with both the literal meaning and the implications.

FIGURE 3.3 ## Planning an Expository Text

A NEW TAX FOR THE COLONIES

After the French and Indian War ended in 1763, Britain was having financial difficulties. The war had been expensive. So the British came up with a plan to make money by taxing the colonists. There had been taxes on the colonists before, but most of them had not been enforced. Britain just didn't collect the money. ❶

The idea of taxes made sense to the British. Since the French and Indian War had taken place in the colonies, they thought the colonists should help pay for it. The colonists did not see it this way. They thought they had paid enough. Many colonists had fought and died in the war. ❷ Besides, they didn't think that the British parliament had the right to tax them for purchases they made inside the colonies. Parliament is Britain's lawmaking body, and the colonists were not represented in Parliament. ❸

In 1765, the British government passed the Stamp Act, which put a new tax on printed materials. They made everyone who bought things like newspapers, calendars, marriage licenses, even playing cards, buy a special tax stamp. The colonists became very angry over this tax. The list of items to be taxed was six pages long! ❹

COLONISTS PROTEST

The colonists began to act against the tax. They decided they would rather do without things than pay Britain. They organized a boycott of British goods. A boycott means people refused to buy anything made in Britain. ❺ Not buying British goods caused hardship for the colonists. They had to do without many items, or make their own. But even though the clothes they made themselves were not as nice as they could buy from Britain, the colonists believed it was worth it. ❻

The colonists also held a meeting to protest the tax. The meeting was called the Stamp Act Congress. Each of the colonies sent delegates to the meeting. Some of the most important leaders of the colonies were there. ❼ Delegates pledged that the citizens of their colony would not buy from Britain. ❽ The Stamp Act Congress also demanded that Britain repeal, or take back, the Stamp Act. They said that Parliament did not have the right to tax the colonists because colonists were not represented in Parliament. ❾

BRITAIN REACTS

The Stamp Act Congress really got the attention of the British. They found it very worrisome. Colonists had protested British laws before, but this was something new. Never had colonists come together to decide and agree on a course of action. ❿ The British wanted to make sure this did not happen again. In 1766, the British responded to the protests and repealed the Stamp Act. But the question of whether Britain had the right to tax the colonists had not been settled. ⓫

(Silver Burdett Ginn, 1993)

FIGURE 3.4 How One Teacher Segmented the Text

1. The teacher chose the first paragraph as a segment because it presented so much information, and she wanted to establish the basic situation that the French and Indian War was over and had caused Britain to seek new funding.

2. The teacher identified the second segment to help students glimpse the conflict being set up before the text presents the complication of taxation without representation.

3. The third segment contains the big idea, taxation without representation. Even though this is a small segment, the teacher wanted to isolate it to ensure students would focus on it.

4. The fourth segment presents some details of the Stamp Act. The teacher wanted students to use the details to build the understanding that the tax affected the colonists' everyday life because so many ordinary things carried a tax now.

5. The fifth segment presents a complex picture in four short sentences. Here the teacher wanted to establish what a boycott is and how that connects to the taxes.

6. The teacher identified the rest of this paragraph as the sixth segment because it adds an important elaboration about the boycott by describing the kind of sacrifice the colonists were making in giving up British goods, which indicated the significance of the taxation issue.

7. The teacher identified the seventh segment to help students understand the Stamp Act Congress, which was important to the unfolding events, and thus worthy of special focus. Otherwise students might interpret it as a get-together

8. The eighth segment, a single sentence, was identified to help students connect the taxes to the boycott discussed earlier.

9. The teacher identified the ninth segment to get the final ideas in place about the activities of the Stamp Act Congress.

10. The tenth segment presents the British perspective on the Stamp Act Congress.

11. The teacher chose to use the rest of the text as the final segment. Here she wanted students to note that the Stamp Act was repealed and the idea that something was left hanging, i.e., "But the question of whether Britain had the right to tax the colonists had not been settled."

Text descriptions such as "The colonists also held a meeting to protest the tax," "Each of the colonies sent delegates to the meeting," and "Delegates pledged that the citizens of their colony would not buy from Britain" may be interpreted as fairly mundane actions. The implications may be difficult for fifth-grade students to grasp. Concepts in the sentences "Besides, they didn't think that the British parliament had the right to tax them for purchases they made inside the colonies," and "Parliament is Britain's lawmaking body, and the colonists were not represented in Parliament" are abstract. The notion that the British found the colonists' actions "very worrisome," and that the protests were "something new" are presented in a vague way and may be interpreted as trivial.

Segmenting the Text

As indicated in the excerpt (Figure 3.3) by the numbers in circles, the teacher identified 11 places where she wanted to stop and discuss the material.

Developing Queries

As stated earlier, a teacher's thinking about Initiating Queries and potential Follow-Up Queries interacts with her thinking about where to stop reading and initiate discussion.

1 For example, at the first stop, this teacher began with a general Query to get the information on the table: *"What has the author given us so far?"* The teacher also wanted students to understand that Britain was going to enforce taxes, which it hadn't done before, so she asked, *"What do you think the author is telling us about what Britain will do this time?"*

2 At the second stop, the teacher wanted to set up the upcoming conflict, so she asked, *"What's the author telling us is going on here between Britain and the colonies?"*

3 At the third stop, to make sure students understand what a "lawmaking body" is and that the one referred to here is in Britain, she asked, *"Who does the author tell us Parliament is?"* and *"So, what was the problem the colonists had with Parliament?"* To move students beyond just repeating text phrases in their answers, the teacher planned a Follow-Up Query: *"What was it about Parliament that made the colonists feel that way?"* And to help students connect the idea of representation with electing officials: *"What does it mean to be represented in a lawmaking body?"*

④ The teacher's Query for the fourth segment was *"How does the author explain this new tax?"* To avoid having students get caught up in the details of what was taxed or that the taxed items were six pages long, she asked, *"What do you think that means about how the tax affected life for the colonists?"*

⑤ To establish the basics of a boycott and its relationship to taxes, for the fifth segment the teacher asked, *"What have the colonists done?"* and *"How does that connect to what we read about the taxes?"*

⑥ To emphasize that the boycott was a sacrifice for the colonists, the sixth-segment Query was *"What's the author told us now about this boycott?"* Having taught the Stamp Act text in previous years, the teacher wanted to reduce students' tendencies to simply reiterate the difficulty it caused, so she used a Follow-Up Query to connect the boycott to the feelings about the taxes: *"So what do you think it means that they would make all this trouble for themselves and give up things they liked?"*

⑦ At the seventh stop, the teacher reread several sentences for emphasis: "Each of the colonies sent delegates to the meeting. Some of the most important leaders of the colonies were there." Her Query was *"What is going on?"* And if students didn't seem to grasp the significance of the event, she was prepared to follow up with *"What do you think the author is trying to tell us about this meeting?"*

⑧ At the eighth stop, she wanted to connect "the pledge" to the boycott discussed in the previous paragraph, so her Query was *"How does this connect to what the author told us before?"* Additionally, the Query *"What do you think it means that the delegates are making a pledge about the boycott?"* could point to the strength of feeling and unified action in the colonies.

⑨ At the ninth stop, the teacher wanted to make sure the students understood the significance of the congress with *"Now, what has the author told us about this Stamp Act Congress?"*

⑩ At the tenth stop, as a way of foreshadowing the trouble to come, the teacher asked, *"What's the author saying about how Britain is dealing with all this?"*

⑪ At the eleventh stop, to prompt students again to note that the text was signaling trouble brewing, the teacher asked, *"What's the author trying to tell us here in this last sentence?"* And she was prepared to probe further by asking, *"So, what do you think that means?"*

Planning as an Integrated Process

We have presented planning by discussing three goals: identifying major understandings and anticipating problems students may have as they try to grasp them; segmenting text based on these understandings and potential problems; and designing Queries to help students build meaning from the text. However, we want to emphasize that planning for a QtA lesson is not a rigid three-step process. These three goals are really interwoven. And all of them are in service of the ultimate goal of helping students build meaning from text. Achieving that goal involves making several kinds of decisions. Thus, in our next example, we will present the planning process in a more integrated way. The planning for reading "The Enchanted Tapestry" starts with the teacher's goals (that is, what she wanted her students to understand in the course of reading), shows the text segments, provides the teacher's thinking about the content of each segment, and indicates the Queries.

"The Enchanted Tapestry"

This Chinese folktale is about a widow with three sons who makes her living by weaving and selling tapestries. When her most recent tapestry, which represents the widow's life, is finished, her two greedy sons want her to sell it; her kindhearted son wants her to keep it. The tapestry vanishes. Eventually, the kindhearted son retrieves the tapestry, and with the help of a fairy's magic, the widow, her son, and the fairy become part of the tapestry and live happily ever after.

We determined that the major understanding for this story is the way certain elements, in particular the sons' differing characters and the mother's special tapestry, evolve and intertwine to create an effective story. Toward the goal of having students construct this understanding, we thought they should consider the sons' attitudes and how those attitudes are reflected in the ways each son handles situations presented by the plot. We also thought they should talk about the tapestry and what it becomes over the course of the story. The text and our considerations about all these aspects follow.

THE ENCHANTED TAPESTRY

A long time ago a widow lived in a small house near a forest in China. Like her grandmother and mother, she made her living by weaving tapestry. Her skillful fingers turned silk yarns of every color into flowers, trees, birds, animals, even people—each was a work of art. Her tapestries always brought the highest prices, and she was able to raise her three sons—Li Mo, Li Tu, and Li Ju—on the gold people paid for her handiwork.

One day she began to weave a picture of a fine house with lovely flower gardens, trees, and peaceful green fields surrounding it. The image caught her fancy. She worked on it day after day, month after month. She added a footbridge arching gracefully over a gentle stream and rich green meadows that swept up toward towering mountains.

Her eldest son, Li Mo, and her middle son, Li Tu, tried to make her stop working on the tapestry.

But the old woman stayed at her loom, working by sunlight and candlelight. When tears came to her eyes from strain, she wove them into a fishpond brimming with sleek goldfish; when she pricked her finger with a splinter, she wove the drops of blood into brilliant red flowers and a glowing sun like a huge lantern above the mountains.

Commentary

Although nothing complex was introduced in this first paragraph, it may be a good idea to stop here. The author has introduced a number of characters and has given information that will be important to the story later on, the notion that the mother's tapestries are priceless and a source of income for the family. A simple Query such as **"So, what has the author told us so far?"** should encourage students to discuss the gist of the paragraph.

Two important points have been brought up in these two paragraphs. The first is that this tapestry is a highly unusual and special one, and the second is that the mother's working on it is causing a problem, as shown in the reaction of two of the sons. The author hasn't explicitly stated that the problem is that it has prevented her from selling her work and making money for the family, but this is implied by the action of the two sons. A Query such as **"What's the author told us about this latest tapestry?"** may encourage students to address the point. A Follow-Up Query such as **"What do you think it means that two of her sons wanted her to stop working on the tapestry?"** should provide an important clue to their characters and to the situation being created by the mother's attention to this tapestry. If students don't understand that the family now has no income, go on, as that idea becomes clearer in the next section.

Although this is a short paragraph, this is a good place to stop because we have learned more about the family's situation now that the mother is absorbed by the new tapestry. This section also sets up the contrast between the attitudes of the older sons and the youngest son, which is a key element in the plot. A Query such as *"What is the author telling us about what's happening with this family?"* should help students understand that Li Ju is now supporting the family and what this shows about his attitude in contrast to that of his brothers. A Query such as *"Given what the author has already told us about Li Tu and Li Mo, how does this information connect?"* should encourage the students to see that the brothers don't really want to work and are content to live off the mother and the hardworking youngest brother.

We learn some important information from the dialogue between the mother and Li Ju. We learn that the tapestry is indeed the mother's dream, and we also learn more about the relationship between Li Ju and his mother. A Query such as *"Hmm, we've already talked about how dedicated the mother is to this tapestry. Now what else does the author let us know about how important this tapestry is?"* should encourage the students to talk about the tapestry as the mother's dream and that she even placed herself in it. This could lead to a Follow-Up Query that addresses the idea that Li Ju was the only son placed in the tapestry with his mother and what that may say about their relationship. A Query such as *"What do you think about the mother also placing Li Ju in the tapestry?"* should address the issue.

Finally the youngest son, Li Ju, became a woodcutter, earning just enough to buy rice for them all. His brothers complained that he made barely enough to keep them alive and urged him to work harder.

After more than a year the old woman said, "I am nearly finished. A few more days will complete my tapestry."

"Mother, it's beautiful," said Li Ju, gazing at the grand house with white walls, blue-tile roof, and huge front doors of red. It stood in a garden of rainbow-colored flowers.

The next morning at sunrise, she wove the likeness of herself, standing at the door of the house, into the tapestry scene.

Li Ju, watching, said, "Mother, this tapestry is your dream, isn't it?" She nodded.

"You must never sell it," her youngest son told her.

She smiled as she silently wove into the tapestry the image of Li Ju standing at her side.

Suddenly Li Mo bustled into the room and cried, "Aren't you done yet? Hurry and finish so we can sell this. Let us turn this into good food and fine clothes right away." But his mother would not let him touch it.

Then she said, "This tapestry is a picture of everything I hold dear in my dreams and in my life. All my children should be in it, but I haven't had time to put you there."

"What does it matter," asked Li Mo. "We're hungry." "And ashamed of our patched clothes," added Li Tu. "We only want the gold this will bring," they said.

Suddenly a gusty wind blew in through the western window, ripped that tapestry from its frame, and whirled it away out the eastern window. They all pursued it, but it swirled away into the distance and vanished.

The old woman fainted. When she had recovered enough to speak, the widow called her eldest son to her bedside and said, "Li Mo, go to the East and find my tapestry, or I will die."

Grumbling, Li Mo set out and traveled east. After a month he came to a mountain pass, where he found a stone hut with a stone horse standing in front of it. A white-haired woman leaned out of the hut's single window and asked, "Where are you going, young man?"

The plot develops here with elaboration on the significance of the tapestry—"everything I hold dear"—and the continuing development of the contrary nature of the two older sons. A Query such as *"What picture is the author giving us here?"* may encourage students to consider how these elements develop. If this Query does not tap information about the sons' attitudes, a Follow-Up Query such as *"How does the information here about her older sons fit in with what the author already told us?"* may encourage students to discuss the sons' greedy nature.

The important point here is that the tapestry has vanished, and unless it is returned the mother will die. This reinforces the notion that the tapestry represents the mother's life. The line "Li Mo, go to the East and find my tapestry, or I will die," may be reread, and followed by the Query *"So, what does the author mean by that?"*

A stop here could focus on what the author's choice of words reveals by rereading the first line "Grumbling, Li Mo set out and traveled east." A Query such as *"So the author tells us that Li Mo is grumbling as he leaves. What does that say about Li Mo?"* may encourage students to talk about how this description fits in with what the author has already told us about Li Mo's attitude. If it doesn't, however, a Follow-Up Query such as *"And how does the author's description of grumbling connect with what we already know about Li Mo?"* may encourage students to extend ideas about Li Mo's attitude, because he's even complaining about having to do something to save his mother's life.

It is likely that most of the students will jump in with something like "He's not going to do all that." They recognize that given the description of the tasks Li Mo must undertake, combined with his attitude, there is little chance he will attempt to go on the journey. If they don't initiate any comments, you may want to encourage them to talk about the idea by asking, **"So, how do you think this journey sounds to Li Mo?"**

Li Mo told her what happened.

"That tapestry was taken by the fairies of Sun Mountain in the East," said the old woman, who was really a powerful sorceress. "They love beautiful things, but they will return it, if you ask."

"However, it is very difficult to get there. First you have to cut your finger and place ten drops of blood on my stone horse's flank so he can move. Then you must ride him through the flame mountains. His magic will protect you most of the time, except when you go through the fire. There you must not make a sound. If you utter a cry or show any fear, you will be burned to ashes.

Then you must cross a sea of freezing waves filled with jagged ice and lashed by terrible winds. My horse will take you safely much of the way. But if you complain once, or even shiver, you will turn to ice and sink to the bottom of the sea. Beyond its farthest shore, you will find Sun Mountain and your mother's tapestry."

A stop and brief Query **"Hmm, blood, fire, and ice, what do you think he's thinking?"** would reinforce awareness of his greedy nature.

Li Mo hesitated, thinking of blood and fire and ice.

The sorceress laughed and said, "If this frightens you, take this gold instead." And she held out to him a bag filled with gold coins.

Li Mo grabbed it eagerly, then ran away to the city to spend it on himself.

A brief pause here would give students a chance to comment on the confirmation of their predictions. It's likely that they will say something about being right.

The old widow grew even more sickly. When Li Mo didn't come back, she said to her middle son, "Li Tu, bring back my tapestry or I will certainly die."

With much complaining, Li Tu set out along the eastern road. After a month's journey he met the sorceress in the stone hut at the mountain pass.

A stop here could briefly touch on the author's description of Li Tu's desire to search for the tapestry by rereading the line, "With much complaining, Li Tu set out along the eastern road" and asking, **"So, what does the author tell us about Li Tu's attitude toward the journey?"**

But when she told him the things he would have to do to get back the tapestry, he, too, took the gold she offered and hurried off to the city to spend it on himself.

This is another place where the students are likely to make comments such as "I knew he'd do that" or "That's mean. I'd never do that to my mother." If, however, students don't initiate such comments, the Query **"So, what do you think of that?"** should encourage them to talk about Li Tu's attitude.

The old mother grew thin as a dried reed. Finally her youngest son, Li Ju, came to her and said, "Let me go and search for the tapestry."

Li Ju was so eager to save his mother's life that it took him only half a month to reach the hut with the stone horse in front.

The sorceress told him what he had to do, then offered Li Ju her gold. But he answered, "No, I must fetch my mother's tapestry, or she will die."

Everything in these three short paragraphs supports what we have already learned about the youngest son, that he loves his mother and would go to any length to save her. A Query such as **"Based on what we already learned about Li Ju, how does this new information connect?"** may encourage students to talk about the relationship Li Ju has with his mother.

The main point here is the dedication the son has to his mother. He is willing to endure such a difficult journey to save her life. A Query such as **"So, what picture has the author created for us?"** should encourage the students to talk about how awful the journey is and what it says about Li Ju's dedication to his mother.

The focus here might be on the point that although the journey was extremely difficult, it appears that it was worth it since Li Ju will be given the tapestry in the morning. A Query such as **"So, what's happened now?"** should allow the point to be made.

So he followed the old woman's instructions and ten drops of blood fell on the stone horse. It came to life with a whinny, shook out its silky mane, and stamped its hooves, eager to begin their journey. Li Ju leaped on its back, grasping its mane, and they galloped away to the East.

Soon they came to the flaming mountains and the icy sea. Though the heat of the mountains blistered Li Ju's face, he made no sound and let himself show no fear. The horse leaped from ice floe to ice floe across the sea, while waves, lashed by freezing winds to a fury, threatened to drown them. But Li Ju did not allow himself the tiniest shiver. And so they passed through in safety.

On the farthest shore, they came to Sun Mountain. Halfway up was a palace built of gold. Beautiful fairies dressed in rainbow silks gathered on the broad steps, staring in wonder at the human who had risked such dangers to reach them.

The most beautiful one of all, dressed in red, came down to meet Li Ju. She greeted him, then introduced him to her sisters.

When he told them why he had come, the one in red said, "We are bound to return the tapestry to you. But you cannot cross to mortal lands at night. Rest, and I will bring you the tapestry in the morning."

But the red-robed fairy had fallen in love with the young man. While her sisters slept, she hung a huge, glowing pearl on a rafter and spent the night weaving a picture of herself and part of her magic into the wonderful tapestry.

The next morning Li Ju took the carefully folded tapestry. Then he galloped back across the icy sea and through the flaming mountains. Soon he returned in safety to the stone hut beside the mountain pass.

"Hurry, young man," said the old woman, "your mother is dying."

Li Ju ran night and day to where his mother lay wasting away.

"Mother! Mother!" he cried, bursting into her room, "I've brought your tapestry back!"

He pinned it to the wall for her to see; eagerly she raised herself up out of her bed, already feeling her health returning.

A ray of morning sunlight suddenly struck the tapestry through the eastern window. The cloth began to grow and grow, until it covered the whole wall. It grew even more, and soon it became a landscape into which mother and son could step.

The focus here could be to discuss why the red-robed fairy spent the night weaving herself into the tapestry. A simple Query such as **"What do you think it means that the fairy wove herself into the tapestry?"** should encourage the students to talk about her love for Li Ju and how by weaving herself into the tapestry she can become a part of his life.

The focus here is again on the idea that the tapestry does represent the mother's life, and now that it has been returned, her health is beginning to improve. A Query such as **"The mother's health began to improve the minute the tapestry was pinned to the wall. What do you make of that?"** should encourage the students to talk about the connection between the tapestry and the mother.

This paragraph has the potential to confuse the students. The tapestry that represented the lives of the mother and son has now become their lives, literally. It may be helpful to reread the last line, "It grew even more, and soon it became a landscape into which mother and son could step," and ask, **"So, what do you think the author is talking about here?"**

The ending ties everything together nicely. The mother and Li Ju get to be together, and the two greedy sons will no longer be a part of their lives. The fairy who had placed herself into the tapestry is now married to Li Ju. And they will all live happily ever after in the wonderful world that had been created for them by the mother's tapestry. A simple Query such as **"So, how does the ending connect with the rest of the story?"** should bring out those major points. If it doesn't come up, the fairy's role in the magical outcome might be realized with a Query such as **"Now, how did this magnificent house and all that come about?"** And, if students respond by saying only "the tapestry," a Follow-Up Query such as **"Her tapestry, yes, but how did it get to be real?"** may encourage them to talk about the role of the fairy's magic. If not, ask students to find that part in the text that described what the fairy did with the tapestry. Have them note that she wove "part of her magic" into the tapestry along with a picture of herself.

Together they walked toward the magnificent house with white walls, blue-tile roof, and proud red doors that lay before them. They crossed a lovely footbridge over a stream filled with shining water; they paused to exclaim over a fishpond filled with sleek goldfish.

And, waiting at the front door, her dress as red as the doors themselves and the great red sun overhead, was the beautiful fairy.

As it happened, Li Ju married the beautiful fairy, and the three of them—mother, son, wife—lived very happily together.

Ending Notes

The following points recap our discussion about planning:

- There are three basic goals in planning a QtA text-based lesson, whether it's for expository or narrative text. They are: identify the major understandings; to segment the text, so as to "chunk" information needed to build understandings; and develop Queries that promote the development of those understandings.

- Identifying major understandings means deciding what you want students to take from the text and anticipating potential obstacles in the text that may impede comprehension.

- Segmenting the text is the process of deciding where you will stop and initiate discussion. These decisions are driven by the content—where key ideas occur or possible confusions or complications arise.

- Developing Queries means deciding how to prompt students' thinking about ideas in the text to initiate discussion.

- Segmenting texts and developing Queries serve as mechanisms that help teachers help students in building meaning of the major understandings.

Frequently Asked Questions

1. What do I use as a guide for segmenting texts?

Once you have made decisions about the most important text ideas that you want students to understand, you segment the text accordingly. That is, stop reading and pose Queries at points where there's a key idea or ideas to be grappled with. Be sure to provide enough content to allow building ideas, but not so much that students are overwhelmed and have difficulty knowing where to begin.

Try not to focus on distracting details and avoid using paragraph or page ends as markers for segmenting. Sometimes a single sentence should be the focus of discussion, sometimes several paragraphs.

2. Should I be concerned that I'm covering less text material in a lesson than I did in previous years?

A natural consequence of dealing with ideas deeply is that it takes time. Not all ideas have to be dealt with deeply. Some material can and should be skimmed, briefly paraphrased, or even skipped over altogether. You can compensate by carefully planning and segmenting so that only important ideas get more time.

3. Why am I having trouble getting through the amount of material I planned for a lesson?

It may be hard to know how much will be covered in a QtA discussion because it is hard to anticipate exactly what is going to happen and how long it will take to see some ideas through. But be on guard that discussion doesn't get bogged down.

For example, watch for students' tendency to repeat and elaborate upon ideas that have already been sufficiently dealt with, as well as their tendency to go off on tangents.

Teachers are often reluctant to cut off student participation. But it's important to balance participation with keeping discussion focused.

4. How do I handle sections of text that aren't that important to what I want students to understand?

Not all portions of text are equal. Sometimes one sentence can be more important than an entire paragraph. Our recommendation is that you skip those portions of text that are less important and either return to them later, or eliminate discussion about them altogether. Those decisions are entirely yours.

5. As a class, how is the text read? Is it always read aloud? Does the teacher always read aloud?

Because we want to talk about the text—and make the text and the talk public— the text is read aloud, generally speaking. Both teachers and students should take roles as readers.

But students should be asked to read only if they want to read. When a complicated or key section is being considered, it is a good idea to call on a strong reader or read the text yourself. When students who are weak readers want to read, it is best to find short portions to assign to them.

On occasion you can assign a short segment for silent reading. A major problem with silent reading is that students have different reading rates. Therefore, it is important that only a brief section be read silently and that discussion follow immediately. The issue is that the group is developing meaning by working through a text together, and different reading rates could interfere with this collaborative process.

6. How do I approach teaching a novel?

A good approach with a novel is to read the opening chapter or section in Questioning the Author fashion. Some subsequent portions can then be assigned for independent reading. Have students mark parts of the text that they have difficulty with or parts that they think merit discussion. Discussion can then proceed based on students' suggestions. Additionally, a teacher's planning for a novel includes identifying parts that call for QtA discussion during the initial reading. Such parts may contain critical plot turns, subtle character development, and the like.

CHAPTER 4

Discussion

JOSEPH: First we agree, then we disagree.

NADA: Yeah, I'm always like, "Darleen, you hear what I'm saying?"

JOSEPH: Then we try to convince each other, and I end up disagreeing with myself!

DALLAS: We go back and forth with each other so much you'd think we were a bunch of lawyers.

This is how several fourth graders responded when we asked them what typically happened in a QtA discussion. We especially like the "bunch of lawyers" comment, and not just because it's amusing. We like that it shows that with QtA, students learn the skill of interrogating a text together and building a case for one another's ideas about the text. With these students' comments, you can just imagine the children leaning forward, participating in the discussion with gusto. Energy, engagement—that's just what ought to characterize reading lessons.

In this chapter, we look at the discussion aspect of Questioning the Author. As we have with the chapters on Queries and planning, we will contrast QtA discussions and more-traditional classroom discussions. Then, we will describe features of QtA discussion and provide examples of the specific ways teachers have promoted those features.

During a QtA discussion, students do the work of building meaning as they first encounter ideas in a text. One way to conceptualize a QtA discussion is to imagine that when students engage in reading and talking about a text, they enter a kind of maze. The ideas in a text make up the maze, and the goal is to reach points of understanding. To do so, students must follow any unexpected twists and turns the text-maze presents, recognize dead ends, and use strategic maneuvers to get through. The QtA teacher has already been through the maze, so he or she knows what students are facing. However, the teacher's job is not to show students the path through the maze, but rather to assist them as they discover their own way through. After all, in most mazes, there is more than one pathway to the destination. QtA helps students find their way through a text, but it does not take away their responsibility for figuring out how to do it.

It almost goes without saying that the effectiveness of a QtA discussion depends on the quality of the interplay between the teacher and the students. The teacher's role is to help students think about the text and develop ideas—she is not there merely to manage conversation or explain ideas. The students' role is to collaborate with the teacher and with one another to build ideas about text during reading—rather than present ideas that have been largely spoon-fed to them by the teacher after reading.

Let us elaborate. In a QtA discussion, the teacher participates as a *co-collaborator* in building meaning. To do so, as we noted earlier, the teacher attempts to develop a sense of a text similar to a young reader's. That means that the teacher spends time closely reading and considering which ideas in a text are most important for students to construct. This up-front work gives the teacher a sense of where in the presentation "maze" students may most likely need some encouragement or other input. During a QtA discussion, the teacher simultaneously keeps watch over two perspectives of the maze: the student's (a ground-level view) and their own perspective (a bird's-eye view). As such, the teacher has to keep in mind that, to students, a text may at first seem confusing, dense, and ambiguous. At the same time, the teacher has to keep in mind the major understandings she wants her students to construct and the actions she can take to help students get there. During the course of a QtA discussion, the teacher strives to facilitate the kind of thinking needed to build understanding of ideas. To facilitate thinking, the teacher often thinks aloud her thoughts as she struggles to get past an impervious section of text. In doing so, the teacher invites students right into the maze. She poses Queries that prompt students to think, question, formulate ideas, and construct meaning for themselves.

Comparing Traditional and QtA Discussions

Let's see how QtA discussions differ from more-traditional classroom discussions. Figure 4.1 compares features of traditional and QtA discussions.

Students' role Perhaps one of the most typical patterns of traditional classroom discussions is that students tend to report information from a text, information they have already more or less figured out on their own. Because students are engaged in retrieval of acquired facts and opinions, participation may be flat. Although students may argue, and debate a peer's conclusion, how those conclusions were reached or how meaning was developed from the author's presentation of information in the text is rarely the focus or purpose of a traditional discussion. In contrast, students in a QtA discussion are expected and encouraged to develop, connect, and especially explain ideas from a text, not just report information. Students are engaged in shared investigation of meaning, not just shared retrieval of information and beliefs, so participation tends to be active.

Teacher's role Teachers' actions in the two kinds of discussions differ as well. In traditional discussions, teachers tend to collect student contributions, one after another, and give each of them equal attention. In contrast, a QtA teacher deliberately attempts to differentiate among student contributions, attending to and using those responses that will help develop ideas and build an understanding. Furthermore, teachers in traditional classroom discussions tend to dominate the thinking while a QtA teacher uses Queries that entice students to participate, and elaborate on ideas, so that they are the predominant voice.

In the next section, we present what we refer to as Discussion Moves and demonstrate how these moves can help a teacher maintain the flexibility and improvisational decision-making QtA requires. To get a better ideas of what Discussion Moves do and how they work, we'll look at some lesson transcripts.

FIGURE 4.1	Comparison of Traditional and Questioning the Author Discussions

Traditional Discussions	Questioning the Author Discussions
STUDENTS	**STUDENTS**
• present ideas they have already built from a text	• build ideas as they are encountered in a text
• engage in retrieval of acquired facts and opinions; participation tends to be flat	• engage in shared investigation of meaning; participation tends to be active
• report information from a text, which may reveal little about their comprehension	• develop and connect ideas from a text to arrive at a comprehensive understanding
• present responses in isolated chunks	• present responses that build on one another's ideas
TEACHERS	**TEACHERS**
• treat various students' contributions equally; the goal seems to be to collect and validate all contributions with little apparent focus	• differentiate among student contributions; the goal is to focus contributions toward building an understanding of text ideas
• dominate the thinking; they do most of the work of developing ideas and signal students to merely react to the ideas they have constructed	• ignite and respond to students' contributions strategically; they advance students' thinking and signal students to take ideas further

Discussion Moves

Discussion Moves are actions that teachers take to help orchestrate students' participation and the development of ideas. We have identified six QtA Discussion Moves: marking, turning-back, revoicing, recapping, modeling, and annotating. The moves are neither sequential nor prescriptive. Rather, they are ways that we have seen QtA teachers keep discussion focused and productive. Let's look at each move in turn.

Marking

Teachers use **marking** by responding to student comments in a way that draws attention to certain ideas. By marking, a teacher signals to students that an idea is of particular importance to the discussion. Below, student comments are marked during discussion of the book *Ben and Me* (Lawson, 1939), told by Amos, a mouse that went up in Ben Franklin's kite.

In the story, Amos describes how he and Ben became fast friends and that Ben had built a kite that allowed Amos to go up and spend time aloft, which he reveled in. However, he then discovered that this all was a deceit, as he describes it, because Ben was really trying to capture electricity. Amos describes how the discovery nearly destroyed their friendship.

At the point at which we pick up the class's discussion, the students were trying to figure out a passage about why the friendship between Ben and the mouse had broken up. Jamie, a student, commented, "It says *deceit*. Umm, that's lying, so it means a lie broke up their friendship." The teacher marked the student's worthy idea by paraphrasing it and adding strategic intonation, saying, "Oh, that's interesting. Jamie said that there was some *lying* going on and that caused a rift in their friendship." By marking the student's comment in this way the teacher attempted to underscore the connections between the friendship breaking up and lying.

Teachers also mark an idea by explicitly acknowledging the importance of a student's comment. For example, later in the discussion of *Ben and Me*, a student, Charlene, commented that Amos, the mouse, was willing to take a chance and go up in the kite. The teacher marked this comment explicitly, "I want to focus on something Charlene said because it's important. She said Amos was willing to take a chance."

Turning-Back

The **turning-back** Discussion Move is associated with two kinds of actions. First, turning-back refers to turning responsibility back to students for figuring out ideas. Second, turning-back also refers to turning students' attention back to the text to clarify or focus their thinking. Let's consider examples of turning-back to text first.

Turning-back to text is a key move that has a number of variations, all aimed at having students take account of the text and use it as their focus in building meaning. The simplest turning-back to text move is used when a student has clearly misread or misinterpreted something in the text and needs to be redirected toward something stated in the text. When this occurs, the QtA teacher simply asks, "Is that what the author said?" The student checks the text and more often than not makes a self-correction. This scenario seems far preferable to telling a student he or she has given the "wrong answer."
It frames the situation as a temporary misstep rather than an outright error, and it is a quick way to clear up confusion.

A turning-back to text move is also called upon when students debate an issue that could be easily clarified by what the author has explicitly presented. In such situations, discussion seems to have moved away from the text. Although a goal in discussions is to have students interact with one another, sometimes students get so caught up in responding to one another that they almost seem to forget that the text is there. For example, in the discussion about *Ben and Me* mentioned earlier, students were commenting that Amos liked being up in the kite. They had just read a segment describing the construction of the kite. It mentioned that a car was added atop the kite. The segment ended, "Enabled to ascend and descend at will, I spent many happy hours at this thrilling sport." But this last part seemed forgotten as students discussed the mouse's feelings with comments such as "I don't think he liked it" and "It doesn't say he was happy but you can figure it out 'cause if there was a car it would be fun." After several more comments that did not consider the text, the teacher intervened, asking, "Does the author tell us if he is happy?" A student checked the text and read: "I spent many happy hours at this thrilling sport." The class was then able to agree that Amos was, indeed, happy flying in the kite.

A turning-back to text move for rereading a portion of the text is called for when students are having difficulty grasping a major idea in a text segment.

Rereading provides the students with another chance to consider the text and reflect on the ideas. We cannot emphasize enough that students often need a second take. Adults, as mature readers, tend to forget that the material we give young students to read is unfamiliar to them, and it may take more than one pass for it to sink in. Here we return to the *Ben and Me* discussion at a point just before Jamie made her comment, described in the section on marking, about the rift in the friendship between Ben and Amos. The text describing this situation is difficult, and students were struggling with it. The text reads:

> **This question of the nature of lightning so preyed upon his mind, that he was finally driven to an act of deceit that caused the first and only rift in our long friendship. I feel sure that brooding on this subject must have seriously affected his mind, for this is the only way in which I can excuse his treacherous conduct.**

After the teacher asked what was going on here, students began making comments such as "He's trying to tell us why he didn't talk about electricity," "He's trying to find out what electricity can do," and "How he feels after he discovers electricity." The teacher stepped in and said, "Let me reread these two sentences to you." She reread and led the discussion back on track with her Query, "What's the author telling us about Ben and Amos?"

The turning-back to text move helps prevent students from going off on tangents and introducing irrelevant information into a discussion. When students are reminded to take account of the author's words and ideas, they can refocus their attention on the more important ideas, and the discussion returns to more-productive meaning building.

Now let's consider the other form of the turning-back move—**turning-back to students**. This form also has several variations, all of which aim to support students' *building on* what they say in service of developing a coherent representation of the text. The examples we will use here are from a fourth-grade discussion of "The Emperor and the Kite," a story in which the Emperor's smallest daughter becomes a witness to his kidnapping, and despite her small size, eventually rescues him (Yolen, 1967).

The most basic turning-back move is used when a student's contribution does not fully respond to the issue at hand—a very frequent occurrence, as Queries ask students to share in-process thinking. So teachers simply turn back to the students to fill out the information provided. For example, when the fourth graders read the beginning of "The Emperor and the Kite," the daughter, Djeow Seow, is described as "tiny, not thought of much—when she was thought of at all." In response to the teacher's Query "What's the author talking about?," Ricky responded, "The girl, she was not thought of much." The teacher then turned back with the following: "What does that mean, 'She was not thought of much?'"

This basic turning-back move is very productive. It helps teachers avoid simply accepting spare responses and then filling in the important information themselves. The teacher fill-in is a kind of occupational hazard. We do it almost reflexively, because, after all, we are there to teach. It is so easy to lose sight of the fact that the best way to teach is to prompt students to do the thinking on their own. And most of the time, teachers find that students can, indeed, do the thinking. For example, in the case under discussion here, another student went on to describe the Emperor's daughter as "insignificant to other people."

Turning-back to students can also prompt them to make crucial connections. For example, after the class read the segment in the story in which evildoers kidnap the Emperor but fail to notice his tiny daughter, the teacher prompted the students to notice that the girl's supposed flaw is now serving her well. He asked, "How does what happened here connect to what we know about Djeow Seow?" And indeed, a student was able to make the connection, responding: "I think that it was a good thing now, her tininess. If it was her brothers or sisters, they would have got caught, and now I think she can help the Emperor." Turning-back for connections appears to encourage students to get involved in reasoning about ideas that were previously presented in the text.

Similarly, turning-back can be used to encourage students to connect their ideas with the ideas of other students. Such an example occurred in the discussion of "The Emperor and the Kite." When Djeow Seow's kite flying is introduced in the story, the kite is talked about as "mounting to the high heavens." A student, Deanna, had commented that this was how the girl was big—her kite reached to the sky, and then maybe she felt important. As the story developed and the students realized that Djeow Seow was going to try to rescue her father, a student said she thought the girl would use her kite to reach the tower where the Emperor was being held. The teacher then asked, "How does that connect to what Deanna said earlier—what was that about her kite?"

The goal of using turning-back is always to turn the responsibility for grappling with text ideas back to students and to help teachers avoid taking over the thinking. Whether the teacher turns back to students for elaboration or to text for students to take better account of what an author has said, the move promotes students' taking responsibility for figuring out ideas and resolving issues.

Revoicing

Another Discussion Move is something we call **revoicing**. By revoicing, we mean interpreting what students are struggling to express and rephrasing the ideas so that they can become part of the discussion. Revoicing is a kind of "in other words" mechanism that helps students to express their own ideas and distill from their comments the most important information or implicit ideas. Revoicing also raises the level of language, giving more-articulate expression to students' ideas. It is also supportive of students—revoicing their thoughts gives them confidence and motivates them.

Let's consider an example from a discussion in which a student was trying to describe reasons behind workers' early efforts to organize for better working conditions in factories. The student commented, "Work was really dirty and stuff in the factories, and so people wanted to pass laws for health and safety and no children." The teacher recognized that the student had the key ideas, but the comment was not phrased very clearly. So the teacher revoiced the comment: "So, you're pointing out that the working conditions could be unsafe or unhealthy, and that people wanted laws made so that conditions were better, and also that they didn't want children working in the factories." This kind of revoicing clarifies the essence of an idea and, as such, allows a student's unwieldy expressions to become part of the discussion. When student comments are made clearer and more focused through revoicing, other students can more easily respond to and build on them.

The revoicing move has a similar function to marking. In both cases the thinking work has already been done by students, and the moves are used to emphasize and set up ideas so they can become a part of a productive discussion.

Recapping

Recapping is a Discussion Move that is useful when students have come to a place in their construction of ideas that seems to suggest they get it. They've grasped the essential meaning and are ready to move on in the text. Recapping allows teachers to summarize major ideas that students have developed so far. For example, a comment such as the following signals to students that they have accomplished something important and it reinforces the understanding they have built:

> So now we know that Washington gave the French leader's message
> to the governor that they didn't plan to leave Pennsylvania. And then
> together we figured out that Washington counted the canoes at the
> fort and made the drawing so he could give the governor information
> about plans the French had and maybe how strong their forces were.
> Good work, class!

Recapping also signals students that it is time to move on to a new or different point in the text and serves to remind them of where they left off. For example, a comment such as the following lets students know that the meaning they have built so far is part of a bigger picture that will only come into focus as they continue reading:

> Now that we've figured out that Granny is trying to tell Dewey that
> she wants to get off the boat, let's see what he's going to do about it.

Recapping does not have to be the sole responsibility of the teacher. We have found that inviting students to recap is an effective way of engaging them in the task of summarizing what has been built so far. In this way, students gain experience in capturing the most important ideas. Recapping encourages a mental organization of the ideas students have been wrestling with and signals that the efforts have indeed produced a coherent understanding.

In addition, there is another pair of Discussion Moves in which the teacher brings himself into the interaction more directly than with the previous moves. The two moves, modeling and annotating, place the teacher at the center. They are usually used when a teacher wants to take her students further than they may be able to go on their own. They should not be used too liberally; students should be at the center of the wrestling and mulling of text ideas, even if they do sometimes struggle.

Modeling

Various forms of **modeling** of cognitive tasks have been around for a long time. The activity of thinking is invisible, and modeling is a way to "make public" some of the processes in which experts or mature thinkers engage. For example, in an algebra class, many of us have heard teachers say something like "Okay, I looked at each side of the equal sign and saw that I could get rid of this x by subtracting it from both sides, so that is what I will do next."

There have been many recommendations to extend modeling to other content domains, including reading (see, for example, Duffy, Roehler, & Hermann, 1988). But what is modeling in reading? When teachers model some of the things they do as they read, they are trying to show students how their minds are actively interacting with the ideas in the text.

Although there are many examples of modeling that work well, there are also some tendencies that consistently reduce the effectiveness of modeling as a teaching strategy. For example, contrived attempts at predicting an obvious event, such as "I think the wolf is going to blow the third little pig's house down," do little to reveal what is involved in working with subtle ideas to make a less than obvious prediction. This example points to a common problem with modeling that we have seen, which is that what gets modeled tends to be the obvious. It also highlights the contrived nature of some kinds of modeling.

In contrast, effective modeling can help students see things in texts they may not have noticed and allows students to observe or overhear how an expert thinks through a complicated idea. Which parts or ideas in a text that a teacher chooses to model is determined by the text ideas the teacher thinks students may need help with, or according to her spontaneous reactions to text. Additionally, a teacher can model what she had on her mind about an issue under discussion as a way to make a point that students seem unable to reach. So modeling should be as brief and as natural in character as possible.

Below, we provide some examples of how teachers have used the modeling move. The examples represent general categories of what teachers chose to model. The first three show how modeling can be used to communicate a teacher's affective responses to text. The remaining examples present instances of teachers' modeling their process of trying to build an understanding of a confusing portion of text.

The following example comes from a fifth-grade discussion of Kate DiCamillo's *Because of Winn Dixie* (2001), a novel that tells the story of ten-year-old Opal, who has just moved to a new town and feels a bit lost. She adopts a dog she finds at the grocery store and together they make friends with an interesting variety of characters in the town. The teacher introduced it as one of her favorite books, and after the class had read the first page, she said,

> I love how she says she went to the store for macaroni and cheese, rice, and tomatoes and came back with a dog! As soon as I read that, I knew I'd like this book.

The next example shows how a teacher brought attention to some exquisitely presented material toward encouraging appreciation of what the author did and how it affected her as a reader. In the course of a ninth-grade class discussion of the beginning of Dickens's *Great Expectations*, in which the escaped convict is described, the teacher said:

> What a frightening man! Mmm, every time I read Dickens I find myself in awe of the effect his use of language has on me. Those sentence fragments, how effective: A man soaked in water, and smothered in mud, and lamed by stones, and cut by flints, and stung by nettles, and torn by briars, who limped and shivered and glared and growled. . . .

The teacher's repetition of text phrases emphasized their cumulative effect on her as a reader. It also provided an opportunity for students to see how that effect was created.

These examples show how teachers can expose their own reactions to what an author has written. Neither of the examples is particularly long or pedantic; rather, they seem to be natural attempts to share a response to the text.

Another way that modeling can be used effectively is to demonstrate how one may work through confusing portions of text. Calling attention to text that is not clear is also an opportunity to reinforce QtA's emphasis on the fallible author.

The following example comes from a fifth-grade discussion of a brief narrative in their social studies book in which Native American children have run away from school and the principal has gone after them. The students seem to think the boys are in a lot of trouble, but the teacher notices that the principal is expressing sympathy for them. So she shares her thoughts, saying,

> What I was thinking as we read that is it sounded as if the principal was making excuses for the boys. I mean, he's telling the teacher that "Yeah, they're just used to open spaces that they've heard the howl of coyotes at night." So it sounded like even though the principal

knew he had to punish these two boys, he really couldn't blame them too much.

It has been our experience that when modeling is briefly folded into ongoing discussions over time, it is a useful way for students to encounter a range of expert reading behaviors. Moreover, modeling in a QtA discussion can reinforce the teacher's role as a collaborator in constructing meaning.

Annotating

The Discussion Move we call **annotating** comes in handy when a teacher needs to provide information to fill in gaps during a discussion. On occasion, authors simply do not provide enough information for students to be able to construct meaning from the text alone. There are gaps in information, and in lines of reasoning, and assumptions about background knowledge that young readers don't have. To deal with such problems, teachers annotate the text.

Let's look at an example from a class of fourth-grade students who were studying the drafting of the U.S. Constitution. The text provided little information about the new Constitution, saying simply, "The Constitution was finally finished. Now it was up to the states to ratify, or approve, it. Ratify means approve. If nine states ratified the Constitution, it would become law" (Macmillan/McGraw-Hill, 1997). So the teacher annotated by adding information to the discussion that was important if students were to construct a deeper understanding of what made this new constitutional law so important:

> What happened in this new Constitution? This is not all in the book, but I want you to understand what actually happened. In the new Constitution, three-fourths of the states have to approve for something to change. But in the old Articles of Confederation, the way these rules were written up, all states had to agree. Look at the contrast. In the old Articles of Confederation, the old rules of the game to running our government, all the states had to agree before there would be a change. With the new Constitution's rules, three fourths of the states would have to say yeah, yeah. Tell me about the contrast. Tell me about what would happen.

Notice that the teacher ends by turning-back to students for their responses to the situation based on the information she has added. Annotating is a way for teachers to step into the discussion and keep it going by providing necessary information that students cannot generate or discover on their own.

Discussion in Action

Now let's look at some lesson transcripts that show the Discussion Moves in action.

Discussion Moves: An Example with Nonfiction

The first transcript comes from a class in which students had been studying the American Revolutionary period. The text excerpt that students read follows below.

> **Benjamin Franklin had hoped that Britain and the colonies would make peace. Yet after the Battle of Bunker Hill, Franklin gave up this hope. He wrote to a friend who was a member of Parliament, "You have begun to burn our Towns, and murder our People. Look upon your Hands! They are stained with the Blood of your Relations! You and I were long Friends: You are now my Enemy, and I am Yours."**
>
> **(Macmillan/McGraw-Hill, 1997)**

MR. K: Pretty strong words, "They are stained with the Blood of your Relations.... You are now my Enemy, and I am Yours." What's this all about?

"Pretty strong words. . . ." The teacher turned back to an important portion of the text by rereading it before posing a Query.

KATE: Maybe, like, they were relatives and one of them moved or something and settled somewhere else, and, um, that's where, like, the war between those two countries was going to be.

MR. K: Okay. I like a couple things that you said. "One of them moved." What is Kate talking about there?

Kate answers, but her response is a little convoluted, so the teacher marks the most relevant part ("one of them moved") and then turns back to the students for clarification.

TODD: Um . . . a colonist from Great Britain wanted to go to the . . . well, what is now the USA to settle in the colonies, and when he or she went there, Great Britain still wanted to rule the colonies and when the Battle of Bunker Hill took place, Benjamin Franklin wrote one of his friends and said you have killed your, like, old friends and you have killed your cousins and your brothers and sisters just because we didn't want to be ruled by Great Britain.

MR. K: And that would be like killing your old friends?

Notice that the teacher turns the discussion back to Todd by creating a Query from part of his response.

TODD: Because they were once all living together in Great Britain.

MR. K: You said a lot, Todd. I think you're right. And now they're on opposite sides. One more thought to add before we move on. Steve, you want to get in on this?

Above, the teacher marks Todd's comment, extends it briefly, and then invites another student into the discussion.

STEVE: Like, he was hoping that they could make peace and stuff that, like, they wanted to be ruled by British as much as British is ruling them. Like, um, they could. . . the taxes, they could vote on it and use the money for the taxes on their own.

MR. K: You're bringing up the idea that Benjamin Franklin had been hoping that Britain and the colonists could settle their issues without a war.

The teacher marked the idea that Steve had introduced. This lets the students know that this is a productive direction for discussion.

KURT: I agree with Todd because, like, they're both, if they're cousins or something, they're both looking at the same place, and if one moved, like, to Great Britain, and the other was still there, and the Battle of Bunker Hill was starting, it was like they were shooting at each other. They'll just kill, like, their best friend or their family.

Notice below how the teacher connects the students' contributions by revoicing and recapping their ideas.

MR. K: I think that we're agreeing that what Ben Franklin is talking about is that these people were family before, and now maybe one person in their family is a British soldier and they're colonists, and now they're on opposite sides and they're each other's enemy.

Discussion Moves: An Example with a Narrative

Now let's look at a transcript that shows Discussion Moves in narrative.

Pettranella (Waterton, 1980) is a story about a young girl whose family moves to America, except for her grandmother, who stays behind. The excerpt we consider below is the parting scene between Pettranella and her grandmother.

Pulling her close, the grandmother said gently, "But I cannot go to the new land with you, little one. I am too old to make such a long journey."

Pettranella's eyes filled with tears. "Then I won't go either," she cried.

But in the end, of course, she did.

When they were ready to leave, her grandmother gave her a small muslin bag. Pettranella opened it and looked inside. "There are seeds in here!" she exclaimed.

"There is a garden in there," said the old lady. "Those are flower seeds to plant when you get to your new home."

"Oh, I will take such good care of them," promised Pettranella. "And I will plant them and make a beautiful garden for you."

MS. F:	"'There are seeds in there!' she exclaimed. 'There is a garden in there,' said the old lady." Now how can this be? What is the author trying to tell us? Hannah?

The teacher began the discussion by rereading an important point in the text and commenting on it in a way that modeled confusion: "How can this be?"

HANNAH:	That there are seeds, and there are so many seeds in there that she can make a big garden.
MS. F:	Okay, a garden is nice but why did she give her these seeds? Nice going-away gift, huh? Wow, thanks, seeds.

Here the teacher kind of revoices Hannah's response by sarcastically suggesting that seeds don't seem like a special going-away gift and turning back to the students for explanation.

ALLEN:	Because the seeds in the bag so the little girl, Pettranella, can remember her grandmother by that bag, and the seeds can make that garden.
MS. F:	Very nice. Allen tells us that those seeds that she's going to plant are going to remind her of her grandmother, who was not able to come there with them.

The teacher marks and revoices Allen's response, which prompts a question from a student.

DENISE:	I want to ask a question.
MS. F:	Okay.

Notice in the exchange below that Denise turns the discussion back to the text and to the teacher, and then the teacher directs the question to the class and revoices Denise's question for them.

DENISE:	When it said, in the paragraph, it said that her grandma said, as she pulled her close and said, "Sorry, but I'm too old to go on a long journey like that." Um, I don't understand 'cause how can a person be too old to go to another place?

MS. F:	Well, can somebody help Denise out? She's saying that the grandmother says, "Oh, I'm too old to make that journey." How can that be? Only people 40 and under are allowed to get on the ship? What's that mean?
ROY:	She is too old to go, because if she, like, she gets there and she only might live a couple days while she's there, so she might as well stay home and pass where she's at, the way she used to be.

The teacher turns back to Denise.

MS. F:	Okay, before we go on, let me ask you a question, Denise. They're [the class] helping us to figure out what the answer to your question is. What does this say about the journey, that she says, "Oh no, I'm too old to make this journey." What's the author trying to tell us about the journey? Jesse?
JESSE:	It's probably trying to tell us it's long, it's real long and she's too old that she can't get on the ship or nothing.
MISSY:	It might be dangerous?
MS. F:	Maybe it's dangerous. What else didn't the author tell us that maybe might help answer Denise's question?

Notice that the teacher responds to Missy by marking her statement and then turns discussion back to the class.

RICKY:	Well, they had to grow crops, crops at the farm, and the grandmother's probably too old to grow crops and she doesn't want to do all that.
MS. F:	Hey, it might be too much work, too. Does that help answer your question?

Finally, the teacher marks and revoices Ricky's final statement.

After a QtA Lesson: A Few Thoughts

As we have emphasized, the focus of QtA is during-reading discussion that builds understanding. A few comments are in order about what may happen after a reading selection has been completed. At the end of a selection, teachers frequently pose such Queries as "Why do you think the author wrote this text?" or "What was the author trying to get across with this story?" or "What did the author want us to think about this character's motivations?" Queries like these prompt students to consider text as a whole and what they as readers can take from it.

QtA does not prescribe a format or further prompts for post-reading discussion. The expectation is, however, that students who have gone through a QtA discussion—thinking, connecting, and integrating ideas—are particularly well equipped to undertake global discussion of text after reading. QtA provides them with resources they need to consider themes, intertextual connections, authorial intent, author's craft, the big idea, and the like.

By well equipped, we mean that they are able to draw on their understanding of a text to discuss larger issues in a way that is grounded in the text rather than in tangential associations. Discussion of an entire piece is essentially an outgrowth of the during-reading discussion. This is illustrated well in the following example of a seventh-grade class working on Robert Frost's poem "The Road Not Taken" (1916). The example also demonstrates how well QtA can be applied to poetry.

QtA in Action: Exploring a Poem

In the example below, note in the first excerpt how the during-reading discussion is proceeding. Students are engaging well with the words and ideas of the poem, aided by the teacher's prompting through revoicing and rereading. Then notice in the second excerpt that the discussion naturally develops into an exchange of ideas. In fact, a student offers a response to the poem as a metaphor before the teacher even has the opportunity to pose a final Query.

In this first excerpt, the class is in the midst of discussing the second stanza of the poem:

> Then took the other, as just as fair,
> And having perhaps the better claim,
> Because it was grassy and wanted wear;
> Though as for that the passing there
> Had worn them really about the same,

MS. T: Let's go back to this line, "Because it was grassy and wanted wear." What do you think the poet means there?

ALICIA: It wanted somebody to walk on it.

MS. T: And what about the line before, who can explain what this means, "And having perhaps the better claim"?

ROCHELLE: It might be a better path.

MS. T: A better claim—so perhaps it was a better path. But as Alicia said, it wanted somebody to walk on it; it had had fewer travelers. Hmmm.

STAN: Maybe a lot of people were going down the wrong path.

MS. T: Oh! Did you hear that? Maybe a lot of people were going down the wrong path. Let's keep that in mind. Now let's take a look at these last lines.

In discussing the rest of the stanza, "Though as for that the passing there / Had worn them really about the same," students concluded that the two paths were physically similar—"they probably had, like, about the same grass and flowers and stuff"—but may have led to different places.

The second excerpt focuses on the final stanza:

> I shall be telling this with a sigh
> Somewhere ages and ages hence:
> Two roads diverged in a wood, and I—
> I took the one less traveled by,
> And that has made all the difference.

As the teacher finishes reading the stanza, Susanna jumps right in:

SUSANNA: For some reason, I don't think this is about a path in the woods, I think it's about a path in life that you have to take.

MS. T: Okay, nice and loud … give me that again.

SUSANNA: I think this isn't about the woods, like a path in the woods, I think this is about a path you have to take in life.

MS. T: Okay, what makes you say that?

SUSANNA: Because he says, "And that has made all the difference." I don't think a path is going to make a very big difference in the woods, but in life you have to take it step by step. If you go to the right path it could lead to something good or something.

MS. T: Okay, so she's saying—and actually you answered my question that I was going to ask—she thinks that the poet is not really talking about paths in the woods. She thinks he's talking about paths in life, or choices in life. And I'm going to come back to you now, Stan, because you're the one who kinda first put that thought out there. Who remembers what Stan said?

ARNETTE: He said that one path might be right but another might be wrong.

MS. T: Okay, one path might be the right path; one path might be the wrong path. Connect that with what Susanna's saying.

EVAN: It means, like, the choices that you make in life. One might be wrong and one might be right.

LAURAL: I think he's saying the people were going down the worn-down path, they went down the wrong path in life; they took the wrong decision. But he did different, and he went down the right path and he guessed he was successful in life.

From here, other students join the discussion, and various thoughts on the theme of life's choices are offered, including that many people choose conventional paths or make the wrong choices in life:

> The other path is wrong because so many people would have took the worn path. A lot of people want to choose the wrong path instead of the right one, which is why the one path may have seemed more worn.

That the poet himself may have chosen the wrong path earlier in life and now is taking a different turn:

> I think maybe like before he chose the wrong path, but I think he chose to do different because he wasn't doing too good, he chose to do different and take the right path this time to be more successful.

And that the poet chose a path that not only made a difference for himself but allowed him to make a difference in other people's lives:

> That made a difference in other people's life for what he did.

In addition to examples such as this one, we also have evidence of students' interpretive ability following a Questioning the Author lesson from a study that compared discussion approaches. Sandora et al. (1999) found that students were significantly better able to respond to interpretive questions with a QtA story reading than with a Junior Great Books discussion. Interpretive questions considered such matters as authorial intent ("Why do you think the author made the Handicapper General a woman, as opposed to making the character a man?) and a character's actions ("Other than killing Harrison, what options might the Handicapper General have considered and why?").

Ending Notes

Here are a few points to keep in mind about QtA discussion:

- Dynamic discussion in which students and teacher work together to build meaning from text is at the heart of QtA.

- A QtA discussion consists of neither a teacher posing Queries and students simply responding to them nor students going off on their own and getting further and further away from the text.

- During discussion, the teacher prompts student thinking about text. Students reveal and share their thinking and through further teacher prompting connect and integrate ideas to build a coherent representation of the text.

- Because the events of a QtA discussion can be unpredictable, teachers rely on some tools to manage discussion and make improvisational decisions. We call these Discussion Moves and have identified six: marking, turning-back, revoicing, recapping, modeling, and annotating.

- Marking involves drawing attention to an idea to emphasize its importance and to use it as a basis for further discussion.

- Turning-back can involve turning-back to text as a source for clarifying thinking and keeping discussion on track or turning-back to students as those responsible for thinking through and figuring out ideas.

- In revoicing, a teacher interprets what students are struggling to express so their ideas can become part of the discussion. Marking, turning-back, and revoicing represent different ways to make productive use of what students have offered in a discussion.

- When recapping, a teacher reviews or highlights major ideas and under-standings developed so far. Over time, students can assume more responsi-bility for recapping.

- The modeling and annotating moves involve greater teacher input. The teacher steps in in a more direct way. Modeling makes public the processes in which readers engage in the course of reading. We believe that modeling is most effective when it is kept short and is folded into discussions to emphasize an authentic response to text. Annotating provides information to fill in gaps or point out sources of confusion in a text.

- Questioning the Author focuses on building understanding during reading. Although QtA does not provide a framework for after-reading discussion of the larger ideas, evidence suggests that, after engaging in a QtA lesson, students are very well equipped to engage in discussion of larger issues, such as themes and universal ideas.

Frequently Asked Questions

1. Should I be using all the Discussion Moves in every lesson?

No. The Discussion Moves are not a recipe for conducting a discussion. They are simply teacher actions that can help you manage and facilitate a discussion. For instance, if you want to draw attention to an important idea, you could use the marking move, or if you think students need to reconsider what the author is saying, you could use turning-back to text, and so on.

The moves themselves do not drive or frame a discussion. Rather, the various situations that arise during a discussion determine the specific moves that can help you maintain focus and keep the discussion meaningful.

2. Whose discussion is it—the students or mine? How "in" it should I be?

Maybe it will help you to figure out your role in a discussion by considering yourself a little more than a collaborator and a little less than a conductor. You need to play the role of facilitator and encourager of discussions—creating an environment in which the focus is building meaning, but without doing all the building yourself.

The teacher's role involves a delicate balancing of being in and staying out. At times, you will do a little more of one and at times a little more of another, depending on what is happening in the discussion and whether students seem to need help in constructing meaning.

3. How do I know when I am leading the discussions too much? And how do I stop doing it?

Probably the best indicator that you are leading too much is that you are doing most of the talking. When you're doing most of the talking, it probably means that you're also doing most of the thinking.

If you are doing a lot of talking because you feel the need to fill in a lot of information, try giving just a small amount of information, perhaps by modeling. For example, "What I was thinking here was that . . . ." Then, pose a Follow-Up Query to prompt students to pick up where you left off.

4. How can I tell when I am not leading discussions enough? And how do I lead the class a little more if I need to?

One sign that you are not leading discussions enough is if students are repeating responses. Another sign is when a lot of time is spent discussing issues that are tangential rather than central to the text. These situations indicate that students aren't picking up the focus and need some help directing their thinking.

Try to lead a little more by developing Follow-Up Queries that restore the focus on important ideas. Also, use turning-back to text and recapping. These moves can help refocus attention on and review the ideas discussed so far.

5. How do I know when a discussion has helped students to construct meaning?

Watch for evidence that students are able to put ideas into their own words, connect ideas within the text, and explain and elaborate on text information.

A further indication is that students will bring up information from previous discussions on their own and draw connections themselves.

6. Do I always have to follow up on what students say?

Your responses are important, and you should be responding implicitly or explicitly to all students who offer responses. But not every response needs an extensive follow-up. When responses sufficiently cover a point, all that's called for is acknowledgment by marking. For example, "Okay, so John just noticed something very interesting" or "Good point!"

In contrast, when a response is not useful for the discussion, you can avoid having to spend a lot of time on it by marking it in a neutral way and then moving on. For example, "Okay, that's another idea."

Finally, another point to be considered is that you are not the only person who should be responding to students. A discussion is most effective and constructive when students address and respond to one another's ideas.

7. How do I handle a response that contains mostly wrong information?

There are several options. If the problem involves misunderstanding or misinterpretation of text information, you might ask the student to reconsider his or her response by using a Follow-Up Query such as "Hmm. Is that really what the author said?"

If students seem to be deeply confused, you may want to use the Discussion Move turning-back to text to direct their attention to what the author actually wrote.

Another approach may be modeling confusion. For example, "This is confusing; the author hasn't really made this very clear." Then, annotate the text by providing information.

8. What if a student comes up with a good idea that I don't want to deal with right then?

If an idea is good but not immediately useful, you may want to ask the student to hold the thought for a while and mention that you will return to it later. In this way, you acknowledge the idea but signal the student that you are going to move on. Making a note on the chalkboard may be a way to remember points you want to consider at another time.

9. What about students who do not participate?

One mechanism that we have found to involve more students is to try eliciting a few quick consecutive responses from a sample of students who are a little reluctant to participate. For example, "What do you think, Ethan? And you, Larry? And, Rosette, what about you? Do you agree with Larry?" or "All of you who agree with Kayla, please raise your hand."

Try to encourage students to piggyback on one another's responses. That way, some of the more reserved students have less information and pressure to deal with. For example, "Rosette told us that she thinks this character hasn't really learned from her mistakes. What do you think of her idea?"

Also, try calling on students who seem to be on the verge of speaking but then shy away from it. Respond with lots of praise and excitement when they do respond. Also, remember that students who are not participating are still benefiting from discussion. They are observing how ideas and meaning are constructed and are probably taking away a better understanding of the text than they would have otherwise acquired on their own.

CHAPTER 5

Implementation

An e-mail from a teacher who had attended a QtA workshop captures one perspective on implementation:

> I attended the workshop this past week. It was my first exposure to QtA. We had some schedule changes today, but I was determined to try [one of the stories planned at the workshop]. I had prepared and highlighted the Queries. I told my [fifth-grade] class we were going to have fun reading a story and I spoke about the author being fallible. All I can say is that they gave me an early Christmas present and they didn't even realize it. When the bell rang to change classes, they were upset. It wasn't perfect but it went well for my first time. I did it with two homerooms and each reacted the same way when the bell rang.

In our early publications about QtA, we included a discussion on implementation as a way of offering some guidelines on how to introduce students to what was likely to be a new way to approach the reading they did in the classroom. What we have learned since, from the vantage point of working with more than 2,000 teachers in schools across the country for more than 15 years, is that considerations of implementation go well beyond the scope of our original guidelines. So here we offer an expanded discussion that we think will help get teachers started. This chapter will address arranging the classroom, preparing students for QtA, knowing what to expect in the beginning, using QtA flexibly, and reflecting on your own implementation.

Arranging the Classroom

Given that QtA uses discussion as the primary tool for collaboratively reading and understanding a text, students need to sit in a configuration in which they can see and interact with one another. A U- shape arrangement or a square or circle is particularly appropriate. The configuration should send students the message that paying attention to and responding to one another's ideas is as important as contributing ideas. Chairs should be placed so no one can hide or take a backseat; it's everyone's job to work through a text.

Even if classroom space does not allow rearranging the configuration, students can be asked to face a central point so they are all focusing together and can look at individual students when they speak. The physical arrangement of the room may seem like a trivial detail, but we have found that it makes an enormous difference. We have observed some teachers having a difficult time getting QtA going in their classrooms for weeks and even months, because they have neglected to arrange desks for discussion. Then when they were finally convinced to try it, they found the difference was immediately obvious. Students were transformed into engaged communicators. Just consider what it would be like to try to hold conversations with colleagues whose backs were turned to you. How long would you pay attention? How hard would you try to make yourself heard? An orientation toward discussion needs to include orientation of the classroom.

Preparing Students

Because QtA engages students in reading and discussing text in a way that is probably different from what they are accustomed to, they need to be sufficiently prepared. In preparing for QtA, there are three general points that we think are useful to address: the notion of fallibility of the author, why authors can be hard to understand, and what the QtA process will be like.

To set forth the idea that an author might be fallible, a teacher might say something along these lines:

> One important idea to remember about reading is that what we read is just someone's ideas written down—someone called an author. Sometimes what authors have in their minds to say just doesn't come through clearly when they write about it. Authors are real people, so, just like real people, they aren't perfect. Sometimes authors do a fine job of explaining something, but other times, they don't do a very good job at all. As readers, we have a job to do. We have to figure out what the author is trying to explain.

Words such as these have a powerful effect on young readers, who may have been spending months and years presuming that when a text is hard to read, it's because they are weak readers. So when you introduce QtA, consider it a major goal to address, in a direct way, students' tendency to blame themselves. We have found it useful to tell students explicitly and repeatedly that it is their job to figure out whether an author's ideas make sense to them. Once students understand this concept, they appear to be more inclined to dig in and expend effort on a text's ideas, because their fear of being wrong is diminished. Understanding a text becomes more an opportunity for a challenge and less an intimidating chore. The result is typically more excitement and cooperation. A related point about the author that is particularly appropriate for readers at middle grades and above is that there is an intelligence behind the text. This may be described to students as follows:

> Authors, just like other people, have prejudices, convictions, beliefs, likes, and dislikes. Often what writers are trying to express through their stories are their convictions and beliefs about society and the

way the world works. So as readers we need to be alert to what a writer may be expressing by the way he develops his characters or portrays the consequences of their actions or resolves plot situations. Watching out for such things as we read is part of figuring out what an author is trying to say.

Point out to students the reasons why authors are sometimes difficult to understand. Students need to know some of the reasons texts can seem confusing and difficult so that they can begin to recognize these problems themselves. An explanation may go something like this:

> Sometimes, when authors try to write down their ideas, they do some things that make it hard for us to understand what they are trying to say. Some authors use words we are not familiar with or describe things in ways we do not understand. Authors don't know what information you know and don't know, so they may have difficulty explaining things to you in clear ways. Sometimes authors leave information out or they tell us so much that it's hard to keep it all straight. These are the kinds of things that make authors hard to understand.

Finally, students need to hear about the new way they will be dealing with text, which might be presented as follows:

> There are some things we will be doing a little differently as we read. First, whenever we read, our purpose will be to build an understanding of what the author is trying to say. We will be reading the text together, taking turns reading sections out loud a lot of the time, and silently some of the time. We will take the text a little at a time, then stop and try to figure out what the author has said so far. When we stop, I will ask you questions to get you to think about the meaning of what we read, like, "What do you think the author has told us so far?" We will listen to one another's ideas so that we can all work on building understanding together. We will have lots of discussions about what the text means as we read it together.

We have found that teachers differ on the question of using the label Questioning the Author with students. Some do and find that it helps students get a handle on what they are being asked to do. Some don't and simply regard this new kind of reading as the way reading is done in their classroom. Either way works—the decision depends on what facilitates getting things done in your classroom.

What to Expect

We have learned from our workshops on QtA that teachers tend to react in one of two ways. Some respond, "Isn't this what I already do?" and tell us that QtA is really what they have been doing in their classroom all along. Others have an overwhelming feeling of having so much to think about and manage that they are not quite sure where and how to begin. Teachers in the first group often quickly come to change their minds. Of course, every thoughtful teacher wants his or her students to make sense of what they read, tries to ask questions that make students think, and sometimes creates discussion in the classroom. But it is very difficult to carry that off in a systematic and ongoing way. To do so requires planning and resources to turn to when things are not going well (as when students don't respond or get off on the wrong track). We think this is what the QtA framework offers. And we think that unless teachers try to implement QtA in a systematic and ongoing way, they will have little more than sporadic success with promoting meaningful discussion.

For teachers who are overwhelmed, we suggest some starting points to focus on in the beginning. These are (1) lesson focus (2) Initiating Queries and (3) turning-back to text. Having a focus to your lesson, a strong major understanding to guide you, really helps you keep discussion on track. It also helps you develop Follow-Up Queries spontaneously because you are aware of the direction in which you want the discussion to go. So many teachers have told us that as long as they keep their focus in mind, they always have a decent lesson. Initiating Queries are a good starting point because they can be prepared ahead of time and provide an overview of the lesson. Turning-back to text is a good starting move to work with, because the text is always there. You don't know what response you may get from students, but you can always turn to the text and do rereading to spur thinking and discussion. And you can prepare just what portions you might reread ahead of time. One further point that teachers have drawn our attention to is the importance of really listening to what students say. In QtA, students' responses are much more in their own language, so they may not sound like what you've come to expect. That means you may have to listen harder to recognize the thinking that may be there.

Using QtA Flexibly

Questioning the Author was developed as a whole-class approach in which the text is read aloud, by teacher or students, in segments. Between segments, Queries are posed by the teacher, and whole-group discussion follows to build meaning. But QtA can also be used in other formats, and QtA principles can be applied in other situations. Most simply, for example, QtA can succeed for a teacher working with small groups of students.

As far as text materials go, QtA works with content-area texts as well as with narrative material, as we have shown in the preceding chapters. In fact, we first developed QtA using social studies material and then quickly saw how well it worked in language arts classes as well. Many teachers have told us how much they enjoy using QtA with poetry. Some have said they find QtA especially well suited to poetry because it seemed to free their students to share their perspectives on a poem and not feel they had to get some secret message that was hidden there. We have had many teachers use QtA in science as well, with great success. Successful implementation in science takes a teacher who is familiar and comfortable enough with the content to stray from the textbook questions and answers.

QtA even finds uses beyond text! It can be used in hands-on science as well, as teachers demonstrate events or reactions and ask, "What's going on here?" or "What was that all about?" A couple of art teachers have even taken to using QtA to get their students involved in discussing their perspectives on works of art—something like "What's van Gogh trying to say?"

A number of teachers have pointed out to us how easily QtA hooks up with writing. They see that QtA pushes students to lay out the thinking about their ideas and also allows them to see the thinking of other students. This laying out and piecing together of ideas to build meaning is very similar to the writing process that teachers try to get students to engage in as they compose. Teachers find that QtA makes that process come more naturally. Also, if students are asked to write about what they have read in a QtA lesson, they have much more to go on, having been involved in a discussion in which ideas were examined and meaning was built.

QtA can be used to seed student writing in some easy ways. One is to have students write their response to a particular Query. For example, you may devise a Query that addresses a major point in the text, and then ask students to stop and write their response. Then several responses might be read aloud to spur some discussion. A writing task may also be created by asking students to respond in writing to a final Query at the end of a piece. Queries such as, "Why do you think the author wrote that story?" or "What message was the author trying to give?" serve such a purpose.

The ultimate goal of QtA is, of course, to have students internalize the process of building understanding as they read. We want them to use this process when they read on their own. Having practice with QtA as a whole-class endeavor helps them do this, but it also helps guide students to a more independent process. A first step is to remind students often that the QtA process is the same one they should use when they read on their own—pause occasionally during reading, ask themselves what is going on, consider what they have read, reread sections as needed, consider what connects to what and whether it all makes sense.

Another step is to make the QtA process more student run. Teachers have done this in a number of ways, but the key to success is that QtA must be strongly in place in the classroom first. Students cannot begin to take ownership of a process that is not already fully familiar and productive for them. A common way to begin is to provide a story with stopping points marked and Initiating Queries provided. The class begins the lesson together for a text segment or two, then divides into groups. Each group reads, stops, discusses, and then writes their response. Some teachers choose to have students write individual responses and then discuss, others to discuss first and develop a group response. As students work, the teacher circulates, helping with issues that arise and keeping students on track. Typically, teachers have groups come together at the end for a brief discussion of what they have read and discussed.

An issue that complicates implementing QtA for many teachers is that some of the material that students read is too long to be dealt with solely in the classroom in a whole-class manner. Independent reading needs to be assigned to get through entire text, but it precludes the collaborative meaning building that is at the heart of QtA. The process of meaning building can still be encouraged in a couple of ways. One way is specifically to assign students not only to read as they do in a QtA lesson, but to mark places in the text where they stopped to think about what the author was saying, or where they weren't sure whether things made sense, or where they made an important connection. Then, a discussion can be based on places in a text that students marked. Of course, this, again, assumes that students have become sufficiently accustomed to QtA that they can recognize such points in their own reading process.

A way to encourage meaning building after students have completed an independent assignment is to conduct a QtA lesson based on key passages in the reading. Read the passages, pose Queries, and discuss the ideas and how they fit into the text.

Neither of these formats should dominate in a classroom where QtA is being implemented. As much as possible, text should be read aloud and meaning should be built together. Students need a great deal of practice before they will truly be able to build meaning so productively on their own.

Implementation Feedback

Learning anything new takes practice, and that practice is more effective and brings about improvement more quickly when the learner receives feedback. This is true whether one is learning to play tennis, speak Chinese, or do science experiments. Teaching is no different. As we have worked with QtA, we have provided follow-up, including feedback, to teachers as they implement the approach.

The training process for QtA has consisted of a workshop and subsequent in-school follow-up. The follow-up included observations of a teacher conducting a QtA lesson and receiving feedback about the lesson. Of course, there is no way to provide such assistance in this volume. But we do have an alternative we can offer, in the form of a Planning Guide for before the lesson and a Reflection Guide for after the lesson. They both appear on the following pages. The Planning Guide (page 126) simply lays out the planning process outlined in Chapter 3 and includes some suggested wording for Queries. This is just a way to keep the structure and reminders for planning a lesson in place so that you have the best chance of success as you begin.

The Reflection Guide (page 127) provides a series of questions to spur your thinking about the various aspects of QtA and how they played themselves out in a particular lesson. We think such a format may be helpful. It is difficult to consider the lesson as a whole and ask oneself, "How did that go?" and come up with a useful response. It may be a more productive reflection to consider various aspects separately.

Even with the Reflection Guide, it can be difficult to recall how specific things went. It is not easy to conduct a lesson and, in a sense, observe it too. We have suggested to teachers that they tape-record their lessons and listen to the recording as they respond to the Reflection Guide. Although some teachers resist—so many of us just don't want to listen to ourselves—those who have recorded themselves find it more valuable than they had imagined. Teachers have found the recordings hold great surprises as well. Many things occurred that they hadn't recognized at the time—including excellent student responses, their own bad habits they swore they never had, and some hints of Queries and moves that worked particularly well.

Ending Notes

Here are our key points that wrap up our discussion of implementing QtA:

- The first step to implementing QtA is to arrange the classroom in a configuration fit for discussion where everyone can see everyone else's face. A U-shape arrangement or circle shape is ideal.

- Teachers need to prepare students for QtA by describing reading as a process of figuring out what an author is trying to say and whether it makes sense to them. Help students keep in mind that authors are people who write down their ideas—and they are as fallible as the rest of us.

- Implementing QtA can be made less overwhelming by focusing on a few aspects at first. A lesson focus is key to keeping discussion on track, as are planned Initiating Queries. If students have a hard time at first expressing full or clear ideas, turn to the text to reread.

- QtA is a flexible approach that can be used with the whole class or small groups and with any kind of text—narratives, content-area texts, even poetry. QtA can also be used to move students into writing about what they read.

- Students should be guided to incorporate QtA into their own independent reading processes—this is the ultimate goal of QtA. Achieving this goal begins with telling students that this is how they should read when they read on their own—stopping and thinking about what an author says and making connections. Teachers can also turn QtA over to students and have them work together to Query text and build meaning in groups. The process of becoming independent needs to build on a strong familiarity with QtA.

- Implementing a new process successfully takes practice and feedback. The Planning and Reflecting Guides are resources that can support those functions.

Frequently Asked Questions

1. How much oral reading and how much silent reading should occur with Questioning the Author?

Much of the time, texts are read orally in Questioning the Author discussions, especially in the beginning. A major goal of Questioning the Author is to expose text ideas, potential sources of confusion, and connections. That's easiest to do if text is made public from the start, through oral reading. Presenting text orally is especially important for readers whose decoding difficulties may interfere with their ability to get a general sense of the text's content.

However, many teachers have found ways to incorporate silent reading into Questioning the Author lessons. Sections of text that have less content to contend with (for example, descriptive passages in narratives) may be good candidates for silent reading. You may want to keep the silently read passages short, so that differences in students' reading rates do not become a problem. Older, and perhaps more skilled, readers can handle more-frequent silent reading opportunities.

The main point to keep in mind is that the decision about whether to use silent or oral reading depends on both the content and the skill of your readers.

2. How do the activities that usually introduce a text lesson, like setting a purpose and introducing vocabulary, fit in with doing Questioning the Author?

In Questioning the Author, attention is focused on what happens during inter-action with the text. So before-reading activities assume less of the burden for enhancing students' experience with text. That doesn't mean, however, that you should forget about preparing students for reading. For example, it is basic good instructional practice to provide or activate prior knowledge and set a context for the text to be read. It is also helpful, and sometimes even necessary, to introduce some vocabulary.

But students don't need to be prepared for everything they may possibly need before they read a text. In a Questioning the Author discussion, issues related to background knowledge or vocabulary can be addressed in the course of reading. You can plan Queries around the use of vocabulary, for example. Most important, given the structure of a QtA lesson, students have opportunities to ask questions in the course of reading about words or ideas that are not familiar to them.

3. Where do using strategies like predicting and summarizing fit in with doing Questioning the Author?

Perhaps the key to understanding the relationship between Questioning the Author and strategy approaches is that when you use QtA, you will see students doing things like predicting, finding main ideas, making inferences, and questioning in a more natural way, within the context of ongoing reading and discussion.

The purpose of teaching students to use strategies is to enhance their ability to construct meaning. Questioning the Author shifts the focus from dealing with the strategies to grappling directly with the ideas in the text.

4. Should I still use after-reading activities when we finish a story or lesson?

Traditional after-reading activities usually consist of questions that assess and assist students' reconstruction of what they understood from reading. The during-reading focus of Questioning the Author makes it unnecessary to use traditional post-reading questioning to check comprehension. However, it is good practice to provide opportunities for students to use what they have learned. For example, teachers may want to encourage students to write responses to what they've read or use ideas from reading as a basis for independent or small-group research projects.

5. How often should I be doing Questioning the Author?

That is mostly up to you. However, we recommend that you be persistent and consistent—both for your sake and the students. The more you use Questioning the Author, the better you will become. And the more accustomed your students are to Questioning the Author, the more they will improve in their ability to construct meaning.

Planning Guide

1. Identify major understandings and potential obstacles

What do you want students to understand from the text?

Are there potential obstacles to that understanding? How will the text strike students?

_____

_____

2. Segment the text (and develop Queries)

Where do you want to stop to initiate discussion?

Consider what you want students to take from each discussion point. Stops should be guided by the content. The segment should hold:
- Enough to provide grist for discussion
- Not so much as to cause confusion about what to discuss

3. Develop a Query to initiate discussion at each stop

Keep the wording open:
- *What's the author trying to say?*
- *What's going on?*
- *What just happened?*
- *What is the author letting us know?*
- *What is all that about?*

_____

_____

Consider what students might miss, and anticipate follow-ups:
- *With all that, what do you think the author wants us to know about . . ?*
- *How does that connect with what we already know about . . . ?*
- *Does the author give us any clues as to why that might be important?*

Underline text portions to reread.

_____

_____

Reflection Guide

Provide an overview of the lesson, considering:
- To what extent was it generally a success/a disappointment?
- What were the high points/low points?

_____
_____

What indications were there that students understood the major ideas?

_____
_____

What indications were there that students had some problems understanding some of the major ideas?

_____
_____

To what extent did your Initiating Queries effectively get things off the ground? Any examples come to mind?

_____
_____

To what extent did your Follow-Up Queries help students make connections and grapple with ideas? Any examples?

_____
_____

How would you judge the overall quality of the students' comments and ideas? Any examples?

_____
_____

How satisfied are you with the number of students who participated? What might have increased student participation?

_____
_____

If you could go back and change something in this lesson, what would it be and why?

_____
_____

Implementing QtA: 25 Classroom Cases

The last chapter of Section 1, on implementation, may be viewed as a response to "Now that I've read and thought about Queries, planning, and discussion, what do I do Monday morning?" In contrast, Section 2 provides 25 mini-cases of authentic classroom situations and issues that go far deeper and much further than "Monday morning" for teachers who have already started to implement QtA. The cases were developed to help teachers deal with a variety of problems and issues that come up in the classroom, especially when a new instructional approach is being implemented: What can I do when . . . ? How can I handle . . . ? What if some students don't . . . ? The cases were designed as resources that teachers could draw on over time in the course of using QtA in their classrooms. The materials in the cases come from authentic situations that arose in QtA classrooms.

We saw the need for these cases from our years of developing QtA in close collaboration with teachers. We came to understand the complexity of the teacher's role in fostering classroom discourse that leads to building meaning. With the QtA framework, lessons no longer consisted of reading straight through a text, then asking questions aimed at retrieving text information. We learned firsthand what Cazden (1988) observed: "It is easy to imagine talk in which ideas are explored rather than answers to teachers' test questions provided and evaluated. . . . Easy to imagine, but not easy to do" (page 54).

Early on we were collaborating with teachers to learn about and solve problems in the implementation of QtA, so our contact with them was very close. We addressed their difficulties by providing extensive, ongoing firsthand support, such as lesson observations and feedback, demonstration lessons, and brainstorming meetings to consider specific problems and issues. Thus, we were confronted with the situation—one that has often been described in the literature—that what is learned from such efforts is in the form of anecdotal accounts of face-to-face collaborations among teachers and between researchers and teachers (e.g., Palincsar, Magnusson, Marano, Ford, & Brown, 1998; Saunders & Goldenberg, 1996). Although much of value resides in such accounts, it needs to be transformed before it can be useful to other teachers. So we undertook the task of transforming the detailed and exquisite content of our face-to-face interactions in a form that other teachers could use on their own.

We began the process of developing cases by analyzing the documentation of the first three years of implementation (see Beck et al., 1996; McKeown et al., 1996, for details on these implementations). The documentation included notes from meetings with teachers, teachers' journal entries, classroom observation notes, and transcripts of 125 videotaped sessions.

As we analyzed the material, we noticed a pattern of development that seemed to typify the implementation process. The pattern began with the teacher moving from conventional retrieval questions to open-ended Queries. As the teachers became adept at opening up their questions, they then started to realized that student responses to open questions needed to be addressed with follow-up questions that invited elaboration, clarification, and the like. After follow-up questions became a more natural part of the teacher's repertoire, we noticed that often a series of follow-ups was needed to build important text ideas during a discussion segment, but it was difficult for teachers to sustain a focused discussion beyond the first couple of student responses. Within this pattern, we worked to identify specific difficulties and issues.

From our databases of QtA lessons and our analysis, we created 25 cases. Each case has the same format. It begins with a "Classroom Snapshot," an excerpt from a lesson transcript, or a teacher's journal entry that illustrates the particular issue to be addressed. Next a section called "What Happened and Why" gives a brief explanation of what happened in the snapshot or was recorded in the teacher's journal, and why it might have happened. Then a section called "Dealing with the Problem" suggests ways the problem might have been handled differently. This is followed by several examples of ways that other teachers have dealt with the same kind of issue, along with our commentary. Most cases also contain an additional example of the target issue, in a section called "Your Turn," that provides an opportunity for teachers to design a solution on their own. Finally, we offer a "Recapping" of the issue and ways to handle it.

Our field-testing of the cases indicated that the case-based support yielded positive results comparable to that of face-to-face support (McKeown & Beck, 2004). The teachers in the study, as well as many other teachers who have subsequently used the cases, have told us that they learned a great deal from them, that they relied on them for direction and support, and that often they were surprised to find how relevant the cases were to their own issues. As one teacher told us, "It's wonderful to see other teachers having the same problem I do. It makes me feel that I am not the only one. And the discussions of solutions to certain problems are terrific."

We see the cases as playing a unique role in professional development. We believe that the most effective professional development provides means for teachers to understand to what extent their actions correspond to principles they are aiming to enact, and provides strategies for increasing that correspondence. The cases provide substantive content about the principles and actions of QtA, and how the two connect. The content is consistent and based on extensive documentation from previous implementations.

We have arranged the cases in an order that we think will be the most useful. Our experience has suggested that certain issues take priority earlier than others. We hope that as you use the cases, you'll feel free to question the authors. Read, mull over what's there, jot notes on the pages, and underline as you go, making what's there meaningful to you and your classroom, in the best tradition of Questioning the Author.

Getting Discussion Going
Why Do Initiating Queries Sometimes Fall Flat?

Several teachers have told us that when they were first getting started with QtA they sometimes found that their Initiating Queries seemed to fall flat. Students just didn't have much to say, and it was a struggle to get discussion going.

CLASSROOM SNAPSHOT

Ms. C and her class are reading the novel *Mama's Bank Account* (Forbes, 1971). Ms. C wants to focus the discussion on the complications of a family problem that Mama and her sisters were trying to solve. But, as you'll see below, that is not how students respond to Ms. C's Query.

In the text segment that the class is reading, Mama and her sisters talk about how to care for their aunt, who is elderly, deaf, and now needs a place to live. The final sentences of the segment reveal a key issue:

The Aunts agreed and explored the subject endlessly. Each one was more than willing to offer their aunt a home—but would she accept? They remembered her stiff, unyielding pride.

MS. C: What problem has the author presented here?

BART: Aunt Elna, and she's, like, deaf.

JANET: She's the aunt of the aunts, like a great-aunt, and she's really old.

What Happened and Why?

Bart's and Janet's responses picked up small aspects of the text situation, but they didn't get to the heart of the matter—the question of how the family is going to deal with Aunt Elna. Why might this have happened?

Students may have difficulty recognizing which ideas are most significant when text material is complex or offers several possible ideas to discuss. A Query posed about such material may fall flat, with students providing minimal responses, as was the case with Bart and Janet.

Initiating Queries may fall flat because of the differences between Queries and traditional questions. When teachers develop questions, they tend to have a specific response in mind, so there's not much room for a question to fall flat—it just gets answered correctly or incorrectly. Queries, on the other hand, are supposed to provoke thinking and consideration of ideas. But because Queries leave room for thinking rather than pointing to a direct answer, students may be puzzled about how to respond, and it can be a struggle to get discussion going.

Dealing with the Problem

A key to dealing with discussion that falls flat is to develop Initiating Queries that leave room for students to think but also give enough direction to overcome their puzzlement. Although the intent of QtA is to get students to think about what the author is trying to get across, Initiating Queries such as "What is the author trying to say?" or "What problem has the author presented here?" may not always hold sufficient cues to direct students' thinking.

Working to prevent an Initiating Query from falling flat starts with anticipating the kind of response that it may elicit. Below are two examples in which teachers anticipated that an Initiating Query might fall flat if it were phrased too generally. The teachers then were able to plan Initiating Queries that were tailored to focus students' thinking.

EXAMPLE 1. In this first example, the class is reading a selection about young Native Americans in a school on a reservation. The story began with a scene in which the school's principal was transporting some students back to school after they had wandered off. The principal explained to Bob Woods, a teacher at the school, that staying put in school was sometimes difficult for these students because they were so used to wandering the wide-open spaces of the reservation. Here is the next segment of text:

> "Yesterday I saw Grandfather Laughter with his flock of sheep and goats. I knew the older boys saw him. And I thought we might have a few stray students this morning. Excuse me, Bob. I'd better see that these fellows get back to the classroom."
>
> As the principal left, Bob thought of his visit to Johnny's hogan. It helped him to understand why some of the students were restless. "I should give them more of a chance to tell about their life on the desert," he said to himself.
>
> When class began that afternoon, Bob Woods asked, "Did any of you see Grandfather Laughter yesterday?"
>
> "I did," Roger Lee said. "Grandfather Laughter is one of the best sheepmen of our tribe. Someday I hope to be as good as he is."

The teacher's goal for this segment is to signal her students to continue with a line of thinking begun in discussion of the previous text segment, which was the issue of the young Native Americans' restlessness in school. The teacher has a sense that asking a general Initiating Query like "What is the author telling us here?" may invite students to focus on less important text ideas, such as the character of Grandfather Laughter. So, the teacher phrases an Initiating Query to direct attention to the young Native Americans' feelings of restlessness in school. Notice the response it draws:

MS. W:	How did the author settle this restlessness that was opened up? How does the author let us understand that?
JANET:	Well, Bob Woods went to Johnny's hogan and we read about that already, and he's thinking, well, after I see these two boys, I'm not spending enough time asking these kids about their lives in the desert, I'm not, like, paying much attention to their lives, and I think that that's sort of what it is.

Janet took the teacher's cue and provided a good explanation of how Bob Woods decided to address the needs of his students. Capturing this kind of student thinking might have been less likely if the teacher had simply asked, "What is the author telling us here?"

EXAMPLE 2. Below is another example that accomplishes the same kind of student focusing. In this example from a social studies lesson, the class is reading about the colonization of North America. The text passage introduces the concept of a joint-stock company to describe a financing plan for future colonies. Here is the text:

> Sir Walter Raleigh had lost a fortune trying to start a colony on Roanoke Island. His experience showed that trying to plant a colony was too risky for one person. So in 1606 a group of English merchants decided to share the costs of starting a colony by forming a joint-stock company. In a joint-stock company, instead of one person's putting up all the money, a number of people each put up part of the money and share ownership. Each owner receives a certificate called a stock, or share. If the company makes money, all the stockholders share in the gains. If the company loses money, all share in the losses. But no one risks everything.

The teacher's goal with this segment is to help students make sense of the notion of a joint-stock company. Yet, the teacher does not want to ask the obvious direct question, "What is a joint-stock company?" because he is concerned that it could too easily result in students simply repeating a statement from the text.

The teacher is also concerned that a general Initiating Query such as "What is the author trying to say?" may not be sufficient to get the students started. So the teacher handles the situation by posing an Initiating Query and then constraining it by mentioning some of the key words from the text to help direct students' thinking:

> MS. M: What is this all about? The joint-stock company and
>   sharing—what is that about?

The teacher's approach appeared to be effective. The first student called on began by saying that people wanted to start a colony and "decided to share the cost," thus setting in motion a productive line of discussion.

Your Turn

Try to develop Initiating Queries for the text segment below with two considerations in mind. First, you mainly want students to understand that New England is rich in forests and that the wood provided an important resource for industries that developed. And second, you don't want to spend too much time on the concept.

EARLY USE OF TIMBER

The forests and woods of New England have long been an important natural resource for the people in the region. When the first English colonists came here, they were thrilled by the many tall, straight trees. These fir trees were perfect to use for the masts of the English sailing ships.

Although New England is today one of the most populated regions of the United States, much of the land is still forested. Many different kinds of trees are found there, including fir, birch, spruce, pine, oak, and maple. Timber became one of the earliest raw materials for New England industry.

➡ *Write & Compare* Jot down your ideas for Initiating Queries on a sheet of paper. Then, compare your Queries with those below.

To encourage students to focus on the general idea of the importance of timber to New England rather than talking about "tall, straight, trees" or "sailing ships," Initiating Queries such as these may be useful:

- What big idea do you think the author is trying to tell us about?

- With all that, what do you think the author wanted us to know?

Recapping

It may be a struggle to get discussion going if Initiating Queries don't help students figure out where to focus their attention, especially if the text segment contains difficult content or several ideas that could capture their attention. In such cases, a general Initiating Query such as "What is the author telling us?" may not give students enough to go on. Queries that are tailored with a focus may be more productive. The key here is to provide focus while taking care to leave room for student thinking.

Segmenting Text
How Do You Decide Where to Stop Reading and Start Discussing?

QtA teachers have found that segmenting text—making decisions about where to stop reading and begin discussion—is not an easy task in the beginning. Teachers have told us that certain decisions can make it difficult for students to focus on meaningful ideas.

CLASSROOM SNAPSHOT

Mr. W's class is reading a social studies unit on United States geography. The goal that Mr. W has selected across the unit is for students to develop a bird's-eye view of the geography of the United States. For the text segment below, about the Appalachian Mountains, Mr. W wants the class to understand that although the mountain range has different names in different states, it's all one range. Here is the final paragraph of the segment on the Appalachian Mountains:

The Appalachian Mountains have different names in different states. In New York they are called the Adirondacks. In Virginia and North Carolina, they are called the Blue Ridge Mountains. And in Tennessee they are called the Great Smoky Mountains. The highest point in the Appalachian Mountains is Mount Mitchell, which is in North Carolina. It has an elevation of 6,684 feet (2,037 m).

Notice below that Mr. W's Initiating Query has a general focus, in contrast to the response it draws:

MR. W: What is the author telling us here about these mountains?

DONNA: The highest one, in North Carolina, is 6,684 feet.

What Happened and Why?

Donna responded to the final sentences in the segment, which provided very specific information, rather than to the general concept. Mr. W's decision to include these final sentences in the segment, though they were unrelated to the general concept, resulted in distracting attention from the main point.

Dealing with the Problem

In segmenting a text, be clear about what it is you want students to understand from a text segment. An important part of that is considering what information is available to students to construct a response. Sometimes if a segment is very long, or if it is dense with ideas or details, students may be unable to focus on a key idea, such as occurred in Mr. W's class. On the other hand, if a segment is too brief, there may not be enough information for students to build a meaningful response.

EXAMPLE. Now, let's pick up on the next part of the text in the geography unit, which is called "A Flat Land." We'll look at segmenting decisions that take into account the content that students will have available as they respond. The teacher's major goal for the material that follows is to have students build into their geographical view that the vast expanse of the middle of the country is flat land known as plains.

The information in the section includes characteristics of plains: that there are two types, their geographical extent, and their form. Because this information is scattered among the three paragraphs, the teacher decided that it would be best to keep all three paragraphs together as a single segment. Stopping after the first or second paragraph could put more focus on facts about the cities mentioned and less on the overall concept of plains. Following is the text and commentary on the segmenting decisions.

A FLAT LAND

Moving westward across the Appalachian Mountains, we reach the Central Plains regions. This region has two major parts. The first part lies just west of the Appalachian Mountains. It is called the Interior Lowlands. Chicago, Illinois, is the largest and most important city in the Interior Lowlands.

The temptation may be to stop at the end of this first paragraph since the idea of plains has been introduced and two types set up. But no content has been provided about the distinction between the two types, so the responses are likely to be limited to retrieving the fact that there are two parts to the plains. And that is not building meaning.

The second part of the Central Plains lies to the west of the Interior Lowlands. This area is called the Great Plains. The largest city on the Great Plains is Denver, Colorado. That city lies at the western edge of the Great Plains. Together the Interior Lowlands and the Great Plains stretch about 1,500 miles (2,414 km) across the United States.

Why not stop here since both types of plains have been characterized? The decision to go on through the next paragraph allows some more characteristics to accumulate, to help students see the bird's-eye view.

Here and there on these vast plains are some hilly areas. There are even a few small mountains. But mostly the Central Plains region is flat. Standing on these plains, one can see straight out to the horizon, where sky and land seem to meet, without a single rise in the land to interrupt the view.

At this point, the material is available for students to put together their view of a big, flat expanse at the center of the United States. A Query such as **"What's the picture here that the author is trying to create?"** may help them do that. If students respond with more specific information, a Follow-Up Query may be: **"How does that help us understand our country's geography?"**

Your Turn

A section on rainfall follows the section in the textbook that introduces plains. In the "Rainfall" section, the distinction between the two types of plains is explained. That is, they differ in the amount of rainfall they receive and consequently in the type of vegetation they have and their potential for agricultural use. The text, marked with a teacher's decisions about where to segment it, follows on the next page.

➡ *Write & Compare* Jot down your ideas about the teacher's decisions for segmenting the text in the space below. Then, compare your ideas with those on pages 142-143.

_____

_____

_____

_____

_____

_____

_____

_____

_____

_____

_____

_____

_____

_____

_____

_____

RAINFALL

The main difference between the Interior Lowlands and the Great Plains is the amount of precipitation each gets. The Interior Lowlands receives 30 to 40 inches (76 to 102 cm) of precipitation a year. That is more than enough precipitation to support the growth of tall grasses, which are often as tall as a person.

To settlers first seeing the Interior Lowlands, the tall grasses were a welcome sign. They knew that if there was enough rainfall for tall grass to grow, there would be enough for farming.

In contrast, many parts of the Great Plains receive only 20 to 25 inches (51 to 64 cm) of precipitation a year. Also, precipitation is not the same each year. While the average yearly precipitation for an area might be 20 inches (51 cm), that same place might get more precipitation in some years and less in others. For example, it might get 5 inches (13 cm) of precipitation one year, 20 inches (51 cm) each of the next two years, then 30 inches (76 cm), and finally 25 inches (64 cm). The five-year average would be 20 inches (51 cm), but precipitation the first year would have been too low to support grasses and trees.

As a result there are almost no trees on the Great Plains. There is hardly enough rain from year to year for short grass to grow. When settlers first arrived on the Great Plains, they took one look at the short grass turning brown in the summer sun and decided that this was no place for them.

In time, Americans did settle on the Great Plains. As you will read later, they learned how to farm with little rainfall. They also found the short grasses of the plains ideal for grazing cattle and sheep.

Even though this paragraph implies that one kind of plain has enough rainfall and the other does not, keep going—the information is made explicit and explained in the following paragraph.

Stop here because the contrast between the types of plains has been stated, and the details in the paragraph beyond this point may complicate establishing the basic contrast.

Stop here to discuss the general idea that the amounts of rainfall on the Great Plains wouldn't be sufficient for farming. Getting this information is tricky because the reader has to wade through the particulars about rainfall from year to year before being able to establish the point of the segment. So it would seem best not to let students leave this paragraph without grappling with the information to make it meaningful.

RAINFALL

The main difference between the Interior Lowlands and the Great Plains is the amount of precipitation each gets. The Interior Lowlands receives 30 to 40 inches (76 to 102 cm) of precipitation a year. That is more than enough precipitation to support the growth of tall grasses, which are often as tall as a person.

To settlers first seeing the Interior Lowlands, the tall grasses were a welcome sign. They knew that if there was enough rainfall for tall grass to grow, there would be enough for farming.

In contrast, many parts of the Great Plains receive only 20 to 25 inches (51 to 64 cm) of precipitation a year. Also, precipitation is not the same each year. While the average yearly precipitation for an area might be 20 inches (51 cm), that same place might get more precipitation in some years and less in others. For example, it might get 5 inches (13 cm) of precipitation one year, 20 inches (51 cm) each of the next two years, then 30 inches (76 cm), and finally 25 inches (64 cm). The five-year average would be 20 inches (51 cm), but precipitation the first year would have been too low to support grasses and trees.

As a result there are almost no trees on the Great Plains. There is hardly enough rain from year to year for short grass to grow. When settlers first arrived on the Great Plains, they took one look at the short grass turning brown in the summer sun and decided that this was no place for them.

In time, Americans did settle on the Great Plains. As you will read later, they learned how to farm with little rainfall. They also found the short grasses of the plains ideal for grazing cattle and sheep.

Stop here and connect what the settlers saw and concluded with what was presented previously. That is, the settlers reached the conclusion that growing things would be very difficult on the Great Plains, which connects to the previous information about lack of rainfall.

Don't include this paragraph in the segment with the above. The discussion of people's eventually settling and learning to farm there muddies the issue of the Great Plains' distinction from the Lowlands. So it makes sense to establish the notion that the Great Plains lacked rainfall and the consequences before discussing that the consequences were overcome.

Your Turn Again

Moving along across the country, we reach the Rocky Mountains. Where would you segment this section of the text in order to promote the bird's-eye view of United States geography? Explain your reasoning.

➡️ **Write & Compare** Mark where you would segment the text and note your reasons on a sheet of paper. Then, compare your decisions with those on page 145.

HIGH, RUGGED MOUNTAINS

As you reach the western end of the Great Plains, the land rises quite sharply. You'll recall that Denver, Colorado, is a city at the western edge of the Great Plains. Its elevation is 5,280 feet (1,609 m)—exactly one mile above sea level. But just about 100 miles (161 km) west of Denver is a peak of land called Mount Elbert. The elevation of Mount Elbert is 14,433 feet (4,399 m)—nearly 3 miles above sea level!

Mount Elbert is the highest point in the broadest chain of mountains in our country. These are the Rocky Mountains. The Rocky Mountains are about 3,000 miles (4,827 km) long. This mountain range runs like a giant spine, or backbone, down the North American continent from Alaska to New Mexico.

Some peaks in the Rockies are so high that their tops are often hidden in the clouds. The snow never melts on some of these peaks. That is because as a general rule, the higher a place is, the cooler it is. In fact, a mountain peak as high as Mount Elbert is about 45° colder than another place at the same latitude but at sea level.

HIGH, RUGGED MOUNTAINS

As you reach the western end of the Great Plains, the land rises quite sharply. You'll recall that Denver, Colorado, is a city at the western edge of the Great Plains. Its elevation is 5,280 feet (1,609 m)—exactly one mile above sea level. But just about 100 miles (161 km) west of Denver is a peak of land called Mount Elbert. The elevation of Mount Elbert is 14,433 feet (4,399 m)—nearly 3 miles above sea level!

Mount Elbert is the highest point in the broadest chain of mountains in our country. These are the Rocky Mountains. The Rocky Mountains are about 3,000 miles (4,827 km) long. This mountain range runs like a giant spine, or backbone, down the North American continent from Alaska to New Mexico.

Some peaks in the Rockies are so high that their tops are often hidden in the clouds. The snow never melts on some of these peaks. That is because as a general rule, the higher a place is, the cooler it is. In fact, a mountain peak as high as Mount Elbert is about 45° colder than another place at the same latitude but at sea level.

Stop here to focus on the significance of the difference in elevation from Denver to Mt. Elbert. Recognizing the enormous difference here provides a good basis for understanding the geographical pattern of this part of the country. To go on to the next paragraph in the same segment may lessen the impact of the elevation difference, lessening its usefulness as a hook to understanding the geography.

Although this paragraph is fairly short, it is incredibly dense! Even though none of the information is particularly difficult, the sheer number of ideas suggests a need to stop to let students sort it out:
• highest point
• broadest mountain chain
• 3,000 miles long
• spine of the continent
• Alaska to New Mexico

Again, there is quite a density of information in this paragraph! Even though the paragraph revolves around a single concept, that of cooler temperatures at higher elevations, quite a bit of information is offered. It would probably be helpful to stop and allow students to make sense of it all.

Recapping

The point at which a text is segmented—where reading stops and discussion begins—should help students focus on key ideas and avoid drawing attention to distracting information or less significant details. A segment should provide enough grist for students to build meaning, but it should not be so dense that students don't know where to focus their attention.

CASE 3

Responses in the Right/Wrong Mode
How Do You Let Students Know That It's Thinking You're After?

Teachers have told us that as they began using Queries to guide discussion of text ideas, students persisted in responding as if they were being asked merely to retrieve correct information from the text. As one teacher put it, "The students were still in the right/wrong mode!"

CLASSROOM SNAPSHOT

The students in Ms. T's class are reading about the development of the steel and coal industries in Pennsylvania in the late 1800s. The text describes a new and better process for heating iron, which is used in steelmaking. Ms. T expects students to respond to her Initiating Query with ideas about why the new process would be preferred, but as you can see below, that's not what happens:

Toward the end of the 1800s, the open-hearth process was being used in a large number of steel mills. In the open-hearth process, a bowl-shaped furnace was used to heat iron. The iron could be heated to greater temperatures in this type of furnace. Samples could be taken from the furnace and tested for quality. Although it took longer to make steel this way, a better kind of steel was produced. By 1908 more open-hearth steel was made than Bessemer steel.

MS. T: What's the author just told us?

TIM: That the furnaces were shaped like bowls.

SAM: That by 1908 there was more open-hearth steel than Bessemer.

What Happened and Why?

Ms. T opened with a general Query meant to elicit the overall message of the text, but Tim and Sam responded by simply reiterating pieces of information from the segment. It seemed as if they were deliberately looking to the text for "right" answers. One of the reasons this may happen is that students are not used to the idea of considering meaning and grappling with text ideas.

Dealing with the Problem

To develop a meaning orientation, reinforce that focus frequently and make it explicit. There are several ways this can be done. Use the Discussion Moves of marking and turning-back. One way to turn back responsibility for thinking to students is by probing their responses to direct their thinking toward meaning. Another way is to mark student responses when they do demonstrate thinking and grappling with ideas. Examples of both follow.

Turning-Back Responsibility for Thinking to Students

The first set of examples below shows how Ms. T is able to turn back responsibility for thinking to students by probing student responses to elicit more thinking.

EXAMPLE 1. Ms. T responds to what Sam said in the Classroom Snapshot with a Follow-Up Query that explicitly indicates to students the kind of meaning that may be built from the segment. Look at what happens:

MS. T:	Does the author give us any idea what's behind that— *why* would there be less Bessemer steel?
JULIA:	The Bessemer steel wasn't as good as the open-hearth steel, so people went for the better stuff.

By turning-back responsibility for thinking to students, Ms. T's Follow-Up Query helped direct students' attention to *why* the process of making steel was changing, and Julia's response provided the reason for the change.

EXAMPLE 2. As the lesson proceeds, the class reads the text segment below:

> Coke was made by heating soft coal. It was used for heating furnaces to make steel. New kinds of ovens made coke more quickly than before. These ovens also captured gases given off by the coal as it turned to coke. The gases could be used to make materials such as fuels, fertilizer, and cleaning fluid. The person who owned most of the new coke ovens was Henry C. Frick of Fayette County.

Again, Ms. T begins with a general Query and draws a response from Barbara that shows little consideration of meaning:

MS. T: What has the author told us now?

BARBARA: Coke ovens, that Mr. Frick owned.

Given the limitations of Barbara's response, Ms. T then poses a Follow-Up Query to focus attention on the importance of the coke ovens:

MS. T: Okay, Mr. Frick did own most of them, but what about those coke ovens, what do you think the author wants us to know about them?

The Query seemed to work as students went on to describe how coke was used not only to produce steel but also other products such as fertilizer.

EXAMPLE 3. The next example is based on the following text segment about worker strikes:

> Striking was one way that unions tried to make working conditions and pay better. When workers strike, they stop working. When a company did not give its workers what they thought was fair, the workers went on strike. Some strikes were violent. However, many strikes did make gains for the workers and their unions.

Although Ms. T poses a Query aimed to help students generate an overview of what a strike is and what it does, a student responds with a narrow definition.

MS. T: What has the author told us about strikes?

JOHN: That in strikes, workers stop working.

Ms. T then issues a challenge by echoing the short response as a question:

MS. T: They'd just stop working?

Notice how Betty picks up on Ms. T's challenge by filling in some important parts of the picture. However, she ends with a literal rendition of a key consequence of strikes:

BETTY: Because if they didn't think work, like the rules, were
              fair, they stopped going to work anymore. And they
              could make gains for the workers.

Finally, notice how Ms. T follows up by turning-back to students the responsibility for explaining the meaning of this point:

MS. T: What does the author mean by "many strikes made
              gains for the workers"?

Marking by Acknowledging Student Focus on Meaning

Probing student responses is one way to develop a meaning orientation. Another way is by marking, or acknowledging, student comments that demonstrate an effort to build meaning. The following examples show ways to recognize such efforts.

EXAMPLE 1. The exchange below comes from a discussion in a social studies class about a text segment that describes how the invention of the Conestoga wagon solved a problem in moving west. The segment ends as follows:

> The wagon rode on four large wooden wheels. These had bands of iron like tires around the rims. The wagon could carry 2,500 to 3,500 pounds of material. Because the wagon was first made in the Conestoga Valley, it was called a Conestoga wagon.

The teacher asks students to consider what problem this new wagon solved, and a student presents a nicely reasoned explanation. The teacher then marks the response by providing the kind of acknowledgment that can encourage students to think about meaning.

MR. D: So, what was the problem? I mean, these farmers had wagons all along. Why couldn't they just use them to go west?

MICHAEL: Well, what if they happened to hit a large stone and it might have hit the wheel and the wheel broke? With the steel bands around it, it'd be easier and the wheels wouldn't break as easy.

MR. D: Okay! So, Michael has given us a problem here that might have come up if they used the regular wagons, and it would be solved with these new wagons. Good thinking!

EXAMPLE 2. In this next example, the class is reading the novel *The Whipping Boy* (Fleischman, 1987). At this point in the story, the runaway Prince Brat and his friend Jemmy have been captured by two lowlifes who want the King to pay a ransom for the Prince's return. The Prince, however, is refusing to leave and deliver the ransom note to the castle. Included in the segment is the following dialogue between Jemmy and the Prince:

"I've already thought it. Once you're up and gone, I'll slip away. Out in the forest, I'll be harder to catch than a flea."

"But I'm not leaving," said the Prince firmly.

"Gaw! But why? Is it your Pa you're afraid of? Is that why you won't go back?"

The prince scoffed. "He won't miss me."

"Course he will!"

"Let him wait. And mind your own affairs, whipping boy."

As the class explores the developing situation, Ronnie makes the following comment:

RONNIE: While Prince Brat and Jemmy were arguing, Prince
               Brat thought his father wouldn't care if he was gone
               because he didn't think he would like him because
               he was so bad and didn't treat him with respect
               or anything.

The teacher, recognizing that Ronnie has grasped a key to the Prince's situation, marks his comment and invites him to repeat it:

MS. G: Ahh! Ronnie's figured out something very interesting
               about the Prince. I'm wondering, did anyone else
               pick that up? Repeat what you said, Ronnie, because
               that's important.

Marking Ronnie's comment focused attention on building meaning.

Your Turn

The paragraph that follows is from a social studies unit on transportation that describes the completion of the first transcontinental railroad. The teacher's goal was to encourage students to consider the importance of being able to get from one part of the country to another in terms of trade, settling the West, unifying the country, and so on. Given the student response that is first elicited, how would you follow up to help students focus on these bigger issues? Generate as many Follow-Up Queries as you can.

> **On May 10, 1869, the two lines of track met at a place called Promontory Point near Ogden, Utah. A golden spike was driven into the last rail to show that the first transcontinental railroad had been completed. People could now travel from California to New York City on the railroad.**

MS. D: What's the author telling us here that's so important?

STUDENT: You could now go from California to New York
               by train.

➡ Write & Compare Jot down your ideas for Follow-Up Queries on a sheet of paper. Then, compare your Queries with those below.

- That's right, you could go across the country, but why is that so important?

- Okay, you could take a long train ride, but why is that a big deal?

- Right, you could travel across the country by train. But why would this even be important to people who would never make this trip?

Your Turn Again

Now suppose that a student picks up on the meaning focus as indicated below:

STUDENT: It seems like life would get more modern, because you could start getting things easier from all over instead of having all, like, local stuff only.

➡ Write & Compare What Follow-Up Queries would you use to mark the thinking the student has done? Jot down your ideas for Follow-Up Queries on a sheet of paper. Then, compare your Queries with those below.

- Oh, what an interesting observation! More modern. What kinds of changes does that mean?

- That's a neat way to think about it. So, let me ask, how does a railroad going from one part of the country to the other make things more modern? What kinds of things is [student] thinking about?

Recapping

When students respond to Queries as if they were answering traditional questions that have right or wrong answers, it may be because they are not used to using ideas and building meaning from what they read. To develop a meaning orientation, try turning back responsibility for thinking to students by following up their responses with probes that direct their thinking toward meaning. You can also try marking student responses that do show thinking and grappling with ideas.

Too Little Text Covered
How Do You Move Faster?

Some teachers have expressed concern about covering too little text material when they use QtA. They have told us that even though they are satisfied with the way their students are grappling with ideas and building meaning, they sometimes do not finish lessons and worry about not having covered enough text.

Below is Ms. C's journal entry describing her concern about covering text.

> I feel like I'm not moving fast enough through my texts when I am using QtA. The kids are really grappling with text ideas—they are saying and doing things I would have never thought possible. They've even connected ideas we were talking about in social studies to something from science. They are questioning me, interacting with each other, and more and more there is evidence of their deep understanding of what we read. But, all these things take a lot more time than traditional lessons. We're moving through the texts so slowly that I keep wondering how much we can cover by the end of the year.

What Happened and Why?

Covering less text is a natural consequence of dealing with ideas more deeply. And QtA teachers have consistently found that in dealing with ideas more deeply, students understand and "keep" the material they learn. Deeper knowledge is built, and there's less forgetting. Yet we certainly want students to encounter and learn as much information as they can. But *what* information is dealt with deeply is central to understanding the issue. The key is that not all information in texts should be treated equally. Problems can occur when all text information, even less important and less difficult ideas, are given equal treatment.

Dealing with the Problem

Two keys to dealing with the problem of not covering enough text are planning how to handle the text before instruction and pacing yourself during instruction. In handling the text, a QtA teacher has to decide which portions of texts are more and less important. Some portions contain information that is essential to building understanding of the major ideas. Conversely, other portions may be less important or even irrelevant, because they do not support the major ideas of the text. The other key is attending to the pace and progression of discussion. Concerns here include moving on at appropriate times so that discussion doesn't drag and preventing students from going off on tangents.

In this case, we present some ideas on both handling the text and pacing the discussion.

Handling Text

Even though the basic idea of QtA is to grapple with ideas in text, not all text needs extensive grappling. Consider, for example, the text excerpt below, which introduces a unit of study on New England in a social studies textbook:

> **New England is a place of beautiful rocky coastlines, green valleys, many rivers and lakes, and mountains covered with tall trees. The region includes some large cities such as Boston, Massachusetts, and Providence, Rhode Island. New England also has small towns, busy fishing villages, and peaceful farms.**

This introductory paragraph provides a broad overview of what New England is like. As such, there are not a lot of ideas to probe or grapple with. The goal here would be to deal with this portion of text quickly, because devoting time to discussing the features that are mentioned would not really lend itself to building understanding. Below are some ways of dealing with less critical portions of text efficiently.

Signal Students. When a segment of text does not require much attention, signal students that a long discussion is not called for with Queries such as the following:

> So, what we need to know here is really pretty simple. What is the one point the author is making?

or

> All this is really the author's way of saying what? Who can give me just one sentence?

Recap. After a segment has been read, instead of posing a Query, simply recap it yourself:

> We really don't need to spend much time with this, so let me just sum it up. What we want to know from this is that . . .

Provide Overview. Prepare an overview, perhaps as a graphic organizer or outline, that summarizes the most important points of passages you feel the students do not need to take time to read for themselves, but which nonetheless contain some facts you may like them to know. Then work with the overview in the lesson instead of the text itself.

Silent Reading and Student Recaps. Particularly for longer portions of text that contain few important ideas, have students read the segments silently and then call on several students to recap the major points.

Skip It! You may find that some portions of text don't seem worth spending time on. It's better to make a deliberate choice to omit such material along the way than to get to the end of the school year and realize there is material that you will be unable to cover. In these situations, simply tell students that the next several paragraphs of text aren't necessary for the discussion and that you are going to skip them.

Pacing Discussion

The key to pacing discussions to cover text is to avoid getting bogged down in talk for talk's sake—conversation that doesn't build ideas. Sometimes students tend to belabor simple points in a discussion because it's easy to do and provides a way for them to be involved. Thus, it can be difficult for a teacher to cut off participation. However, too much of this kind of talk takes attention away from real learning. Below are some ways of keeping up the pace of discussion while acknowledging students' contributions.

Signal Students. Signal students that it is time to move on in a discussion by saying something like this:

> I think we have some very good ideas, but we need to move ahead and see what else the author has to say.

Quick Responses. To maximize the opportunities for response when lots of students want to contribute, use quick classroom surveys to allow students to signal or quickly respond to the ideas being discussed. For example:

> How many of you agree with what Sam just said?

or

> How many of you think the mystery is about to be solved? How many think it's just another trick?

Recap. When enough attention has been given to a point but students are still eager to discuss it, recap the discussion points, being sure to acknowledge the contributions that students have made. For example:

> Lots of people seemed to have figured out that . . .

or

> You've done a good job on coming to a conclusion about this.
> So, I think we all pretty much agree that . . .

Recapping

Although the amount of text covered is a concern for some teachers, equal coverage of all text is not the goal of a QtA lesson. Rather, a kind of "*un*coverage" is; that is, we want students to dig in and wrestle with important ideas, with the goal of understanding them. Some portions of text can be quickly read, summarized, or skipped altogether. That saves time and attention for more important text ideas.

Follow-Up Queries
How Do You Improvise on Your Feet?

The aspect of fostering a QtA discussion that teachers have found most challenging is improvising good Follow-Up Queries on their feet, or during discussion.
When a student gives a limited or confused response, the teacher has to improvise
effectively if he or she wants to keep the discussion moving.

CLASSROOM SNAPSHOT

Mr. W's social studies class is reading a text segment about people who
agreed to work as indentured servants in order to pay for passage
from England to the New World. As you'll notice below, when Mr. W
poses a Query to get discussion going, a student responds by rereading
from the text. The text segment begins as follows:

**Indentured servants were people who agreed to work for five
or seven years for whoever paid for their passage to America.**

MR. W: Okay, what does the author tell us in this paragraph about
            indentured servants?

DANTE: He said that "Indentured servants were people who
            agreed to work for five or seven years."

What Happened and Why?

Dante's response, as he read from the text, did not even include the complete definition of an indentured servant. His response gave little for Mr. W to go on for developing discussion.

When a student's response doesn't facilitate moving the discussion forward, teachers need to consider how to follow up, how to work with what the student has provided. In a traditional lesson, a teacher would often simply say "No" to a response that was not on target. But in a QtA lesson, the idea is to use student comments to further the discussion. Following up student comments is often not a straightforward process, though, and it can be especially difficult when students give the teacher little to work with.

Dealing with the Problem

Being able to improvise Follow-Up Queries is a new skill that has to be developed. It consists of being able to evaluate a response quickly in terms of what the student has said and the direction of discussion, and then formulate a Query that can move the response in that direction. The goal of the Follow-Up Query is to prompt a more appropriate, meaning-oriented response and to turn back the responsibility for doing so to the students.

Let's look at some examples of how teachers responded to students and the kinds of Follow-Up Queries they developed. Here, we'll be particularly concerned with responses that have limitations, such as being inaccurate, too sparse, or unfocused.

EXAMPLE 1. In this example, a student responds in a way that is inconsistent with information in the text. The text segment concludes with the following:

> But all was not peaceful in the kingdom, just as the wind is
> not always peaceful. . . . The evil men took the emperor to a
> tower in the middle of a wide, treeless plain. The tower had
> only a single window, with an iron bar across the center.
> The plotters sealed the door with bricks and mortar once
> the emperor was inside. Then they rode back to the palace
> and declared that the emperor was dead.

MS. B: Okay. What has the author told us has just happened?

BRYAN: Um, some evil dudes kidnapped the emperor and they
            killed him.

Notice below that in framing his follow-up to Bryan's comment, the teacher echoes the comment and then uses the Discussion Move of turning-back to text by asking whether "the author tells us that."

MS. B: Kidnapped the emperor and killed him? Does the
            author tell us that?

The teacher's Follow-Up Query encouraged students to check the information given in Bryan's response, as evidenced by the following comment from Doreen, which clarifies the text event.

DOREEN: I disagree with Bryan because they said, um, there was
            some evil men, and they didn't like the emperor and
            so, um, they took him to the treeless plain and they
            put him in this, like, a little cage, and then they sealed
            him up, but they didn't kill him.

EXAMPLE 2. In this example, students in a social studies class are reading about the lifestyle and environment of the Plains Indians. Following are the final sentences of the text segment:

> But most of the land that makes up the Great Plains is dry
> and hard. There are almost no trees. The land is covered by
> short grass with tough roots, making it almost impossible to
> dig up the soil without metal tools.

Notice below, in response to the teacher's Initiating Query, Shirelle presents some verbatim text information:

MR. J:	What has the author just told us in that paragraph?
SHIRELLE:	He told us that, um, most of the land is, um, hard and dry.

The teacher then asks the Follow-Up Query below to encourage students to think about the meaning behind the author's words.

MR. J:	Ah, the author told us that the land is hard, and dry, but what does the author mean by that?

Notice that by asking students to think about what the author means, the teacher encourages several students to consider the deeper meaning, the consequences of "hard, dry land."

CURT:	That the Indians can't grow crops or nothing.
MOIRA:	There weren't many trees neither 'cause there's not enough water to make them grow.
ALETHA:	And because the ground is too hard, they can't farm and they can't plant nothin'.

EXAMPLE 3. In the following example, a class is reading *The Gift* (Coutant, 1983), a story about the friendship between Anna, a young girl, and Nana Marie, an elderly woman. The text segment portrays a conversation between Anna and Nana Marie's daughter-in-law, Rita. Rita tells Anna that Nana Marie has become blind and that she is about to come home from the hospital. Then, Rita invites Anna to a party for the old woman. The segment ends as follows:

> **"So you'll come!"** Rita repeated, her voice rising.
>
> Anna couldn't answer. She pulled back, nodding, and turned away. She walked carefully around the puddles in the road. Her whispered "good-bye" floated up unheard by Rita, who was already going in the house, shivering from the February cold.

The teacher poses a Query about the segment which draws a lengthy, unfocused response from a student:

MS. B: Okay. What's the author saying about Anna here?

LORETTA: That, um, they was at the hospital and, um, Anna didn't know that she was going to come home, Anna didn't know. And Rita told Anna that she was blind, and Anna was surprised because she was totally blind. And they was throwing a party for her. So this afternoon she just asked her to come back. And Anna is worried about, um, Nana Marie, 'cause it's her friend and she was thinking about when they met.

Notice that in responding to the array of facts Loretta has given, the teacher focuses on the idea that is key to the segment and pursues its meaning:

MS. B: Okay, you've said a lot of things. Let's kind of sort this out. First of all, Loretta says that Anna is very surprised and shocked to find out that Nana Marie is blind. So what does that mean?

Your Turn

In the following example, a class is discussing how farm animals were transported in pioneer days. Evaluate the student response and decide what Follow-Up Query you would use.

> **Many of the farm products of the West go to eastern markets on the hoof. Since we started, we have passed 6 droves of cattle, 22 droves of sheep, and a flock of 300 turkeys guided by a father and 4 small boys. At one place, the road was a living mass of hogs being driven to Baltimore—4,000 head, we were told.**

MS. R:	What picture is the author creating for us here?
PAUL:	Driving animals to market. The animals were raised in the West, and they're being taken to the East.

➡️ ***Write & Compare*** Jot down your ideas for a Follow-Up Query on a sheet of paper. Then, compare your Query with the one below.

> But how were the animals driven? What does the author mean by "on the hoof"?

The Follow-Up Query above involved turning-back to text.

Recapping

Following up on student comments is a demanding task that involves evaluating what students say and figuring out how their responses can be used to further discussion. Follow-Up Queries can turn the responsibility for developing more appropriate or meaning-oriented thinking back to students. Challenge them to deal with the meaning behind an author's words or suggest they turn back to text to reconsider their response in light of text information. When students offer unfocused responses, Follow-Up Queries can also focus attention on the information that relates to the most important text ideas.

Student Responses That Contain Wrong Information
How Do You Deal with Misconceptions?

Dealing with student responses that are wrong is a concern for QtA teachers. In particular, is it possible to efficiently deal with misconceptions without taking the discussion off track?

Ms. D's journal entry below illustrates the problems misconception can create.

Today in class, we were reading about the Bering Strait and how land between Asia and North America was once connected by what the author called a "land bridge." The word "bridge" became an unexpected source of confusion— with the students not understanding that the word was used metaphorically. The students took the author's words literally, thinking that people had once built a bridge between the two continents so that they could walk across it. I tried to lead them to understand that the author did not intend the word to be taken literally, but I could tell that my Follow-Up Queries were not working, and students kept returning to the bridge idea. I ended up yelling at them, "There's no bridge!" They looked at me in confusion, the discussion halted, and I felt bad. I don't know what to do when kids get these kinds of misconceptions.

What Happened and Why?

Constructing meaning from text during reading involves some unraveling of ideas and words. So it's natural that there will be times in discussions when students misinterpret or misunderstand an author's meaning. Clarifying misconceptions with Follow-Up Queries can be time consuming and even distract from the goals of a discussion. In addition, such responses need to be handled with care to avoid signaling that only "right" answers are permitted, which can discourage participation.

Dealing with the Problem

Most important is not to leave students with misinformation. There are a number of ways that you can use the Discussion Moves of turning-back to text, modeling, and annotating to step in and steer things in the right direction without changing the tone of the discussion. Selecting the most appropriate move depends on the extent and source of the problem, as discussed below.

Turning-Back to Text. Use turning-back to text to help students clarify misconceptions when you determine that paying closer attention to what the author has said can clear them up. Returning to text gives students an opportunity to reread an author's words and reconsider their thinking. For example, in the situation that Ms. D described about the land-bridge confusion, she might have said something like this:

> Okay. We seem to have some confusion about this "bridge" thing. Let's read again what the author actually wrote, and when we do, think about what the author meant by a *land bridge*.

In this way, you can cue students that they probably are misunderstanding something, and that they have a chance to use the text as a resource to ground their rethinking. It is also helpful to emphasize any aspect of the text that may help clarify the issue, such as stressing the word *land* in the term *land bridge*.

Modeling. Modeling the students' confusion can be an effective way to draw attention to a misconception and to the idea that it can be difficult to understand ideas in a text. For example:

> This is very confusing about a bridge across the Bering Strait. How could people back that long ago build a bridge over that much water? It doesn't make sense. What do you think the author meant by using the word *bridge*?

Modeling is probably most effective when followed by turning-back the responsibility to students. Invite them to identify the source of misunderstanding themselves and to correct it.

Annotating. If confusion persists, and the text doesn't offer enough information to clarify the matter, annotating the text may be the appropriate Discussion Move. In a straightforward manner, provide information that will either fill in the gaps or clarify the idea or wording that students are struggling with. For example, Ms. D might have used annotating in the land-bridge discussion as follows:

> When the author used the term *land bridge* in this paragraph, I think he confused us a little. It sounded like he might be talking about the kinds of bridges we all know, the ones that people build. But he used the word *bridge* to describe the narrow piece of land that connected the continents back then—to help us picture it in our mind.

Recapping

Sometimes authors do not provide enough information, or they use difficult language. When this happens, students can easily develop misconceptions. Teachers deal with misconceptions by stepping into discussions and keeping them moving in the right direction. Turning-back to text gives students a chance to reread and reconsider what the author said and meant. Modeling confusion encourages students to dig in and correct their own misunderstandings. And finally, annotating the text provides necessary information that students cannot generate or discover on their own.

Ideas Going Astray
How Do You Get Students to Turn-Back to Text?

Teachers have told us that sometimes students seem to ignore the author's ideas even though they are relevant to the issue at hand. Of course, the point of QtA is for students to construct meaning themselves, but they sometimes seem to forget that the text is a source of ideas.

CLASSROOM SNAPSHOT

Ms. T's class is reading about the growth of cities and towns in Pennsylvania. After reading and discussing a segment about Philadelphia, the class reads the following text segment:

As time passed, other towns began to appear in Pennsylvania. Farmers needed a place to sell their goods. The places where they met became small towns. Soon blacksmiths, shoemakers, and other craftsmen began to do business in the towns.

Ms. T's goal is to have students understand that many towns originated as places where farmers gathered to market their goods. This idea is pretty clear in the text, but notice below that students begin to go in other directions:

MS. T: What's the author telling us in that short paragraph?

BETH: That blacksmiths and craftsmen, um, work in the towns.

MS. T: But why did those craftsmen come to the towns?

RICKY:	Well, whenever we had that filmstrip about they were right on the water, and you could get to all the streets by water.
MS. T:	Okay, you're remembering what we learned from the filmstrip about Philadelphia. But we want to know how just any old town might have started.
MIKE:	The church, like the Quakers.
MS. T:	No, we're not just talking about Philadelphia. This could be any town in any of the colonies.
JASON:	Religion.

What Happened and Why?

As Ms. T pursued the point of generalizing about how towns began, the students seemed to lose sight of the fact that what they were seeking was in the text. As soon as Ricky brought the filmstrip about Philadelphia into the discussion, it seemed to take over as the source for students' responses. Ms. T tried to get students back on track by guiding them away from the specific case of Philadelphia. But confusion between "specific" and "general" was not the only problem. At least part of the problem was that students were no longer dealing with the text.

Dealing with the Problem

Dealing with the problem of students wandering from the text begins by realizing that at times students may actually forget that it is ideas from the text that are under consideration. When students respond to an issue by contributing what they know about it from other sources—prior knowledge, a film, for example—they can lose sight that a primary source is the text in front of them.

Of course, bringing in information from other sources is good and often very useful. The problem arises, however, when students don't first take account of what has already been given in the text. The most direct and effective way to deal with this problem is to use the Discussion Move of turning-back to text. Simply ask students to reread the text itself.

EXAMPLE 1. The class in this example is reading the story "Tonweya and the Eagles" from the book *Tonweya and the Eagles: And Other Lakota Tales* (Yellow Robe, 1992). The class has read that a young Native American boy, Tonweya, spotted baby eagles in a nest and wanted to capture them. He began by making a rope from buffalo hide. The next paragraph then describes how he uses a rope to get to the eagles' nest:

> **Coiling this about him, he made his way to the tip of the cliff right above the eagle's nest on the ledge. Fastening one end of this rawhide rope to a jack pine, he let the other fall over the ledge. Looking down he saw that it hung within a few feet of the nest. His plan was to slide down the rope and tie the eaglets to the end. Then after he had pulled himself up again, he could draw them up after him. Great honor would come to him. A pair of captive eagles would supply feathers for many warriors.**

For this segment, the teacher wants to establish how Tonweya plans to capture the eaglets, because the demise of his plan is the basis for the plot of the story. But notice that rather than summarizing the author's ideas about Tonweya's plan, Teresa's comments take a different direction:

MS. A: What's the author describing for us now?

TERESA: The author's telling what Tonweya's gonna do with the eaglets, their feathers, when they grow up.

The teacher tries to get the focus back on Tonweya's plan, but Mona follows the line of thinking that Teresa started instead of taking the teacher's lead:

MS. A: Right, Teresa. But the author really told us about why he wanted the eagles before. What new information did we get about what Tonweya's up to?

MONA: He might, um, just take them and kill them, the baby eagles. Probably they don't know who their mom or dad is.

The teacher tries again to reestablish focus on Tonweya's plan. But notice that this is not enough to direct attention to the text until she explicitly directs students back to the text:

MS. A: But what did we learn about the kind of plan that Tonweya was making?

NORMAN: He coulda been planning to, like, take them and use their feathers and maybe, I don't think he'd kill them, but maybe use them for other things, like help him hunt.

MS. A: I think you're making guesses about what Tonweya might do. But the author told us some details about his plan. We better go back and check it out again. Who can read us what the author told us about Tonweya's plan to get the eagles?

By explicitly turning-back to text, she finally succeeded in getting the discussion back to the information that the author offered about Tonweya's plan.

EXAMPLE 2. In this example, the class is reading about the Southern colonies and beginning to focus on the concept of an indentured servant. Here are portions of the text segment that the class has just completed:

> Nearly all the workers in the South in colonial times were unfree. . . . There were two main groups of unfree labor. They were indentured servants and slaves.
>
> Indentured servants were people who agreed to work for five or seven years for whoever paid their passage to America. . . . Indentured servants received food, shelter, and clothing, but they got no wages for their work. At the end of their term they would sometimes receive land and a chance to start out on their own.

Notice below that discussion begins as one student describes what she understands an indentured servant to be, and then a disagreement emerges.

> BRITTANY: They get to come to America, but then they gotta work for whoever paid their way for five years.
>
> CARLA: I disagree! They work—how can they come to America without working? They work for five years and then get to come to America.
>
> MALLORY: But if they didn't get paid they wouldn't be able to go to America.

As students argue the issue, they seem unaware that referring to the text could resolve their question. At this point, the teacher intervenes:

> MS. K: Wait a minute! We have a disagreement about whether these people are working in England before getting to come to America or already in America. We better bring the author back into the conversation here; I think we already have that information. What does this tell you: "Nearly all the workers in the South in colonial times were unfree. . . . There were two . . . groups. . . . indentured servants and slaves"?
>
> MALLORY: Oh! They were workers in the South—they were already here, doing their work.

The teacher's comment about "bringing the author back into the conversation" is a nice way to point out that discussion should be grounded in the information provided in the text.

Your Turn

In the example below, the class is reading about sheep shearing. The teacher wants students to understand why sheepherders need to shear the sheep when spring comes. But students go off in a different direction.

Describe your take on what's happening to the conversation. Why doesn't Ms. C's Query work? How would you intervene and refocus the discussion?

> **The spring weather gets hotter and hotter. The sheep begin to get uncomfortable in their thick wool coats. They start to rub themselves against rocks. If we don't shear them soon, all the good wool gets left behind on bushes and rocks.**

MS. C: So, what important information has the author told us about here?

JONATHAN: They shear the sheep in the spring because they get so hot.

MARLENE: The sheep start rubbing on rocks and they could hurt themselves.

MS. C: You've said a lot about the sheep, but what about the sheepherders?

ANTHONY: My mom has a coat with sheepskin for winter. It's like a real heavy fur thing on the inside. The sheep would be wearing that in the spring, so the sheepherders cut it off so the sheep don't die of the heat.

➡️ **Write & Compare** Jot down your idea for refocusing the discussion on a sheet of paper. Then, compare your idea with the one below.

The teacher's Query about the sheepherders provided a cue directing students back to the text, but it wasn't explicit enough, as evidenced by Anthony's comment. To get the discussion back on track, a teacher may need to explicitly ask students to go back to the text:

> I agree that the sheepherders don't want the sheep to die. But there's something else the sheepherders are concerned about. Let's go back and read what the author tells us about why the sheepherders are eager to shear the sheep.

Recapping

Sometimes students wander away from the text to talk about or question ideas that the author has already explained. When this happens, students need to be reminded to return to the text to bring the author back into the conversation. The turning-back-to-text move is an effective way to do this.

Focusing Comments
How Do You Make a Discussion More Than a Collection of Comments?

Teachers have told us that sometimes the comments of students seem scattered. Getting the focus on important ideas and themes seems difficult. A characteristic that may underlie this problem is a tendency to "collect" students' comments rather than using them to build understanding.

CLASSROOM SNAPSHOT

Ms. D and her class are finishing the story *The Wreck of the Zephyr* by Chris Van Allsburg. Ms. D's Query is meant to focus on how to interpret the story's ending.

"A remarkable tale," I said, as the old man stopped to relight his pipe. "What happened to the boy?"

"He broke his leg that night. Of course, no one believed his story about flying boats. It was easier for them to believe that he was lost in the storm and thrown up here by the waves." The old man laughed.

"No sir, the boy never amounted to much. People thought he was crazy. He just took odd jobs around the harbor. Most of the time he was out sailing, searching for that island and a new set of sails."

A light breeze blew through the trees. The old man looked up. "Wind coming," he said. "I've got some sailing to do." He picked up a cane, and I watched as he limped slowly toward the harbor.

MS. D:	What's the author told us about the man who's been telling this story?
SARAH:	He was the boy.
MS. D:	Oh, okay. Robert?
ROBERT:	That nobody believed him, that he sailed like that.
MS. D:	Oh, no one believed him.
CERINA:	The guy who he told the story to didn't believe him either.
MS. D:	What makes you think that?

What Happened and Why

What's happening here is that Ms. D has collected three different comments, and then followed up on only one—in fact, the one that does not seem on target in terms of the Initiating Query. What is likely to follow is a discussion of whether the narrator believed the tale, which is not key to this story. In addition, the significance of whether the man telling the story was the boy himself goes unexamined. Many children in the class may not have figured that out. Moreover, because the teacher seemed to ignore it, students may figure that it was not the case. So even if they had formed the hypothesis that the old man was the boy who had sailed the boat, they may now doubt it. The student's comment about no one believing the boy, which also had merit, met with the same fate.

Dealing with the Problem

Teachers often tend to collect comments from several students without responding to the *content* of the comment itself. Perhaps they want to give other students a chance to respond before revealing the direction of the discussion. Or perhaps they feel that other students will recognize when a student gets the important point, so little more is needed. But lack of acknowledgment leaves questions in the air for students. They most likely take it to mean that the comment was either incorrect or not important. So the next student tends to take the discussion in a new direction.

In general, the teacher needs to deal with responses to guide students and establish the direction of the discussion. This can be done through marking and Follow-Up Queries that provide a thread for the discussion. Let's look at some examples.

EXAMPLE 1. How could Ms. D have responded to Sarah's comment about the end of the "Zephyr" story? Sarah's response, that the man telling the story was the little boy who had sailed the boat, is a good interpretation. Consider how the following response could open up discussion:

MS. D:	Oh, Sarah! How interesting! How did Sarah get to that idea, do you think?
DAVID:	'Cause he walked away with a limp.
MS. D:	And what does that tell you?
DAVID:	Well, the boy who sailed got a broken leg after he crashed. So it could have been left over from that.
ALVIN:	But just because you get a broken leg you don't have to limp.
MARLA:	But it just really seems like it connects. Why would he say that at the end about him limping then?
MS. D:	That is a very interesting observation, Marla. Jeffrey, what do you think of that?
JEFFREY:	Well, like, he didn't have to limp because he broke his leg, maybe, but I think Marla's right. It just seems like those things that authors tell you. It, like, has to be a big deal for the story.

By following up Sarah's seemingly complete comment, Ms. D prompted an insightful discussion about the story.

EXAMPLE 2. In the following example, the class is reading the book *The Talking Eggs* (San Souci, 1989). Notice that when the teacher's follow-ups don't focus on the content of the students' responses, students receive an unintended message about the direction in which to take their responses.

One hot day the mother sent **Blanche** to the well to fetch a bucket of water. When the girl got there, she found an old woman wrapped in a raggedy black shawl, near fainting with the heat.

"Please, child, give me a sip of water," the old woman said. "I'm 'bout to die of thirst."

"Yes, aunty," said Blanche, rinsing out her bucket and dipping up some clean, cool well water. "Drink what you need."

"Thank you, child," said the old woman when she'd taken swallow after swallow of water. "You got a spirit of do-right in your soul. God is gonna bless you." Then she walked away down the path that led to the deep woods.

When Blanche got back to the cabin, her mother and sister hollered at her for taking so long.

MS. K:	What is the author letting us know here?
DOLORES:	That the old woman knows Blanche is a good person.
MS. K:	Okay, what else?
AARON:	The mother and sister are still yelling at her.
MS. K:	Do you have something to add, Joyce?
JOYCE:	She had to get the water, like, do everything for them.

At this point, Ms. K realizes that her Follow-Up Queries are inviting students to merely list events from the story rather than to connect ideas toward building an understanding. So she changes tactics:

MS. K:	Okay, you're all telling me about things that happened in this section. Let's go back to what Dolores first said, though. She said that this old lady knows that Blanche is a good person. Well, how does that fit in with the rest of Blanche's life?
EDWARD:	The old lady sees good things in her, but her mother and sister don't.

MS. K:	Okay, she sees Blanche differently. And do you think that's important here?
JEREMY:	Yeah, 'cause then she says, "God is gonna bless you."
MS. K:	Hmmm, I see. What do you think that means?
FRANCINE:	I think the author is, like, setting up something. The old lady really knows she's gonna do something nice to her.
MS. K:	Ah! Well, let's watch and see. Gabby, continue reading.

So by pursuing the theme Dolores introduced—the old woman's view of Blanche—Ms. K prompted a focused discussion.

Your Turn

The text that follows is about William Penn's founding of the Pennsylvania colony as a haven for religious freedom. What Follow-Up Query would you use to focus the discussion and prevent it from becoming a collection of comments?

Quakers in England were treated badly for their beliefs. Many, including William Penn, were sent to prison. Quakers were also unwelcome in most American colonies. Quakers who tried to settle in Massachusetts were told to leave. Penn longed for a place where Quakers could follow their beliefs in peace.

As it happened, the king of England owed a large amount of money to William Penn's father. When his father died, William Penn asked the king to settle the debt by giving him land in America. King Charles agreed. Penn named the new colony Pennsylvania after his father. Pennsylvania means "Penn's Woods."

Penn said his colony would be a "holy experiment." He invited people of all religions and from all countries to live there.

MS. F:	What has the author told us? Why is Penn's colony different?
STACEY:	It was a kind of holy experiment.
MS. F:	Okay, Jordan?
JORDAN:	The name of it meant Penn's Woods.

➡️ ***Write & Compare*** Jot down your ideas for Follow-Up Queries on a sheet of paper. Then, compare your Queries with those below.

- Okay, its name was one difference. And, as Stacey said, Penn called it a holy experiment. What did he mean by that?

- So Penn's Woods was to be a holy experiment. Why? What made it an experiment?

Recapping

When teachers don't respond to the *content* of students' comments, students have little direction about the focus of discussion. The result may be a collection of unconnected comments. A teacher needs to give some guidance to students by dealing with the content of responses to establish a focus. Marking and Follow-Up Queries can provide a thread that connects comments and directs them toward building understanding.

Not Getting Anywhere
What Do You Do When Discussion Is Stuck?

Some teachers have described getting stuck as they try to follow up student responses to get a discussion moving. These situations seem to arise when a student's response has potential but may be incomplete or confused, or doesn't go in the direction that the teacher intended.

CLASSROOM SNAPSHOT

Ms. D and her class are reading a text segment about how animals adapt to the climate of the Alaskan tundra. Ms. D wants students to understand that animals adapt by growing thicker fur and changing color in winter. Here is the text and how the discussion begins:

Some animals are well suited to life in the cold parts of Alaska. These animals have bodies that help them live where it is cold. Their bodies are covered with fur. During the coldest parts of the year their fur gets very thick. The Arctic fox has fur that changes from brown to white in the winter.

MS. D: What's the author's message here?

MONA: The fox's fur changes to white in the winter, because it has lots of snow and might be cold.

Mona had parts of the two ideas that Ms. D wants to target, and Ms. D figures that she can get the two separated and the missing pieces filled in pretty readily, so she simply invites students to add on. But notice what happens:

AARON: I think it was changing colors because the brown color might be skinnier, not as thick.

MS. D:	Okay, well, you're talking about the fur getting thinner or thicker. Can anyone add to that or suggest a different idea?
LAUREEN:	I think the author's trying to say when it turns white it gets thicker, and brown is thinner.
MS. D:	Okay. Does anyone have a different idea?
ANGEL:	The animals' coats protect them in cold places.

What Happened and Why?

Ms. D's students apparently thought that the thickness of the fur and its color were related. Asking students to come up with "a different idea" or to "add to" what had been said was not enough to help them pull apart the two ideas on the table.

Dealing with the Problem

When students seem stuck in an incomplete or confused idea, they often need to be pointed to the ideas that are missing. Teachers can create such pointers by marking important content, revoicing what students have said to clarify ideas, or providing information through annotating or modeling. Let's look at some examples where teachers were able to use these Discussion Moves to point students in productive directions.

EXAMPLE 1. The discussion in Ms. D's class has turned to what life is like in Alaska today. Students are reading a section of text called "The Last Frontier." The discussion gets stuck because students do not fully understand the idea the text is trying to communicate. In the example, the class grapples with the following text sentence:

Much of the tundra and the interior of Alaska are not settled.

MS. D:	What is the author talking about by saying *not settled?*

HOLLY:	I think that would be, like, the land is, you're kind of getting ready to build houses.
MS. D:	Hmmm, okay. Diedra, what do you think?
DIEDRA:	I think they're gonna start out and begin and then build it up.

At this point, Ms. D sees that the discussion may be getting stuck on what *not settled* means. So she revoices the responses of Holly and Diedra, adding some direction before turning it back to the students again:

MS. D:	Okay, let's think this through. Holly and Diedra are saying it means they're getting ready to build houses, maybe, but there aren't any there yet. If it's an area that's not settled, no houses, no buildings yet, what picture is the author giving you of this area? What's it like?

With Ms. D's comments to guide them, students begin to come up with descriptions such as "open," "empty," and "wild," which help lead them to the idea of a frontier.

EXAMPLE 2. Sometimes discussion gets stuck because the students don't seem to be on the same wavelength as the teacher. This next example illustrates such a situation. The class is reading an introduction to *The Cricket in Times Square* (Selden, 1970). The introduction concludes as follows:

> **Chester's friends Tucker Mouse and Harry Cat also live in the subway station. When this story begins, Tucker talks Chester into letting him sleep in the cricket cage. Tucker uses dollar bills for blankets because they make him feel rich.**

As a way of setting the context, the teacher wants to bring attention to the fact that this is going to be a very imaginative story:

MS. D:	What kind of a story is the author telling you this is going to be? There's this mouse who uses dollar bills for blankets—what's that tell you?
SHARON:	They make him feel rich when he sleeps on dollar bills.

MS. D:	But what do we know about the *kind* of story it is?
KELLY:	He's probably sleeping on the dollar bills so nobody can take his money.

It is becoming apparent to the teacher that the students don't know where she is going with her question. So she uses the Discussion Move of modeling to let students in on what she is thinking:

MS. D:	Well, what I thought about was not so much what things might happen in the story, but I thought, well, we've got these animals talking, and a mouse who likes dollar bills, so it's gonna be an unusual story—it's a story of imagination.

In this example, it was clear that the students did not understand what the teacher had in mind. Seeing that, the teacher intervened rather than have the students continue to grope around for a response.

EXAMPLE 3. A situation can occur when teachers try to prompt students to attend to a particular text phrase or statement. In this next example, the class is reading *McBroom Tells a Lie* (Fleischman, 1976), a story that features much descriptive language and wordplay. The teacher wants to draw students' attention to a phrase that the author uses to describe a new character. Below is the text under discussion:

> **And along came our foxy-eyed neighbor, Heck Jones. You never saw such a spare-ribbed and rattleboned man. Why, he was so skinny he could slip through a knothole without tipping his hat. He wore a diamond stickpin in his tie and was swinging a bamboo cane. Our dog, Zip, stood barking at him.**

Because the phrase *foxy-eyed* foreshadows Heck Jones' intentions in the story, the teacher wants students to explore its meaning. But notice below how she begins and what happens:

MS. Y:	How does the author describe Heck Jones, the neighbor?
TONYA:	He's very skinny. He's so skinny, he could fit through a knothole.

MS. Y:	Imagine that! He'd fit through a knothole, without tipping his hat! What else does the author tell us?
MARIA:	He's spare-ribbed and rattleboned.
MS. Y:	Okay, and how about this, what is the author telling us about Mr. Jones when he calls him the "foxy-eyed neighbor"?

When the teacher realized that the phrase she wanted to highlight was not what students were attending to, she presented it explicitly and asked the students to respond to its meaning. That may seem pretty straightforward. But what we've seen happen is that teachers frequently allude to the phrase they want students to attend to, rather than explicitly providing it.

Your Turn

In the example that follows, a class is discussing the law that would allow British officials to inspect the homes of American colonists to search for smuggled goods. The students seem to get stuck on the colonists' dislike for the law even though the teacher tries to direct their attention to *why* the law was so hateful to the colonists. What would you do to get the discussion moving again?

> **Colonists hated this new law. They still thought of themselves as "Englishmen." One of the important "rights of Englishmen" was that a person's home was safe from searches by the government. Now the British government was taking this right away from them.**

MR. W:	What has the author told us about in this paragraph?
MONICA:	The colonists, they're mad.
SANDY:	The colonists hate the law about searching because it's not fair.
MR. W:	Yes, the colonists are quite angry about the new law. What makes the law so hateful to them?
NED:	It's not fair to have your house searched.

RONNIE: How would you feel if somebody just knocked at your door and could come right in anytime they wanted to?

SONJA: It's not right to have the power to just bust into your house.

TARA: When you have a place, it's yours and you decide who you let in.

➡️ **_Write & Compare_** Jot down your ideas for moving the discussion along on a sheet of paper. Then, compare your ideas with those below.

To get students to focus on *why* the colonists were particularly upset by the search law instead of continuing to restate the idea that the colonists thought the law was unfair, the teacher decides to use the Discussion Move of turning-back to text.

> Okay. You're talking about how unfair the colonists thought the law was. I think we all agree that it must be awful to have your house searched, but what information did the author give us to let us know why the colonists thought this law was particularly hateful? Go back into the text to find the explanation the author gave us.

Recapping

Sometimes discussions seem to get stuck because students are focusing on only one aspect of a situation instead of thinking about the bigger picture. At other times, students may not be on the same wavelength as the teacher. They just are not thinking about the idea or information the teacher wants them to focus on. In such cases, a combination of the Discussion Moves of revoicing, turning-back to text, modeling, and annotating can be used to get things moving in a more productive direction.

Unanticipated Student Comments
How Can You Expect the Unexpected?

QtA teachers have told us that their students sometimes come up with responses they never expected. Getting caught off guard by unexpected responses can sometimes cause a teacher to temporarily lose the focus of the discussion. They asked us: What can I do to expect the unexpected?

Ms. K poses a general Initiating Query she has developed to start a discussion of a text segment about how the ancestors of the Eskimos had traveled from Asia to North America. But as you'll see below, that's not what a student focuses on.

The Eskimos are thought to have come to Alaska from Asia. Between Alaska and Asia there is a narrow body of water called the Bering Strait. Many people think that about 6,000 years ago the Eskimos came by boat or walked on the ice blocks that sometimes jammed the Bering Strait. Other people think the Eskimos came much earlier, when there was a land bridge between Asia and North America.

MS. K: What's the author talking about here?

DARLENE: He's trying to tell us that some people came, they came, um, different ways to get to Alaska. He's trying to say, like, they now live there.

What Happened and Why?

Darlene seemed to have difficulty recognizing or articulating the text's major ideas. The response she offered caught Ms. K off guard because it didn't focus on the key points of the text segment. Why did that happen?

When Queries bring unexpected responses from students, it may be that during planning the teacher did not fully consider how text ideas may appear from a student's viewpoint. Often a line of thinking in a text that seems obvious to a mature reader is not so clear to young students. Key ideas may not stand out or may not be easily explained.

Dealing with the Problem

Take another look at the text segment from the Classroom Snapshot, and as you do, consider the density of ideas in the segment:

> **The Eskimos are thought to have come to Alaska from Asia. Between Alaska and Asia there is a narrow body of water called the Bering Strait. Many people think that about 6,000 years ago the Eskimos came by boat or walked on the ice blocks that sometimes jammed the Bering Strait. Other people think the Eskimos came much earlier, when there was a land bridge between Asia and North America.**

Just a brief accounting of the ideas in that short segment includes:

- Eskimos came to Alaska from Asia
- Between Asia and Alaska is a narrow body of water called the Bering Strait
- Eskimos may have come 6,000 years ago
- Eskimos may have come by boat
- Eskimos may have walked over on ice blocks
- Some say Eskimos came earlier
- There was a land bridge between Asia and North America

With so much information to deal with, it would be a good idea to phrase the Initiating Query so that it alerts students to the complexity of the material and focuses their attention. For example, "The author is giving us a lot of ideas about something that happened a long, long time ago. But what's he saying that these people did way back then?"

It also would be helpful in this instance to segment the text so students are not faced with all the material at once. But developing thoughtful Initiating Queries and carefully segmenting the text may not be enough, given the difficulty and density of the material. Planning should also include thinking about how students may respond and effective follow-ups. So, let's do that now.

EXAMPLE 1. Let's consider a plan for the Eskimos text that divides the content into two segments and anticipates students' responses.

It may help to stop before the last sentence of the paragraph, because that sentence, about the land bridge, greatly complicates the picture. Below, then, is the proposed first segment:

> **The Eskimos are thought to have come to Alaska from Asia. Between Alaska and Asia there is a narrow body of water called the Bering Strait. Many people think that about 6,000 years ago the Eskimos came by boat or walked on the ice blocks that sometimes jammed the Bering Strait.**

Discussion could be initiated with this Query:

What's the author telling us about the Eskimos?

Now, let's consider how students may respond to that Query and some possible follow-ups. Suppose a student said something like this:

The Eskimos came from Asia to Alaska.

A Follow-Up Query may help students think about how it might have been possible to travel from Asia to Alaska 6,000 years ago. For example:

And how could they have done that?

Students may respond by saying something like this:

The Eskimos came by boat or walked on ice blocks.

A Follow-Up Query may encourage students to consider that what's being talked about is a journey from Asia to Alaska. For example:

Okay, well, whether they walked or came by boat, what was it that was happening?

A potential snag is that students could misconstrue "coming to Alaska" as simply traveling or commuting rather than as a permanent migration. The following Query may uncover this problem:

We think of Eskimos as always living in Alaska, but the author is telling us that if you go back long enough, what do you learn about those Eskimos?

If students have difficulty responding, a useful Follow-Up Query might turn students' thinking back to the first sentence of the segment:

What did the author mean when he said, "The Eskimos are thought to have come to Alaska from Asia?"

Now, let's assume it's time to move to the second text segment, the final sentence of the paragraph, which offers an alternative explanation for how the Eskimos made the journey to Alaska:

Other people think the Eskimos came much earlier, when there was a land bridge between Asia and North America.

A potential snag here is the term *land bridge*. The meaning of the word *bridge* as a human-made structure is so strong for young students that the notion of a natural bridge-like formation can be quite puzzling. Given the potential for confusion, it may be helpful to begin with a Query such as this:

The author mentions a "land bridge." Hmmm, what do you think a land bridge could be?

Once it's established that the author means that a strip of land once connected Asia to Alaska, discussion can continue, possibly with a Query such as this:

So, what's the author telling us about how this land bridge might have been used?

Suppose a student said something like this in response:

> The Eskimos could have come across this land bridge to get to Alaska.

A Follow-Up Query could help students understand that this is an alternative explanation, and that no one knows exactly what happened that long ago:

> How does that fit in with what we read in the first part of the paragraph about the Eskimos?

If students don't seem to understand that the text is providing two possible explanations, using the Discussion Move of turning-back to text could encourage that understanding:

> What do you think the author means by "The Eskimos are *thought* to have come" and "Other people *think*"?

EXAMPLE 2. In getting ready for a lesson, trying to expect the unexpected is important, but no plan is foolproof. Unanticipated responses will occur and need to be handled on the fly.

In the Classroom Snapshot, Darlene's response to Ms. K's Initiating Query did not include any of the important ideas in the text segment. Ms. K was unsure how to use Darlene's response. As you will see below, her Follow-Up Query is a very general invitation to add to what has been said.

> MS. K: Good. Darlene said that the author's telling us that there are different ways. Can anyone add to that?
>
> ALVIS: The author is trying to tell us how the people traveled back and forth from Alaska, like, if somebody was traveling, they lived in the suburbs and they were traveling to the city.

Because Ms. K's Query was so unfocused, Alvis's response moved the discussion even further away from the major issue. A more effective Follow-Up Query might have directed attention toward the issue of Eskimos migrating from Asia. The follow-up could include revoicing to incorporate some of Darlene's contribution. For example:

> What is the author telling us about—as Darlene put it—these people who came to Alaska and live there now?

If such a Follow-Up Query fails to take discussion in the right direction, Ms. K may use the Discussion Move of turning-back to text and ask students to focus on a key sentence:

> What does the author mean by "The Eskimos are thought to have come to Alaska from Asia"?

But let's imagine Alvis still offered the response about traveling to the suburbs. Ms. K can handle this by challenging Alvis's comment with a Follow-Up Query to direct students to turn back to text:

> Well, you're talking about one kind of traveling. But is that what the author is talking about? Let's look again at what the author says. He begins by telling us, "The Eskimos are thought to have come to Alaska from Asia." What is he talking about?

Your Turn

Think about how to prepare for the unexpected for the text segment below. Begin by making notes about the ideas the text presents and any difficulties students may have in building an understanding of them.

> **Like all living things, trees need food to grow. The leaves make food for the tree. They use the water and minerals which the roots take from the ground. The leaves also use sunlight and a gas from the air called carbon dioxide. A green substance in the leaves, called chlorophyll, mixes the gas, the sunlight, the water, and the minerals to make the food. The food passes from the leaves to the rest of the tree.**

➡ ***Write & Compare*** Jot down the text ideas and possible difficulties on a sheet of paper. Then, compare your notes with those below.

Text ideas:

- Trees need food to grow

- Food for trees is made within the leaves

- The process uses water and minerals from the ground, as well as sunlight and carbon dioxide

- Chlorophyll is a green substance in the leaves

- Chlorophyll mixes the gas, minerals, sunlight, and water to make food

- Food passes from the leaves through the rest of the tree

Possible difficulties:

- The idea that leaves "make" food does not coincide with how students usually think of food, which is as a product that humans and animals seek in their environment.

- The idea that a tree makes its own food is something that students may have heard about but probably have not understood. Knowing that leaves are food for animals may interfere with the idea of leaves as food factories.

- How leaves carry out the process of food making may not be meaningful to students, since the process is basically a chemical reaction.

Now, think of an Initiating Query and Follow-Up Queries that would help students build an understanding of the text ideas by addressing the difficulties they may have.

➡️ **Write & Compare** Jot down your Queries on a sheet of paper. Then, compare them with the Queries below.

An Initiating Query that establishes the general topic of how trees get food may be the best way to begin:

> There's a lot of information in this paragraph, but what big idea is the author talking about?

Then, Follow-Up Queries can help to sort out how the process works and identify and clear up confusions.

To get at the unusual role of leaves as food makers:

> Okay, so let's think about how trees get their food. The author says that "The leaves make food for the tree." Does that make sense? How could that happen?

To prompt students to get an overview of the process:

> **The author talks about water and minerals and sunlight. What's that all about? How does this work?**

To help students develop some understanding of the role of chlorophyll:

> **What do you think the author means by saying that [chlorophyll] mixes the gas, the sunlight, the water, and the minerals?**

Recapping

One way to anticipate how students will respond to your Queries is to think about the ideas they have to deal with in the text and how those ideas may influence their responses.

If you take the time beforehand to anticipate the range of responses—and develop Follow-Up Queries to address them—you won't be faced with the unexpected nearly as frequently in class.

Making Connections
How Do You Help Students See
How Ideas in a Text Fit Together?

An important part of building meaning from what one reads is seeing how the ideas connect. Some teachers have found that students need help making connections and, more generally, realizing the important role that putting ideas together plays in understanding something.

CLASSROOM SNAPSHOT

The students in Ms. C's class have just begun reading the book *Ralph S. Mouse* (Cleary, 1983). At this point, students have been introduced to Ralph, the motorcycle-riding mouse, and his struggles to keep from having to share his precious motorcycle with his relatives. The text segment below continues the theme in its description of where Ralph has chosen to live:

Above Ralph the clock began to grind and grind and strike, bong ... bong, as if it had to summon the strength for each stroke. Ralph dreaded the sound, even though it was the reason he lived under the clock. The noise terrified his little relatives who thought the clock was out to get them. As long as they feared the clock, Ralph's motorcycle was safe.

Ms. C's intent is to have students understand why Ralph chose to live under the clock by connecting his relatives' fear of the clock with Ralph's desire to keep them away from his motorcycle. But notice that the connection is not as straightforward for students as it may first appear.

MS. C:	What's the author telling us now about Ralph?
SAMANTHA:	His motorcycle is under the clock so it will be safe.
MS. C:	All right, he was worried about his motorcycle. And what did it mean, the reason he lived under the clock and that the noise terrified his relatives? How does that connect?
TIFFANY:	Maybe because he didn't want the clock to, like, scare them or anything.
MS. C:	Ralph *didn't* want the clock to scare his relatives? Is that what the author is saying?
TIMMY:	I think he lived under the clock because the motor-cycle was a going-away present for him. We saw the movie about Ralph, and he kept it there so no one would get it.

What Happened and Why?

Students apparently did not see the connection between Ralph's keeping his motorcycle under the clock and his relatives' fear of the clock. Making such connections is hard for some students. Being able to connect information means seeing the whole picture, which requires keeping track of a lot of information at once. This gets to be an easy task for expert readers, but young readers may need help gaining such facility.

Dealing with the Problem

The key to dealing with students' ability to connect ideas is to help them build a habit of noticing how things are tied together. We have seen teachers use a range of methods to address the issue. They range from using modeling that demonstrates noticing connections to posing Queries that spur students to notice connections, to calling explicit attention to student comments that implicitly contain connections.

EXAMPLE 1. Later in the *Ralph S. Mouse* discussion shown in the snapshot, Ms. C uses modeling to show students a connection between new information and what was already going on in the story. At this point in the story, Ralph is waiting for things to quiet down at the inn where he lives so that he can ride his motorcycle. The segment that the class is reading ends with the arrival of guests at the inn:

"Never mind," said one of the guests to Matt. "We can find our own room." The pair picked up their luggage and stepped into the elevator, leaving behind puddles of melted snow.

"Cheapskates," muttered Matt. Guests at this hotel often insisted on carrying luggage to avoid tipping him.

After the elevator door closed, Ralph worried that the puddles might dry before he had the lobby to himself.

MS. C: What's this—Ralph is worried that the puddles will dry? Why would he be worried about puddles? I'm not sure what the author is up to here. . . . Wait a minute, now I get it! Ralph is waiting to ride his little motor-cycle. Ah, I'll bet he wants to zip through the puddles on his motorcycle! Oh, how funny!

BECKY: Oh, yeah! Like whenever we go to Playland, and it's hot and all, we go on the log-jammer ride—it's a roller coaster where everyone gets wet. So Ralph is gonna ride and splash through the puddle!

Ms. C's modeling made students aware of the connection between puddles and Ralph's motorcycle riding and got them involved in talking about it. Also, by pondering "what the author is up to," Ms. C modeled that a reader expects connections and, upon finding an odd piece of information, begins a process of trying to hook it up to what has already been presented.

EXAMPLE 2. In this example, a teacher promotes connecting ideas by asking students to think about the role of information in the text. The class has been reading about the Eastern Woodland Indians. The following text segment describes how they build their homes:

> In building their homes, the Woodland Indians first made a frame with poles cut from young trees. They tied these poles together with vines. Then they covered the frame with bark, branches, and leaves.
>
> The Eastern Woodland Indians built two kinds of homes. One group of Woodland Indians, the Algonquins, made small single-family houses that were called wigwams. Another group, the Iroquois, made houses in which eight or ten families lived. These were called long houses.

In discussing this segment, the teacher wants to draw students' attention to the connection between how the Indians' homes were built and the information presented earlier about how the Indians developed ways to meet their needs from the forest environment.

MS. D:	What did we learn? Why did the author tell us about how the Indians built their houses?
BRYAN:	I think why they build their houses long is they have a whole bunch of Indians living with them, in their tribe.
MS. D:	Okay, but couldn't the author have just said "they built big houses for big families"? Why did he go into this long explanation of what they used for their houses?
SHERI:	Because before, the author said they got most of their stuff from, like, the woods, all they needed. And now it showed how they use leaves and stuff, branches for the frame of their house.
MS. D:	Yes. It all connects.

The teacher's probing helped students examine how the specific information about the materials these Indians used for their houses fit in with the ideas the author was trying to get across.

EXAMPLE 3. In this example the class is reading about the colonization of North America. Here is the text segment under discussion and the teacher's Initiating Query:

> **The Plymouth colony never became rich. But it did survive. Spanish conquerors like Cortes and Pizzaro had won a continent with their courage in battle. The Pilgrims gained their success with courage of a different kind. It was the courage to stand by their religious beliefs in the face of hardship. In doing this they left their mark on America's history.**

MS.V: What is the author telling us about the Pilgrims?

As the class begins to discuss the text, Beth makes a comment that implicitly contrasts the Pilgrims' aims with those of the Spanish conquerors mentioned in the text:

BETH: They didn't kill people and break down cities and everything to get land. They just believed in their religion all the time.

Notice how the teacher probes to bring this connection to light:

MS.V: Why did you say they didn't kill people and take land?

BETH: Because they didn't want riches or anything. They just wanted to live their own life and do what they wanted to do.

MS.V: Well, who said anything about riches?

BETH: Well, 'cause Pizzaro and Cortes went to other lands and they killed people and broke their buildings because they wanted riches and everything.

MS.V: Oh, so when the author said something about Pizzaro and Cortes, what was he trying to do?

BETH: Compare, and connect up the two because they're different.

The exchange between Beth and the teacher helped call attention to the connection implicit in the text and in Beth's original comment. As such, students were again reminded of the importance of putting things together to make them meaningful.

Your Turn

In the following example, a class is reading *Trouble River* (Byars, 1989), a story about a pioneer family that focuses on the experiences of Dewey, his grandmother, and Dewey's dog, Charlie, as they make their way down river on a raft. It has been a frustrating journey for Dewey. Grandma is stubborn and bossy and keeps telling him what to do. She even accuses him of paying more attention to the dog than to her.

The following segment comes after Grandma has announced that she wants to get off the raft and Dewey has tried but not succeeded in his attempt to land. He can't get the raft to shore. In fact, the raft is turned around as a result of his effort:

> **"Well, let's stop this infernal turning." She was now facing in the direction they had just come from. "I like to see where I'm going, not where I've been."**
>
> **"Yes'm."**
>
> **He plunged his oar into the water almost fiercely. "There," he said.**
>
> **"And remember that I'm wanting to stop. Hear me, boy?"**
>
> **When Charlie, who was restless too, began to whimper, Dewey said harshly, "Hush up, Charlie."**
>
> **"The dog," Grandma said slowly, still tapping her hand against the chair, "wants to get off this here raft."**

MS. P:	Why do you think the author has Grandma say, "The dog wants to get off this here raft?"
JEREMY:	Grandma thinks the dog has to go to the bathroom.
NAT:	Grandma thinks Dewey won't listen to her, but he will stop because he loves his dog.

At this point, how might you probe to guide students to connect Nat's idea to earlier text information about what Grandma has said about Dewey and his feelings for the dog.

➡️ **Write & Compare** Jot down your idea for probing students on a sheet of paper. Then, compare your idea with the one below.

> That's a good idea, Nat. But why would Grandma think that saying the dog wants to stop would help? What information did the author already give us that connects to Nat's idea?

Recapping

Connecting ideas is an important part of building meaning. Students often need help making connections. Some ways to do so include modeling, drawing attention to specific information in a text segment that relates to information in another part of the text, and probing students to make implied connections explicit.

Lengthy Student Responses
How Do You Sort Through a Lot of Information?

Teachers have found that during QtA discussions, students sometimes offer long, rambling responses that include a variety of ideas and confused information. It can be difficult to unravel these lengthy responses on the spot and lift out the good ideas.

CLASSROOM SNAPSHOT

Ms. K's class is reading about characteristics of Hawaii's population. Here is the text:

The Hawaiian Islands have a great mix of people from many places. About one seventh of the people are the offspring of Polynesians—the first people of the islands.

MS. K: What does the author mean here?

JACK: I think it means that some of the people, more people from the Polynesian Islands, came to Hawaii. And there was a mix, people mixed. Some people had stayed, and they just said they would stay there, they wouldn't move to another island or something like that?

MS. K: Stayed on one island? But there are a lot of islands that are part of Hawaii. I don't think that's what the author is saying about the Polynesians. Okay, they were the first ones on Hawaii . . .

What Happened and Why?

In responding to Jack, Ms. K seemed to be getting a little tangled herself. Because Jack's response contained references to relevant ideas among garbled information, using it to create a focus proved difficult. One reason for the tangle that Ms. K found herself in was that she took on Jack's entire comment and responded to each aspect of it.

Dealing with the Problem

A teacher's major challenge in QtA is to use students' responses to build productive discussion. The key to dealing with lengthy, entangled responses is to understand that a response can be used and acknowledged without having to take on everything that the student has brought up. The examples that follow show ways to use the Discussion Move of revoicing to deal with long, entangled responses by selecting aspects to focus on.

EXAMPLE 1. In this example, the class is reading a Chinese folk tale in which the main character is introduced as the youngest and smallest, and generally disregarded, child of the emperor. Later, she becomes the only witness to her father's kidnapping. Below is the final portion of the text segment:

> And only Princess Djeow Seow, so tiny she seemed part of the corner where she sat, saw what happened.
>
> The evil men took the emperor to a tower in the middle of a wide, treeless, plain. The tower had only a single window, with an iron bar across the center. The plotters sealed the door with bricks and mortar once the emperor was inside. Then they rode back to the palace and declared that the emperor was dead.

BONNIE: I think that it was a good thing, her tininess. She was somewhere and she wasn't noticed. It's because if she was big like her brothers and sisters, she would have got caught and they would have been, like, now she knows how to find the emperor. So now I think maybe people will start to believe in her, like the emperor. She'll tell people that the emperor isn't dead, just trapped.

Bonnie has included many ideas in her long response. Notice below how the teacher revoices part of the response, consolidating one important concept that Bonnie brought up:

MS. E: Okay, Bonnie said that the thing that has been so bad for her—never being noticed—is actually going to turn out to be helpful. So what do you see happening here?

By picking and choosing from among Bonnie's ideas, the teacher was able to incorporate some of them without investing a lot of time to explore all of what she had said.

EXAMPLE 2. In this example, the class is reading an excerpt from *The Cricket in Times Square* (Selden, 1970). In the story, Mario's pet cricket has just been caught eating a two-dollar bill. Mario's father then decided that Mario would have to get rid of his pet unless it stayed in a cage. Mario tried to gain freedom for his cricket and offered to pay back the money. The next paragraph of the text presents the solution that Mario and his father developed to settle the issue:

> **Finally it was decided that since the cricket was Mario's pet, the boy would have to replace the money. And when he had, Chester could come out again. Until then—the cage.**

The teacher poses a Query to focus on the settling of the issue, but note that Don's lengthy response covers other territory:

MS. D: All right, this is interesting. Ginger said earlier that
          she saw an argument developing because Mario didn't
          want Chester to have to live in a cage. Now how's the
          author settled the argument for us?

DON: At first the author said, since Mario is the owner of
          the cricket, it was only fair for him to get the money
          back. I think it's a shame because if it wasn't for Tucker
          [a mouse character in the story] leaving the cage open
          and taking two dollars, he wouldn't have to pay for it.
          But since then, Mario has to pay for it.

Don's comment has not really touched on the issue at hand. Notice below that
the teacher mentions part of Don's response, characterizing it as "a piece of" the
issue. The teacher then refocuses the discussion on the settling of the argument.

MS. D: Okay. Well, Don started to tell us a piece of it, that
          Mario has to come up with the two dollars. But what
          about this issue that Ginger had pointed out about a
          disagreement between Mario and his father. How did
          the author work that out for us in what we just read?

By touching briefly on part of what Don had said, the teacher was able to
acknowledge Don's contribution while keeping the focus on the issue of settling
the argument.

Your Turn

In the following example, a class is reading about the American colonial period
during the time when England was imposing taxes on the colonists. The issue of
the time was "no taxation without representation." In response to the teacher's
Query about whether the colonists were represented in the English parliament,
Patrick offers the following response:

PATRICK: No. It's because they even, it's because the author
           even told us. He said that if, he said the only reason
           why people didn't send a representative is because
           if you had a representative and everybody voted on
           you, you'd probably still have to pay all that tax money.
           But if you didn't have a representative there at that
           meeting, you wouldn't have to pay no kind of taxes.
           So the people got so mad because they kept getting
           taxed. They got so mad that they said that they didn't
           want a representative no more. And that's why they
           didn't have to pay no more.

➡️ **Write & Compare** At this point, how might you deal with Patrick's
response? Jot down your ideas for dealing with Patrick's response on a sheet
of paper. Then, compare your idea with the one below.

> Okay. Patrick said that the colonists were not represented in the
> English parliament. And he's right. Now let's move on to think about
> what happened because the colonists were not represented in
> Parliament. How did the colonists react to the situation?

Recapping

In a QtA discussion, students are often eager to offer their ideas even when they
haven't completely thought them through yet. As a result, they may offer lengthy
responses because they are thinking on their feet. One way to deal with such
responses is to use the Discussion Move of revoicing to pick and choose from
among the ideas students offer. Another approach is to use a student idea as a
point of departure or contrast from which you can return the focus to the
important ideas.

Collaboratively Building Understandings
How Can You Get Students to Build on One Another's Ideas?

In QtA, individual student contributions are the content from which meaning is built. But it can be difficult to build meaning if students don't relate their ideas to ideas that are already on the table. Teachers have told us that it is sometimes a challenge to get students to attend to and build on one another's ideas.

CLASSROOM SNAPSHOT

Ms. T's class is reading about the geography of the southeast United States. Ms. T's intent is to encourage students to get the big picture of the topography of the region. Here is the text segment that completed the description of the region.

The third major landform of the Southeast region is the Piedmont. Piedmont is a French word that means "foot of the mountain." The Piedmont lies between the Atlantic Coastal Plain and the Appalachian Mountains. If you stood in this belt of rolling hills, you might be able to look down on the coastal plain and up to the Appalachian Mountains.

MS. T: What's the picture that the author is creating for us of this region?

Notice below that the first student, Lisa, begins to focus on the big picture. But watch what happens when a second student, Zach, is called on.

LISA: If, that you can stand on some hills and look one way and it's down to the plain.

MS. T: Okay! What else, Zach?

ZACH: The author told us that *piedmont* is really a word from French. And it has "foot" and "mountain" in it.

What Happened and Why?

Lisa's response made a good start in identifying the main idea, but Zach introduced a new topic, even though there was a topic on the table that had not been completely addressed. When Ms. T asked, "What else?" Zach interpreted her question as an invitation to bring up something new rather than as a signal to continue with the line of discussion already in progress.

Dealing with the Problem

Students need to learn that building meaning from text often requires putting ideas *together*. Because this may be a new way of operating in a discussion for them, the teacher needs to help them build the habit of working together on ideas.

As students begin to learn about collaborating, a teacher may often need to signal students about what the focus of discussion is, when that focus needs more attention, and when it's appropriate to bring closure to a topic. Let's look at some examples of how teachers established a focus and invited students to build ideas.

EXAMPLE 1. In this first example, the class is reading about how the economy of the Southern colonies developed as farms grew and plantations began to dominate. Here is the text segment that opens the lesson:

> ## FARMS AND PLANTATIONS
>
> **In all the Southern colonies, most people farmed for a living. Before 1700 most of these farms were small and located on the Atlantic Coastal Plain. With the South's long growing season, farmers produced all the food they needed to live. In addition, they usually raised a cash crop, which is a crop they could sell for money.**

For this segment, the teacher wants students to establish that because of favorable growing conditions, farmers in the South began to be able to turn a profit in addition to filling their own needs. Here is the teacher's Initiating Query:

MS. E:	Okay. What did the author start to tell us about in that opening paragraph?

Notice that Debbie responds at a general level, and that the teacher uses what Debbie says to focus on building the idea of a cash crop:

DEBBIE:	He told us about their farms.
MS. E:	What did he tell us about their farms? Jayme?

Next, Jayme's response does focus on farms, but it is still general. Notice how the teacher follows up by working with Jayme's response, and then Alicia's, to further refine the focus:

JAYME:	He told us where they were located, and told us what they did with the crops they made.
MS. E:	He told us—so, what *did* they do with the crops? Alicia?
ALICIA:	Um, they sold, they used a thing called a cash crop and they sell it.
MS. E:	What did the author mean by the term *cash crop*?
TERESA:	They get cash for their crops.

Now, notice how the teacher implicitly signals that repeating Teresa's response as a question needs an explanation:

MS. E:	They get cash for their crops? Robert?
ROBERT:	Cash crops, which is the crops they can sell, like at the grocery store. And they get money, and they just made up the word to mean that those crops you get cash for selling, you don't keep them.

EXAMPLE 2. In this next example, the class is reading a story about a boy, Justin, who goes to visit his grandfather on a ranch. Justin doesn't like sharing in household chores at home, where he lives with his mother and sisters, because he thinks it's not something boys should be concerned with. However, his grandfather surprises him with his fastidiousness about doing the dishes, making beds, and so on. The first segment of the story ends with the following paragraph:

> When he saw his grandfather busy making his own bed, Justin went into his room. His unmade bed and his pajamas on the floor bothered him. But he decided that the room didn't look too bad. He picked up his pajamas and placed them on the bed and sat beside them. He waited.

The teacher's goal is to set up how the situation differed from Justin's expectations and how he seems to feel about it. She begins a discussion of the segment as follows:

MS. F:	What do you think the author's letting us know about Grandpa? Eric?
ERIC:	That, um, his grandpa isn't married, 'cause they would have said something about his grandma. So he's cleaning up like he's a grandma.

Notice in the exchanges below how the teacher keeps the discussion focused by using a conversational style in which she briefly revoices the responses and then invites students to contribute what they think.

MS. F:	Okay, so he's acting like a grandma, cleaning up after himself. Interesting. What do you think, Loretta?

LORETTA: Um, cowboys don't do dishes, so he must not have a wife right now.

MS. F: So you think the wife would be helping with this stuff? Okay, what do you think, Anthony?

ANTHONY: Justin thought he was going to have fun, but now his grandpa is doing all this cleaning up around the house. It's, like, boring.

MS. F: So Anthony is going on the side of Justin here, saying Justin was going to have all this great fun with his grandfather. But his grandfather is doing stuff like dishes and cleaning up. Christina, what's it look like to you?

The teacher's approach was fairly subtle. She didn't directly tell students what to focus on, but her conversational style kept attention on what was said and suggested continuation along that line.

EXAMPLE 3. In this next example, reading and discussion of the story of Justin's visit with his grandfather continues. Students begin to grapple with why Justin seems happy to learn household chores from his grandfather when he fought doing the same chores at home. The teacher continues to manage the focus with a light touch, but one student, Alma, does not pick up on the teacher's cues. Instead, she brings up another topic by asking about a term introduced in the story:

ALMA: What's the author talking about, they're gonna go "riding fence"? Does that mean like riding horses?

Alma's question is a good one, although it doesn't fit in at this point. Notice below how the teacher acknowledges Alma's curiosity but retains the focus of the discussion:

MS. F: Oh, that *is* a funny expression—good question, Alma. But let's hold on to that for now, and see if we can first settle this about why Justin seems to suddenly like making his bed and folding shirts.

Your Turn

Think about how you would respond to the student comments in the examples below. First, evaluate how the student response relates to the understanding being built. Then, decide whether you should provide a focus or maintain or retrieve the focus already established.

In the following example, a class is discussing Conestoga wagons and how they were built to withstand the rough roads pioneers had to follow as they went west. The text segment ends with the information below. What Follow-Up Query would you use to respond to what Mary says?

> [The wagon] was about 16 feet long, 4 feet wide, and 4 feet deep. A canvas top stretched over wooden hoops covered it. The wagon rode on four large wooden wheels. These had bands of iron like tires around the rims. The wagon could carry 2,500 to 3,500 pounds of material.

MS. Q: Alright, the author has told us about this Conestoga wagon. And he said that it solved many problems for the pioneers who were traveling west. How did the Conestoga wagon help the pioneers?

SHAUN: The covering on the wagon kept things covered if it rained.

MS. Q: Good point. The covering on the Conestoga helped the pioneers solve the problem of protecting their belongings.

MARY: The pioneers had to take everything with them when they went west.

➡️ Write & Compare Jot down your Follow-Up Query on a sheet of paper. Then, compare your Query with the one below.

> You're right. The pioneers had to take a lot with them. How did the Conestoga wagon help the pioneers with that problem of taking so many things on their journey?

The above Query related Mary's comment to the focus—ways the Conestoga wagon helped the pioneers—and kept the discussion on track.

Your Turn Again

In the following example, a class is discussing a story in which a boy goes to visit his sister, Jan, who is a botanist studying the Sonoran Desert. How would you respond to Danny's comment?

> **We talked about deserts. Jan told me what defines them—water. A desert, she said, is a place where the rainfall is not more than ten inches a year.**
>
> **Water is the key to the desert. It even shapes it. Cuts out the canyons and rubs the stones smooth.**

MS. C: What has the author told us about the desert in this passage?

BARBARA: The definition of a desert. What makes a desert a desert.

MS. C: What *does* make a desert a desert?

DANNY: Like what we were studying in science about erosion. Like water can wear things down, like canyons. Like the Grand Canyon.

➡ *Write & Compare* Jot down your response on a sheet of paper. Then, compare it with the one below.

> You've made an important connection to what the author said about water shaping things, Danny. But you're getting ahead of us. First, let's think through what Barbara brought up—what is it that makes a desert a desert?

Although Danny's comment provided an important connection to information learned previously, it did not address the more basic issue of what a desert is. In the Follow-Up Query above, the teacher managed to acknowledge the value of the connection Danny had made while also retrieving the focus of the discussion.

Recapping

Building understanding often involves putting ideas together; however, students may not be used to collaborating to construct meaning. Teachers must sometimes provide, maintain, and retrieve the focus of discussion by signaling students that certain ideas are under construction and their job is to work together to build them.

Helping Students Grapple
When Not to Fill in Information

An issue that QtA teachers face is how to refrain from filling in information themselves and get students to work through difficulties that arise. As one teacher asked, "How do I keep the 'thinking' ball in their court?"

CLASSROOM SNAPSHOT

Ms. T's class is reading about struggles between Congress and President Buchanan over the issue of slavery. The text segment ends as follows:

> **In 1857, when Kansas was about to become a state, some settlers in the territory wrote a constitution that would make Kansas a slave state. President Buchanan supported the people's right to make this choice. He urged Congress to accept the constitution. But Congress refused and sent it back to Kansas. Antislavery settlers in the state voted it down. When Kansas became a state four years later, it was a free state.**

MS. T: What has the author told us in this paragraph?

CARLA: The settlers wrote a constitution that it would be a slave state and then they jump to four years later and it's a free state.

MS. T: Yes, and what do you think went on in those four years?

TROY: If you look at the picture on the page, it says, "Because of fighting between proslavery and antislavery groups, Kansas became known as 'Bleeding Kansas.'"

MS.T: Aha, yes. There was a lot of fighting even within states,
          between groups of people who lived there, because some
          wanted slavery and some not.

What Happened and Why?

Troy brought to the discussion some relevant information about what had been
happening in Kansas in the four years between the voting down of the first
constitution and statehood. The information Troy introduced was significant
for understanding the growing national crisis over slavery. However, students did
not get the opportunity to consider its significance, because Ms. T filled in for
the students, explaining the general issue that people within states were fighting
over slavery.

Dealing with the Problem

Filling in information may be done either deliberately or automatically. A teacher
may decide that an issue is not worth pursuing at length or that pursuing it would
be too time-consuming, and so the teacher deliberately provides the information
to students. Sometimes, however, a teacher finds him- or herself filling in information out of habit, rather than considering whether students could or should
deal with it themselves.

The key here is to be reflective—consider whether you are taking over opportunities to have students dig in and reach understanding on their own. Try to
resist immediately filling in information. Give students at least some opportunity
to take a crack at it before adding to the discussion. Sometimes you need to go
further than a single Follow-Up Query to provide enough guidance to get students
grappling productively. In the following examples, teachers use several techniques
to prompt students' thinking about difficult or unfamiliar ideas.

EXAMPLE 1. In this example, the class is reading about how early people from Polynesia traveled to Hawaii. The following sentences conclude the text segment:

> **The Polynesians had to sail thousands of miles or kilometers to get to the Hawaiian islands. The canoes the Polynesians used were made by lashing together pieces of wood with rope. Polynesians made the rope from the outer covering of coconuts. They wove leaves of plants into sails that they used on their boats.**

MS. S: Why do you think the author is telling us this stuff? He tells us that "Polynesians made the rope from the outer covering of coconuts. They wove leaves of plants into sails that they used on their boats." Why would he want us to know this? Doreen?

The teacher's goal is to have students realize that these early people used the resources around them to construct their boats. But notice below that students have a hard time reaching that idea.

DOREEN: They tell us what they used on their boat.

MS. S: And what did they use?

CURT: Rope. They used coconuts and they used wood.

MOLLY: They used leaves. That was the sail.

MS. S: A sail out of leaves and coconut rope. Isn't that strange? Why would the author want us to know this?

ALMA: He's telling us how they got to Hawaii.

MS. S: But why would we have to get all this detail?

GARY: He wants us to know this because he wants us to know how they used all the natural resources.

MS. S: Aha! Wow! They used all the stuff from the land. Boy, Gary, that was terrific thinking.

Notice that getting students to respond to the concept of natural resources was not simple. The teacher focused and guided students' thinking with brief responses that expressed puzzlement, that drew attention to connections between ideas (for example, "a sail out of leaves"), and that challenged students to figure out "why."

EXAMPLE 2. In this example, the class is reading a fictional account of Ben Franklin, supposedly written by his friend Amos, who is a mouse. Discussion is focused on the mouse's description of "an act of deceit that caused the first and only rift in our friendship." Students are having some difficulty understanding what the author was talking about, evidenced by comments such as the following:

DEBBIE: It says their friendship was breaking up.

MARY: But later in the story it says Ben was enjoying the mouse.

A comment by Carl then offers an explanation of how the apparent contradiction might be resolved:

CARL: A break in their friendship doesn't mean they gotta break their friendship.

Notice below how the teacher, rather than jumping in and declaring Carl correct, simply revoices Carl's comment and suggests the class continue with the text:

MS. D: Okay, so Carl thinks that they might still be friends, even though something happened. We're going to continue, because the only way we're going to find out is if we read some more.

> **That deceit could raise its ugly head in such idyllic surroundings and bring to an end these innocent diversions seems particularly painful. I shall pass over as rapidly as possible the unfortunate happenings which almost brought our friendship to a close.**

Now, notice how the teacher guides students to grasp the point but leaves the grappling up to them:

MS. D:	Does that shed any light for us?
SUE:	It says, um, "brought our friendship to a close."
MS. D:	Please read that sentence again.
SUE:	It says, "I shall pass over as rapidly as possible the unfortunate happenings which almost brought our friendship to a close."
MS. D:	Anybody notice anything in what Sue just read?
BART:	Almost.
TIFFANY:	That almost the friendship is over.
MS. D:	*Almost* the friendship is over. So what does that mean?
BART:	That the friendship isn't broken up yet.

At several points in the above discussion the teacher could have simply supplied the information for the students. But instead, she allowed the students to do the thinking. She helped by marking key parts of responses and of the text with emphasis, turning-back to text, and turning-back to students.

Your Turn

In the following example, a class is reading a segment from *The Whipping Boy* (Fleischman, 1987). In the story, Prince Brat and the Whipping Boy have run away from the castle and been kidnapped by two cutthroats. Cutwater, one of the outlaws, is sharing breakfast with the boys. The teacher wants students to understand how differently the breakfast is perceived by the prince and the outlaws, but notice that the student who responds to the teacher's Query only refers to the prince's reaction:

> **The scrawny outlaw sliced off two thick pieces of coarse bread. He draped a salt herring across each slice. "Eat hearty, little fellers."**
>
> **"This smelly stuff!" Prince Brat glared at the bread and herring. "It's not fit for flies!"**
>
> **"Why, we eat it regular, worms and all," said Cutwater.**

MS. M:	What's going on here? What has the author told us about this breakfast Cutwater offers to the boys?
NOREEN:	The prince won't eat it because it's disgusting.

How would you respond to encourage students to notice the contrast between the prince's reaction and Cutwater's? Think of several ways you could guide students' thinking in case they do not pick up on the contrast right away.

➡️ **Write & Compare** Jot down your ideas for guiding students on a sheet of paper. Then, compare your ideas with the ones below.

> Okay. Noreen is right. The prince is really disgusted by the breakfast. But what else does the author let us know in this part of the story?

If students don't pick up on the outlaws' point of view about the food, the Discussion Move of turning-back to text may guide their thinking. For example:

> What does Cutwater mean when he says, "Why, we eat it regular, worms and all?"

Recapping

Teachers often fill in information for students automatically. In QtA discussions, teachers are encouraged to reflect before deciding to fill in information that students can be helped to provide for themselves. Students are often eager to present their ideas, even if they are not completely thought out or connected to larger issues. Teachers can deal with such responses by providing the necessary information or by providing the kind of guidance and support that will encourage students to do the thinking needed to make connections or to figure out the significance of ideas. The Discussion Moves of turning-back—both to the text and to students—and revoicing are particularly effective.

Listening to Students' Responses
When Should You Question a Good Response?

QtA teachers quickly come to realize how important it is to have students understand ideas and not merely respond to questions by retrieving words from a text. But it isn't always easy to tell from students' responses whether they really do understand the ideas. As one teacher put it, "How can you tell when students really understand what they're talking about?"

CLASSROOM SNAPSHOT

Mr. W's class is reading about the arrival of the Pilgrims in the New World. The segment began by stating that the Pilgrims had not landed where they had expected and thus would not be living under the rules of the Virginia Company. The segment concludes as follows:

In the Mayflower Compact, the signers agreed to form a government that would make "just and equal laws . . . for the general good of the colony." All 41 men on board signed the agreement. It established the idea of self-government in America—that is, that people should govern themselves.

After this paragraph, the text moves on to discuss life in the Plymouth Colony and puts aside the ideas about self-government. Because of the importance of the concept of self-government in United States history, Mr. W wants to leave a strong trace of the concept so that students can build on it later. The following is Mr. W's Initiating Query and the response it draws.

MR. W: Okay, they arrived in America, and what did the author tell us they decided to do?

> ANDREW: They had to, 'cause they didn't land where they wanted to, they had to make their own laws and pick their own people for government. So it was like a self-government.

What Happened and Why?

What do you think Andrew understands about self-government? Although he gave a very good summary of what he had read, putting important ideas in his own words, it is not clear what he understands "self-government" to be—or even whether he views it as a good idea, since the text presented it as what the Pilgrims had to do because they had landed in an isolated place.

Dealing with the Problem

Judging whether a student's response represents understanding is always important, but it can be particularly difficult in two cases. The first is when the ideas reflected in the student's response are inherently complex or particularly significant, and the second is when the ideas do not easily fit with students' prior knowledge. In these cases, the chances are that even what sounds like a good response may not represent a solid understanding. So, in these cases, it is worthwhile to reinforce, elaborate, and clarify the ideas. In this case, we offer examples of both situations to show how teachers probed students' responses to find out what their understanding was.

EXAMPLE 1. In the case presented in the Classroom Snapshot, Mr. W decides immediately to follow up Andrew's response by probing about self-government. Even though Andrew expressed himself well, Mr. W feels sure that a concept such as self-government needs more attention. Here's how it plays out:

> MR. W: Okay, so they ended up in an unexpected place. And now tell me about that self-government thing again, Andrew.
>
> ANDREW: It was like they had to do it for theirselves, 'cause, they had to be, like, their own government.

MR. W: Well, you're saying they had to because they were
           pretty much on their own. But where is the author
           going with this when he says, "It established the idea
           of self-government in America—that is, that people
           should govern themselves"?

JOSEPH: That they should, people should be their own
           government. Then you can make the equal laws,
           like they said, and it'd be more fair.

Joseph's response added important information related to the idea of self-government. Mr. W reasoned that having the connections to "equal laws" and fairness on the table would help students remember and build upon the concept the next time it was encountered. Notice that Mr. W didn't pursue a full-blown explanation of the concept of self-government, considering that an unrealistic goal at this point in students' developing knowledge. Rather, he looked for signs of their grappling with the new notion and relating it to ideas that share a conceptual foundation, such as "fairness" and "equal laws."

EXAMPLE 2. This example illustrates that what may seem like a straightforward text statement can cause problems if it does not fit with what students already know. A social studies class is reading about the aftermath of the French and Indian War. The segment of text they are considering, followed by the teacher's Initiating Query and a student's response, is presented below:

NEW TAXES. Great Britain and the colonists had an even bigger quarrel. This quarrel was over taxes. To pay for the war against France, the British government had borrowed a great deal of money. Now it was necessary to pay this money back. Great Britain also wanted to station troops along the frontier to keep peace between the colonists and the Indians. The British government would need money to pay for these troops.

Where was all this money to come from? To Parliament, the answer was clear. The colonists must help pay for all these things.

MR. W:	What did the author tell us?
RICKY:	That war was expensive, so he's gonna, the king needs to get some money because he, like, borrowed a lot. So now he's gonna put on taxes for the people, the colonies to pay.

Ricky's response is an accurate reflection of the text: The king plans to raise needed funds by taxing the colonists. However, the teacher realizes that students may have difficulty integrating the situation with their knowledge of governments, and may assume that it is people in England who would be taxed by the British government. So the teacher follows up Ricky's response to make sure the students understand.

MR. W:	The people in the colonies? That's who he's gonna tax?

In following up by challenging the idea that it is the colonists who will pay the taxes, the teacher drew attention to this potentially difficult aspect. It also allowed him to check if other students had grasped this key aspect. And sure enough, the teacher uncovers problems, as shown by Miriam's response:

MIRIAM:	I think that the king is going to raise taxes in England, because he's king of England.

At this point, several students called out, "I disagree," and a heated discussion ensued about the king's intentions. The teacher intervened by going back to the text to read the lines indicating that the colonists would be paying the taxes. In doing so, he pointed out that despite what usually happens—the English king taxing the English people—the king is indeed planning to tax the colonists. Thus, he dealt directly with an idea that didn't fit with students' prior understanding.

Your Turn

The text excerpt below presents a complex idea, evaporation. Think about what students need to understand about it. Then, evaluate the student's response in terms of the understanding it reveals and develop a follow-up to probe for an elaboration from the student.

> Suppose you place a saucer of water on a windowsill. Later you see the water is gone. Why? When the water dried up in the saucer, it changed to a gas. This change from a liquid to a gas is called evaporation. The gas goes into the air. Water in the form of a gas is called water vapor.

MS. C: What is the author talking about here?

ANDY: Water vapor. Water turns into water vapor, like, if you leave water in a dish, it disappears.

➡️ *Write & Compare* Jot down your idea for a Follow-Up Query on a sheet of paper. Then, compare your Query with the one below.

The teacher wants to be sure students understand that "disappears" represents an important process by which a liquid changes into a gas, so she uses the Query below:

> What do you mean the water disappears? How could it do that?

The Query presses for a more detailed explanation that should reveal how much the students really understand about evaporation.

Your Turn Again

The text excerpt below focuses on condensation. Although students have probably walked through dewy grass or at least know about dew, it is likely that they have not really considered how dew is formed. It is also likely that they may connect dew and rain. Develop a follow-up to the student's response below that addresses this problem.

> Water vapor in the air can change back into a liquid. This happens if the air is cooled. The water vapor will condense on a surface such as a blade of grass. Condensation happens when water vapor changes to liquid water. The temperature at which water vapor condenses is called a dew point. When the temperature of the air falls to the dew point, water forms on the grass.

MS. C: What is the author describing for us here?

TERESA: Dew, like rain, is liquid water.

➡️ **Write & Compare** Jot down your idea for a Follow-Up Query on a sheet of paper. Then, compare your Query with the one below.

> Dew and rain are both liquid water, but what makes dew different from rain? Where does dew come from?

By asking students to differentiate between dew and rain, the teacher explicitly addresses any potential confusion students may have between the text and their prior understanding.

Recapping

When constructing meaning about complex ideas or ideas that may not fit with students' prior knowledge, it is a good idea to follow up initial responses by asking students to elaborate or clarify what they have said. It pays to probe. Even when a student's response sounds good, it may not represent an understanding that's solid enough.

Making It a Discussion
How Do You Get Students to Talk to One Another?

Because QtA uses group discussion as a vehicle for building meaning, it is important that students are engaged in interacting with the teacher and with one another. Some teachers have found that getting students to listen and respond to one another does not happen overnight, and they wonder how it can be encouraged.

Ms. T pondered the issue of student-to-student talk in a journal entry:

> I feel as though I'm taking too big a role in the discussions we have. It seems that the students always look to me instead of talking to the whole class. I try to pull back a bit and not say something after every student's response, trying to promote the idea that they should talk to each other and that every idea doesn't have to go through me. But I find when I do that, the students seem to go off on tangents rather than building on ideas that are being discussed.

What Happened and Why?

Ms. T is finding that taking part in collaborative discussion is not automatic for students as they begin QtA. That is not too surprising—most students are accustomed to directing their responses to the teacher for evaluation. So talking to one another during lessons may be new to them. When Ms. T tries to get students to respond to one another by "pulling back," students may get a different message than the one she intends. They may think that because the teacher did not respond to a student's comment that the comment did not "count."

Thus, they may feel free to initiate a new idea rather than following up on what has been said.

Dealing with the Problem

The problem of getting students to respond to one another's ideas can be addressed—rather readily, we've found—by helping them understand that the goal is a connected conversation, not a string of individual turns to talk. The following are examples of ways teachers have helped students build the habit of working as partners in a discussion.

Explicit Invitation. At first, you may need to give explicit invitations to students to follow up on one another's comments. At times, rather than commenting on a student's response, invite classmates to take up the ideas:

> Anyone want to respond to what Maryanne just said?
>
> Molly, have you got something on this issue that Joe raised?
>
> Good question. Can anybody help us with this?

Reminder of What's on the Table. If a student begins to chart a new path rather than attend to an issue that a previous student has brought up, you may want to help refocus on the first issue. This reinforces the message that it's a connected conversation that you're after. For example:

> Okay, well, you've introduced another issue. But first let's think about what Andrew said.

If students seem to ignore a previous comment, by giving either the same response or an opposite response with no reference to what was said previously, remind them of the connection:

> Oh, so are you agreeing with what Jacob just said?
>
> Well, I guess you're seeing it differently from Manda, then.

Recapping by Naming Names. When several students have contributed to the discussion of an issue, you may want to recap the issue and acknowledge the individual contributions. In this way, students see how individual students contribute to and create a whole. For example:

I think we've got this figured out. Thomas saw that this character was acting kind of sneaky, and then Roberta noticed that it all started that night when he got so mad, and Suzanne reminded us about what the author told us in the very beginning. Good work putting it all together, folks!

Recapping

To build meaning in a QtA discussion, students have to attend to and respond to one another's ideas. This may be novel for students accustomed to a more traditional approach. So, it's a good idea to give students explicit help with their role as partners in discussion. This can be done by inviting students to respond to one another's ideas, reminding them when a peer's comment is the focus of discussion, and illustrating how individual contributions play a part in figuring out ideas and building meaning.

Keeping Hold of Text Ideas
Why Does Building Meaning from Text Slip Away?

Keeping discussion focused on building meaning from text ideas is not a simple task. Sometimes a focus that a teacher thought was readily established can dissolve before her eyes!

Here's how Ms. K expressed the concern in her journal.

> Sometimes discussion seems to go along pretty well, but then when I reflect on what we've done, I feel that the major ideas from the text I wanted students to focus on and understand didn't get talked about that much. It feels like we get a good start on going after meaning. Students don't seem to have trouble responding to my Queries. But then suddenly—where did the meaning go?

What Happened and Why?

Sometimes the focus on meaning in text content can begin to blur during a lesson. And as Ms. K's journal indicates, it can happen rather stealthily. The discussion may be going along pretty well, the content may not seem overly difficult, but suddenly the focus slips away from grappling with meaning of text ideas to raising myriad possibilities of potential meanings. Sometimes the teacher doesn't even notice during the lesson that something was amiss, but only afterward while reflecting on what was accomplished.

Focusing on building meaning from text ideas requires a delicate balancing act. As discussion leader, the teacher does not want to provide the focus too strongly and thus take over the work of thinking through the ideas. Yet, if the teacher doesn't help keep the discussion focused, students may be unclear about where to direct their attention. Here we will explore two kinds of interactions that often cause the focus on building meaning to dissolve. One involves certain phrasings for Queries, particularly the use of "why" questions at certain times, that can lead students in unintended directions. The other arises when student responses are not used to full advantage to establish focus.

Dealing with the Problem

One of the QtA teacher's important roles is to monitor discussion to keep the focus on building meaning. In a group as large as a class, it can be difficult to keep everyone tuned to the same channel! It's not like a one-on-one conversation, where focus is easy maintain. In a QtA discussion, the teacher needs to act as the communal voice making sure that discussion stays on track by underscoring and expressing the focus.

As discussion progresses and as portions of discussion are brought to a close, the teacher needs to develop ways to make the focus clear. Appropriately phrased Queries can help set a focus in motion, and elaborating on and probing student responses when necessary can keep the focus public.

We'll look at a lesson that shows some examples of interactions in which the focus has slipped away, and we'll consider how the lesson could be revised to keep discussion more focused. The lesson covers a text section from a chapter on the New England region. The class reads the first paragraph, below, and then Ms. D poses a Query.

EXAMPLE 1. *Useful Stones from Vermont* Part I

In northern Vermont you can see huge pits dug deep down into solid rock. These pits are stone quarries, and they are among the largest quarries in the United States. The most important stones found in Vermont are granite, marble, and slate. Granite is a very hard stone that lasts many years, through all kinds of weather. It is used for building, statues, and tombstones. Cutting and finishing granite is difficult work.

MS. D: Why do you think the author tells us that granite,
                    marble, and slate are important stones?

With this Query, Ms. D is trying to set up a focus on the three kinds of stones that are discussed in this section of text. However, by using a "why" question at this point, she is essentially asking students to predict the text content. Notice below that the student responses do not initiate a very productive discussion.

ANDRE: Because those are the stones that are important to
                    Vermont?

MS. D: Okay, and why do you think they're so important?

TERESA: They're found in quarries there, and there's probably a
                    lot of them.

At this point, Ms. D makes the good decision to move the discussion to particular information from the text.

MS. D: The author told us some things about granite. What's
                    the author getting at with all this stuff about granite—
                    who can wrap that up for us?

SAMMY: It's a very hard stone.

MS. D: It's a very hard stone; you got it. Ben, read the next
                    paragraph please.

PART I: What Happened and Why

In asking for a "wrap-up," Ms. D's Query communicated that she was not looking for all the details, but the big idea—and she got it. However, the student stated his response so succinctly that the significance could well be missed. Students may not have grasped that the hardness of granite makes it useful for things that we want to last a long time, but that what makes it good—its hardness—also makes it difficult to work with. Because none of this information entered the discussion, an opportunity to set up a focus on the properties of the stone has been lost. Discussion has now moved to the second paragraph of the text on Vermont's stones.

EXAMPLE 2. *Useful Stones from Vermont* Part II

> **Vermont leads the United States in marble quarrying. Marble is another kind of building stone. Most of the marble comes from the western side of the Green Mountains. Quarried marble can be cut and polished to have a beautiful shine. It is used mostly for walls and floors of public buildings and on monuments. Vermont marble was used to build the Jefferson Memorial in Washington, D.C. Why was marble chosen for this memorial?**

MS. D:	Why *was* marble chosen for the memorial, do you think?
DANETTE:	Jefferson might have been from Vermont.
MS. D:	Well, no, Jefferson was from Virginia. Joanne?
JOANNE:	Maybe the architect of the memorial was from Vermont.
SAMMY:	Maybe, like, states take turns, like the Washington monument was built of material from, say, Oregon…

PART II: What Happened and Why?

Here the students have come up with some idiosyncratic ideas about why marble was used. They have not connected its use with its properties. Ms. D was puzzled by these responses. She had thought the relationship between the features of marble and its appropriateness for a monument was rather straightforward. The students may be responding idiosyncratically because the lesson has not succeeded in setting up a focus on the relationship between properties of the stones and their uses. Recall, all we got for the previous paragraph on granite was that it was "hard."

PART II: How the Problem Might Have Been Solved

Ms. D might have been able to capture the intended focus and direct students' attention to the text rather than to possibilities they could imagine if she had phrased her Query as follows:

> Marble was chosen for this important memorial. How does that fit in with what the author is trying to tell us about marble?

With that Query, discussion might have proceeded as follows:

STUDENT: He told us that it's used for monuments.

Note that the student has made a minimal connection, linking the use of marble in the Jefferson Memorial with the author's general mention of monuments. But that is not enough. The point is not to simply connect one idea with another but to explore how ideas fit in to a whole. So, discussion might continue:

MS. D: And why do you suppose that might be the case? Did the author give us any indication?

STUDENT: Because marble can be polished to be very beautiful. And monuments are kinds of places that you'd want to show off and have them be beautiful.

This student nicely links the use of marble to its properties. Discussion now moves to the third paragraph of the text section.

EXAMPLE 3. *Useful Stones from Vermont Part III*

> **Slate is the third main building stone found in Vermont. Slate is used to make long-lasting roof shingles for expensive buildings. It was once used for chalkboards in almost all the classrooms in the United States.**

MS. D: Why do you think the author told us about slate?

Here Ms. D's goal is to have students recognize slate as another important product from Vermont. Note how the "why" phrasing sends students to consider the possible personal motivations of the author rather than the general context of the material.

RODNEY:	In case we need shingles for a roof, we'd know where to go.
HEATHER:	He talks about blackboards, 'cause it might be interesting for kids in school to read about.

PART III: What Happened and Why?

Again in this case the use of a "why" question seems to signal students to consider the author's personal motivations and to make predictions about content. Perhaps a Query that asked, "How does that fit in to what we were reading about?" would have directed students' attention to how slate related to the topic, rather than inviting them to go off on tangents.

After some comments about the usefulness of slate, Ms. D moves to wrap up the entire section:

MS. D:	What does the author want us to know from this section we've been reading?
ROGER:	Useful stones from Vermont.
MS. D:	Okay, yes, Vermont has some very useful stones.

With this comment of Ms. D's, the discussion ends.

PART III: How the Problem Might Have Been Solved

Consider whether the above comment of Ms. D's brings meaningful closure to the discussion. Then, consider the following as an alternate ending to the discussion:

MS. D:	Why did Roger read the title of this section when I asked that question?
NANCY:	Because that's what the author told us about, useful stones from Vermont.
MS. D:	So what's the message there? Did the author just pick out a few stones to tell us about and they happen to be useful?
JESSE:	They're the most useful stones in Vermont.
MS. D:	Is that really it? Did the author just want to talk about the three most useful stones from this state?

MALCOLM:	No! Those are stones that Vermont is known for.
MS. D	Okay, Vermont is an important producer, then, of . . . well, who can wrap it up for us?
TODD:	Vermont has lots of stone resources of these three types. They have granite, marble, and slate.
SERINA:	Vermont makes money from selling them and we can get them if we need granite or marble to build stuff.

In this alternate discussion, without belaboring a fairly simple point, the class sums up the meaning of "useful stones" in terms of their role as products and resources.

Recapping

Successfully focusing discussion on building meaning takes some orchestration on the teacher's part. The teacher needs to see that a focus gets established so students know where to direct their attention, and then monitor the discussion to keep the focus going. Often the focus on building meaning falters because students begin to make a wide variety of associations. Two actions can go a long way toward preventing students' straying from text ideas. The teacher can take care that Queries are phrased to draw attention to text ideas. The teacher can take advantage of students' responses to underscore the focus. It may help to keep in mind that part of the teacher's role is to act as the communal voice in a discussion, keeping track of and expressing the focus so that there is a central point of attention.

Keeping Track of Information
How Do You Avoid Getting Lost?

One of the challenges of QtA is keeping track of a lot of information and interactions that come up in discussions. Teachers have told us that they have difficulty orchestrating the various fast-paced demands of helping students move toward planned goals, handling unanticipated comments, and making on-the-fly decisions about when to recap, move on, and how to keep the discussion focused and constructive.

Below is an entry from Ms. T's journal that describes what happened in one of her lessons. Her description captures very well the demanding nature of a QtA discussion.

> Lately I've been having a problem staying on task during a lesson. It seems that there is so much going on—what I want students to learn, trying to figure out if students are having any problems, encouraging participation, using students' comments. What sometimes happens is that when I really concentrate on what my students are saying, before I know it, I'm way off from where I want to be, talking about something not very relevant to what I planned! Then today, I just completely lost my place. In the middle of the lesson, I couldn't even remember what we were trying to talk about.

What Happened and Why?

Managing a QtA discussion is a challenge because of simultaneous and equally important demands: attending to the goals that you've planned, monitoring whether students are approaching understanding, and considering and responding to individual student contributions. Dealing with all these at once in a fast-paced manner is bound to feel overwhelming at times!

Dealing with the Problem

As we've worked with teachers, several ways of dealing with the problem of losing track amid the demands of a discussion have emerged. Below we describe three techniques that teachers and we found most useful. The first two are ways to limit the demands—by putting some student comments on hold and by developing ways to annotate your text to keep track of goals. The third shows a way to ask for help when needed from your collaborators—the students.

Hold It. Student comments or questions that are interesting but potentially distracting may be handled by establishing a routine of asking students to hold them for later consideration. Here is what you might say:

> I'm going to ask you to hold your question, and we'll get back to it later. Right now, I want to make sure we understand what the author is saying here.

Using a "hold it" routine acknowledges a student's comment but relieves you of having to deal with it immediately, so you can keep the discussion on track.

Solicit Student Help. When you've lost your place and don't know where to go next, asking the students for help can be effective:

> I've gotten a little lost. Can somebody help me out and tell me what we were trying to figure out?

We have found students to be very responsive to such requests. And it helps both to keep them on their toes and to illustrate that they really are partners in the process of building meaning.

Annotate the Text. Another way to help keep track of your goals during a lesson is to annotate your text, or flag it with sticky notes to remind yourself of where you're going with each of your Queries and the ideas you want students to construct. Here's what it may look like:

WHISKEY REBELLION

In 1794, farmers in western Pennsylvania banded together and refused to pay the tax. They threatened tax collectors. President Washington felt that the government must show that it could make people obey the laws. He led 13,000 troops to western Pennsylvania to put down this Whiskey Rebellion. When farmers heard that troops were coming, they dropped their guns and fled. That ended the rebellion. Washington had shown the new government's strength.

> They "threatened tax collectors." What does that remind you of? (colonies vs. British) Why is it different now?

> What does the author mean by "shown the new government's strength?" Why is that important?

Recapping

There is a lot of information to keep track of in a QtA discussion. Occasionally teachers lose the focus of discussion and forget what the goals are. Several ways of securing and/or restoring focus have seemed to work effectively: establishing a "hold it" routine, annotating your texts to remind you of where the discussion should be going, and turning to the students for help. The key is to prepare as best you can for potentially problematic places and to remember that there are ways to recover if you do lose the focus.

When Discussion Gets Repetitive
How Do You Get Out of a Replay Loop?

QtA teachers have noticed an inclination to let students repeat already established ideas. The discussion turns into a replay loop, and lots of time is spent rehashing the same points.

CLASSROOM SNAPSHOT

Ms. D and her class are reading a story called "The Day That Nothing Happened" (Redding, 1977). Ms. D wants to focus the discussion on the boredom of two children in the story as they were taking a walk in the Arctic tundra. As you'll see below, students establish that fact, but Ms. D solicits several repetitions of the same idea. The following text paragraph initiates the discussion.

Naput and Nadeen ambled along. They studied the frozen snow and wondered why it made a crunching sound under their *mukluks*. They thought of exciting things to see on television. Naput remembered his favorite program would be on that evening. The day wouldn't be entirely lost.

MS. D:	Now what is the author trying to let us know by saying, "The day wouldn't be entirely lost?"
DEBBIE:	That they had something fun to look forward to later even though they were bored on the walk now.
TIFFANY:	He means that they wouldn't be bored the whole day— it would just be boring when they walked.
MS. D:	Okay. The day wouldn't be *all* boring. Zach?

ZACH: The author means the day isn't over yet and even though they are bored right now, they still have TV.

ASHLEY: Um ... they were hoping for some action, but, um, they were bored on the walk and knew that the day wasn't over so they would have something fun later.

What Happened and Why?

Debbie's response captured the essential idea that Ms. D was looking for, but instead of acknowledging it and moving on, Ms. D persisted in calling on more students. Most of the subsequent responses were variations of Debbie's original, and so several minutes of discussion were devoted to something students seemed to understand. Why might this have happened?

Conversations with teachers suggest that there are two general reasons that teachers get stuck in this "replay loop." One reason is that teachers want to make sure that students really hear and grasp the ideas being expressed. So, even though a student's comment is sufficient, the teacher continues to elicit "more of the same" to keep certain ideas in the spotlight a little longer.

Another reason is that teachers want to encourage as much participation as possible. Teachers told us they found it difficult to turn down eagerly waving hands. So sometimes they called on students, knowing that they had already dealt sufficiently with the topic.

Dealing with the Problem

Both of the impulses that give rise to a replay loop have merit, but teachers have found ways to reinforce ideas and allow student participation without the repetition. An idea can be reinforced effectively with the Discussion Moves of marking and revoicing—revoice the student's comment, mark the most important aspects, and then move on.

Student participation can be maximized without creating unnecessary repetition with "quick responses." In this case, we'll look at examples that show teachers heading off a repetitive loop by using these techniques.

EXAMPLE 1. The class in this example is reading about the characteristics of ice-cap lands. The text is addressing the nonintuitive fact that very little snow falls on these lands, although they are always snow- and ice-covered. The text segment being discussed follows:

> **Only about five inches of snow falls in the ice-cap lands in a year. The snow that does fall, however, keeps piling up.**

MS. C:	What does the author mean in those two sentences?
DAVID:	It never stops piling up when it snows. A little snow comes down, but it's so cold that it probably won't melt and stuff.

David's response captured the concept well. Yet the teacher is not ready to leave the issue, wanting to make sure that the students do grasp the concept. Notice below how she marks an essential part of the idea and then revoices it.

MS. C:	Yes! Isn't that interesting? Boys and girls, what happens to snow after a while where we live?
STUDENTS:	It melts.
MS. C:	Right, we have snow for a little while and then it gets warm and the snow melts. In ice-cap lands—David hit it right on the nose—it's going to snow maybe five inches a year, but *that snow is never gonna melt.* Then it will snow another five inches and *that's* never going to melt.

In this example, the teacher wanted to focus on why the snow piles up in ice-cap lands. She could have called on other students, but David's response was so complete that she didn't need to. Instead, she accomplished her goal of emphasizing an important point by using the Discussion Moves of marking and revoicing.

EXAMPLE 2. The example below illustrates how a teacher avoided the repetitive-loop syndrome by offering an alternative for student participation. The class was reading a folk tale about a mountain. Here is the opening paragraph and the initiation of discussion:

> There was once a mountain made of bare stone. It stood alone in the middle of a desert plain. No plant grew on its hard slopes, nor could any animal, bird, or insect live there. The sun warmed the mountain and the wind chilled it, but the only touch the mountain knew was the touch of rain or snow. There was nothing more to feel. All day and all night the mountain looked only at the sky, watching for the movement of the billowing clouds. It knew the path of the sun that crossed the sky by day, and the course of the moon that crossed the sky by night. On clear nights, it watched the slow wheeling of the far-off stars. There was nothing more to see.

MS. C: What is the author trying to say about the mountain in what we've read so far?

CINDY: It's a lonely mountain because it doesn't have any company to talk to or see, feel, or anything.

Facing a sea of waving hands, the teacher calls on another student, and then a third student jumps in:

JAMES: It's really lonely since no animals or birds live there.

TERENCE: There aren't any plants, and it just feels wind, and that makes it lonely.

At this point, the teacher sees that students are offering replays of the same idea. With many students still eager to add their comments, she intervenes and takes a slightly different tack.

MS. C: How many of you agree that this is the author's main message here—a lonely mountain? Okay, we've already got no plants, no animals. When I get to you, tell me just two words about why this mountain is lonely.

The teacher then called on quite a few students, who gave brief replies such as "no sun," "chilly wind," and "no friends." The teacher acknowledged the students understanding and awareness of how loneliness was described and then moved on to the next text segment.

EXAMPLE 3. A repetitive loop can occur when a text raises an issue on which it's possible to take sides. All students may want to announce their preference and argue why their side is right.

In this example, students are reading the book *Mama's Bank Account* (Forbes, 1971). It's the story of a woman whose former fiancé married someone else. The spurned woman then ran away with her ex-fiancé's horse. He pursued, at breakneck speed, and ended up dead. The issue is whether the woman killed him or if it was a tragic accident. As it becomes clear to the teacher that most of the class wants to weigh in on the issue, she decides to take a quick response poll:

MS. D: I see that people have a lot to say about this. Here's what we'll do. As I come to you, tell me if you think what happened to Peder was the result of a murderous scheme or a tragic accident. I'll mark each vote on the chalkboard.

After the vote, the teacher allowed one student from each side to sum up the evidence in support of that position and then concluded that part of the discussion as follows:

MS. D: I think those are all good thoughts and could be very well supported by what the author has given us. Now let's pick up where we left off in the book.

Teachers don't want to dampen enthusiasm for participating in discussions, but sometimes students' persistent attention to certain ideas makes for unproductive discourse. With quick-response formats, teachers can have lots of students take part without derailing discussion.

Your Turn

In the example below, a class is reading a story set in Klawock, Alaska. The discussion about the text segment below falls into a replay loop on the importance of canned food. How might you have avoided the loop? When and how might you have tried to refocus the discussion?

> **Sometimes the weather in Alaska is so cold, things freeze quickly. Since the Klawock soil doesn't have the right minerals for vegetables to grow, we order lettuce and things like that from a city called Seattle. . . . When the weather is real cold, the vegetables we get from Seattle freeze before we can eat them. We eat canned food a lot because it never freezes or goes bad.**

MS. L:	What has the author let us know here?
RONNIE:	The people in Alaska eat canned food a lot.
SUE:	The canned food won't freeze.
SARAH:	They have to eat canned stuff because they can't grow vegetables.
MS. L:	Okay, canned food is very important to the Alaskans. Mark?
MARK:	Food in cans won't spoil.
CAROL:	They get food in cans that they can't grow.

➡️ **Write & Compare** Jot down your ideas for refocusing the discussion on a sheet of paper. Then, compare your ideas with those below.

One place to step into the discussion and prevent a loop is right after Sarah's comment. What she, Ronnie, and Sue have said includes the important information in the text segment, but the ideas need to be connected. Instead of repeating the information, the teacher might have focused student participation by asking for a summary of the information. For example:

> Okay, we have three important ideas here from Ronnie, Sue, and Sarah. Who can put them all together and sum up what we learned?

Another option is for the teacher to mark and revoice the comments herself.

> Okay, I think we've pointed out the problem and the solution the author has described for us. The problem is that vegetables won't grow in the Alaskan soil and that sometimes when vegetables are brought in, they freeze and spoil. Canned vegetables don't freeze or spoil, so Alaskans use those.

If the discussion were to continue beyond Sarah's comment, another place to step in would be after Carol's comment. For example, the teacher might have focused student participation by saying something like this:

> We seem to be referring to the same ideas over and over again. Who can connect the ideas for us, sum up what the author has told us about the problem the Alaskans have and how they solve it?

Recapping

In an effort to emphasize certain ideas or to encourage more students to get involved, teachers sometimes allow discussions to get into a repetitive loop. One way to avoid such a loop is by using the Discussion Moves of marking and revoicing the important ideas and moving on. Another way is to elicit student participation with a quick-response format, such as having students take sides by voting on an issue, or calling on students to provide brief examples or reasons related to a particular point.

Classroom Participation
How Do You Maintain a Balance?

Teachers have expressed concern to us about unequal classroom participation in QtA discussions. Sometimes a small group of students will dominate discussions, and conversely, a small group of students never participates at all.

In the following journal entry, Ms. K expresses frustration about uneven participation in her class.

> I'm having a problem with a few kids dominating the discussion. I can't seem to get them to stop talking and yet I don't want to stifle their enthusiasm by asking them to be quiet. For example, yesterday, Alvis, Darlene, and Tony kept raising their hands and were practically falling out of their seats to be called on. Alvis even hit me on the arm several times to be called on. It was hard not to call on them. Some of the other students just sat there and let them do all the work!

What Happened and Why?

Often a few students end up doing the work of the entire class because of teachers' tendency when first implementing QtA to call on students who are "safe" and can be counted on to keep the discussion's momentum going. Naturally, these are students who tend to be more confident and talkative. Once that pattern gets established, however, it is a hard one to break.

Dealing with the Problem

Achieving balance in student participation can be done in a number of ways, ranging from discussing with students the role of participation to offering ways for students to respond that may help them come to feel comfortable contributing to the discussion. We describe below some ideas that teachers have found effective. They fall into three categories. The first sets forth explicit expectations about participating in QtA discussions. The second suggests ways to draw participation from some of the more reluctant students, and the third suggests new roles that may rechannel the energies of students who want to be constantly participating.

Be Explicit About Participation. Remind students before a discussion begins that all their ideas and comments are important. Explain that taking part in discussion is an important part of their schoolwork because it helps them learn the ideas they read about.

Encourage Participation. The following are several techniques for encouraging active participation from more reluctant students.

[1] **Target students.** To widen participation, select two normally quiet students and make a point to call on them during discussions over several days. Do this several times with different sets of students over subsequent lessons to draw more and more students into the discussion.

[2] **Start small.** Give reticent students opportunities to join the discussion by "starting small," with contributions that don't require elaborate responses or a great deal of risk taking. For example, ask for confirmation of what someone else has said:

> What do you think about Andrew's idea?

or

> Do you agree with what Heather said?

Or ask a student to reiterate what has already been brought up:

> What new information did Beth just bring to our attention?

or

> Okay, so all we really need to know from this paragraph is—what?

[3] Whole-class responses. Engage students in some quick whole-class surveying, saying something like this:

> How many agree with what Ginger just said? Now how
> many disagree?

or

> Who thinks this was a good move for this character to make?

After the survey, call on a less talkative student to explain his or her position.

New student roles. Assign the more talkative students a different task or role during a few discussions. For example, give them an observer role, or ask them to write recaps of the various point of discussion to be read at the conclusion of each lesson. Their temporary absence from the discussions may encourage others to participate.

Recapping

Widespread and evenly distributed classroom participation is an important goal of QtA. Yet expecting 100 percent participation is probably unrealistic. Students who are not directly participating are still gaining from listening to the discussion, because in QtA discussions thinking is exposed. However, steps can be taken to encourage students to participate in ways that promote more widespread classroom interactions.

Telling students that participation is an important part of learning, finding nonthreatening ways to involve quieter students, and getting the assistance of the more verbal students are several effective techniques.

Evaluating Student-Initiated Ideas
When Should You Follow Their Detour?

As students become accustomed to QtA, they tend to introduce more of their own questions and issues into the discussion. This can add richness to discussion and give the teacher insight into their thinking and understanding. On the other hand, figuring out how to deal with an issue that a student brings into discussion can be tricky.

CLASSROOM SNAPSHOT

Ms. D's students are reading about Pennsylvania just before the start of the French and Indian War. The segment ends with the following paragraph:

At that time, French soldiers had a fort in Pennsylvania. The fort was near where the city of Erie is today. The French hoped to own Pennsylvania. England said she owned Pennsylvania. The Governor's message told the French to leave Pennsylvania.

Discussion of the text segment has begun with a focus on how both the French and English could claim the land. But Cheryl has something else in mind. Notice her comment and where it leads in the exchange below:

CHERYL: I have a question. What do they mean by "England said she owned Pennsylvania." What does it mean, *she*?

MS. D: The pronoun *she*? That's a good question. Does anyone have an answer for Cheryl?

CASEY: The queen of England.

MS. D:	No, at that time the king was the one in charge. What is the pronoun referring to?
LEAH:	Mother England.
MS. D:	Mother England! Ooh, what does Leah mean by that?
TONY:	Because it was like the first one, the first state?
MS. D:	But England isn't a state, though.
DANA:	It's a country, but it rules all the states.

What Happened and Why?

Cheryl's question was a useful one, providing an opportunity for Ms. D to enhance students' knowledge of a language convention—that of using female pronouns to refer to nations. However, attention to the issue took more time and moved a greater distance from the main ideas than Ms. D had anticipated. Ms. D pursued students' responses, thinking each time that the issue was nearly resolved. Finally, attention to this tangential issue began to get extensive. Ms. D ended up filling in the information simply by telling students that people often assign a gender to things, and that it's a custom to call countries *she*.

Dealing with the Problem

Dealing with ideas that students initiate presents a threefold challenge. First, how do you decide whether to follow a student's issue? Second, if you do, how much attention should you give it? Third, how do you get back to the major issues of the discussion? Making the initial decision depends on the relevance of the student's issue, its significance, and a judgment of whether it can be handled efficiently.

There are occasions in which a student-initiated issue is of such significance and interest that the teacher decides to take it up as the main focus of discussion. We won't be dealing with those situations in this case, however. Rather, we will look at examples of trying to balance attention to students' ideas with the main flow of discussion. The examples deal with all three parts of the challenge: whether to follow student ideas, how much attention to give, and how to get back to the main focus.

EXAMPLE 1. Ms. D's class continues to grapple with how the French and English claimed the same land. As the students talk, they bring in some additional players not specifically referred to in the text under discussion, namely the king and William Penn. A student, Kathryn, poses the following question for one of her classmates about this:

> KATHRYN: Why—I have to ask Tasha this—why did you say about the king when the author says *the governor* had a message for the French?

Apparently Ms. D saw this as an opportunity to try to sort out the players in the conflict, as she entertains the issue Kathryn brought up by turning the question back to Tasha:

> MS. D: Tasha, she wants to know why you brought up the king when the author talked about a governor?

> TASHA: The king was the one who gave William Penn the land, so now William owns most of the land. But I'm bringing up the king because we don't know how the French got there in order for them to think that the land was theirs. The English were there first. And really I don't think it is the king's because he has his own land to worry about.

Tasha's response didn't really address why she brought up the king and how he relates to the governor mentioned in the text. So now, Ms. D intervenes to directly address the issue of who's who, using the follow-up below:

> MS. D: Okay, but what about this governor? Who is the governor that the author is talking about?

Discussion then established that it was the governor of Virginia, who is British, who wanted to send a message to the French. So, in this example, the teacher first steered discussion toward a student's comment, but when that direction did not pan out, she moved to recover the focus of discussion.

EXAMPLE 2. In this next example, we see Ms. D dealing with a comment by postponing directly addressing it. The topic under discussion now is that the governor asked George Washington to deliver his message telling the French to leave Pennsylvania. Amid discussion, Larry poses the following question:

LARRY: Why did the governor pick George to go?

The author has not yet provided the answer to the question, and thus discussion of it would be based on guesses and speculation and probably would not contribute much to understanding. So Ms. D responds as follows:

MS. D: Hmmm, that's an interesting question, but it's hard to
know from what the author has told us so far. Let's
hold on to that, Larry, and see if we get any more
information as we read.

Subsequently, the issue is, indeed, addressed in the text. Here is the first paragraph of the next text segment:

> Young George Washington was a good person to send on
> this trip. He had learned about the forests from the Indians.
> Washington asked a man who spoke French to go with him.
> He asked a man of the woods to be the guide. Washington
> and the two men went on foot and on horses.

MS. D: Okay, Larry, has the author given you some ideas
about what you were wondering before?

Ms. D judged Larry's comment to be a worthwhile one but not one that needed to be taken up when it was asked. By asking Larry to "hold on to" his comment, she managed to address the comment, acknowledge its value, and keep the discussion on track.

EXAMPLE 3. In this example, a class is reading about the arrival of the first settlers in Hawaii, the Polynesians. The discussion focuses on the following text paragraph:

> **The Polynesians had to sail thousands of miles or kilometers to get to the Hawaiian Islands. The canoes of the Polynesians were made by lashing together pieces of wood with rope.**

Amid discussion of the Polynesians' long journey and the boats they traveled in, Andre raises another point:

ANDRE: Did they stop at every island along the way or something?

The teacher judges Andre's comment as not relevant to the ideas being discussed. After first checking whether Andre thought that was what he had read in the text, she moves to sideline the comment. Below is the exchange that followed Andre's question:

MS. S: Did the author explain something about that?

ANDRE: No.

MS. S: Do you think it matters to what we're learning here about these people?

STUDENTS: No.

MS. S: Okay, let's go on then. The author really can't include every little detail, and for now we need to figure out what the big picture is here.

The teacher in this example decided that Andre's comment might distract the discussion and allow it to break down into speculation about the fine points of the Polynesians' ocean voyage. So she deferred it, suggesting that it was a detail not helpful to the discussion at hand.

Your Turn

In the following example, students are reading *The Cricket in Times Square* (Selden, 1970), a fantasy about a cricket named Chester who ends up in New York and finds a home in a newsstand owned by the Bellini family. The text segment being discussed describes an incident in the story in which Chester has a dream about eating a willow leaf but wakes up to find himself at the cash register in the newsstand. Below is the end of the text segment the students read and the exchange that follows between the teacher and the students. Decide what you would do next in response to the discussion that Corinna's comment inspires: cover and recover, hold it, or send it to the sidelines.

> **Chester looked down at his two front legs, half expecting to find the willow leaf. But it was no leaf he was holding. It was a two dollar bill and he had already eaten half of it.**

MS. D:	How do things look for Chester now?
FRANK:	Awful. He just ate the Bellinis' money and they don't have that much! Mama Bellini is really going to be mad.
CORINNA:	But maybe they can take the two-dollar bill to the bank and get the money.
MICHAEL:	Yeah, I've heard of that before. You go to the bank if your money gets ripped.
CORINNA:	How much money would they get? A half of two dollars is one dollar. Would they just get one dollar, or two dollars, or what?

⮕ Write & Compare Jot down your idea for a follow-up on a sheet of paper. Then, compare your idea with the one below.

> Wait a minute! Let's think about what Corinna just said. What do you think would really happen if the Bellinis took half of a two-dollar bill to the bank and asked for their money back?

The teacher decided to use a cover and recover move. She knew that the issue of the two-dollar bill was intriguing the students, so she decided to deal with it. She also knew that dealing with it would allow students to understand even better how much trouble Chester was in. After students decided that the bank would not give anything for one half of a two-dollar bill, the teacher returned to the major issue of what the destruction of the two-dollar bill meant for Chester and the Bellinis.

Your Turn Again

The following example comes from the same lesson described in the example above. Now the students are reading about Chester's reaction to eating the two-dollar bill. How would you respond to Kristin's question?

> "I just ate half of a two dollar bill," said Chester.
>
> Tucker stared at him in disbelief. "You did what?" he asked.
>
> "Yes," said Chester, "look." He fetched the ruined two dollar bill from the cash register. "I dreamed it was a leaf and I ate it."
>
> "Oh oh oh oh," moaned Tucker Mouse. . . .
>
> "What am I going to do?" asked Chester
>
> "Pack your bags and go to California," said Tucker
>
> Chester shook his head. "I can't," he said. "They've been so good to me—I can't run away."

MS. D:	What's going on here? What's the situation the author has described for us?
KRISTIN:	I don't think a cricket could eat a two-dollar bill, not even one little piece of it. His mouth is, like, small.

➡️ **Write & Compare** Jot down your idea for a follow-up on a sheet of paper. Then, compare your idea with the one below.

> Remember, we're not talking about a real cricket here. Chester can talk and do lots of things a real cricket can't do. But what problem does he have to face and how does he seem to want to handle it?

Kristin's comment could have taken the discussion far off course, so the teacher decided to send it to the sidelines rather than pursue it.

Recapping

It takes a lot of skill to balance paying attention to students' ideas and maintaining the main flow of discussion. Dealing with a student's idea involves three things: deciding whether to pursue the idea, considering how much attention to give it, and working out a way to get back to the main focus. Some options are cover and recover, or taking the time to address the issue and then recovering the discussion focus; hold it, or asking students to bring up the idea at a later time; and send it to the sidelines, or letting students know that the issue is not one that is relevant or worth pursuing.

Constructing Meaning
What if Texts Don't Seem to Lend Themselves to It?

When teachers first begin using QtA, they find that some texts just don't seem to work with QtA. Some portions of texts, especially social studies texts, don't seem to offer enough information about major ideas to provide grist for discussion.

Here is how Mr. W described the issue in his journal.

> I've been looking over the social studies chapter that we'll be starting next week, and I'm having a really hard time figuring out how to use it to build anything like understanding. The chapter is on the New England region, and the material is kind of an odd collection of information about the area—some of it seems unimportant and even silly. There really isn't a big concept running through it. Statements are presented without enough detail to dig into. And ideas that seem to be related aren't presented together. An idea might connect to something a page and a half later! I don't know how QtA will work with this kind of text.

What Happened and Why?

Mr. W has identified several problems that teachers have found with textbooks. In some cases, it's clear what the topic is, but the information about the topic is very shallow. There doesn't seem to be enough explanation or content to provide grist for constructing an understanding. In other cases, it is hard even to know what the main topic is. The material presented is little more than a list of facts that don't seem to have a larger idea connecting them.

There can be other problems as well. For instance, information that is related may be scattered throughout the text, and important information may be mixed in with information of little significance.

Dealing with the Problem

Dealing with problematic texts calls for thoughtful consideration. That is, you really need to "question the author" to figure out what meaning may be constructed. Then, you need to decide what you want students to understand. Even if all the information students may need for developing an understanding of the topic is not provided in the text, and even if it is not clear what the major idea is, you need to decide what it is that *you* want students to gain from interacting with that particular text.

Second, you need to organize your planning around the understanding you've identified rather than relying solely on explicit text statements and the order in which they're presented.

Two examples are presented of thinking through a text that is difficult to plan for, either because of unclear focus or a lack of information on the focus. In both cases, the teacher's planning also had to confront how to handle information that seems out of order and ideas that seem less than important.

EXAMPLE 1. The text section in this example, "Historic Towns and Activities," is from a chapter on the New England region, similar to the one Mr. W wrote about in his journal. The teacher's goal is to have students develop some sense of New England's place in the country's history. Ways to reach the goal and ways in which the text presentation obscures the goal are both reflected in the commentary. The main problem is that the section provides some references to the historic aspects of New England, but does not do so in a coherent or explanatory way.

The subtitle, "A Whaling Community," has no relation to the first two sentences, nor do those two sentences relate to each other. The first sentence relates, obliquely, to an important concept, that is, New England's role in the settling of our country. This point is never discussed explicitly, but some other parts of the text do relate to it, both earlier and later in the text. A plan for dealing with this idea might be to pose a Query to see if students are aware of the historic significance of New England. For example, *"What does the author mean that New England is famous for its historic towns?"* If students are not aware of the history, it might be best to table the idea until later in the text. (See ** on page 262.)

This paragraph and the following one discuss whaling—but only by kind of backing into it. That is, the text introduces Mystic and says it was an important whaling center. Students may have no background about whaling as an important industry, and thus this description may make little sense until the next paragraph is read and examined.

This paragraph provides information about why whales were hunted. The way the information is presented does not, however, make it easy to understand that it was a big and important industry. Focusing on the third sentence in the paragraph, about whale oil being burned to provide light, may develop such an understanding, pursuing and emphasizing the idea that there was no electricity at that time.

Historic Towns and Activities

A WHALING COMMUNITY New England is famous for its historic towns and villages. Many families enjoy visiting the museums and old buildings in the region to learn about the history of our country.

One such historic town is Mystic, in Connecticut. In the 1800s this town was one of the world's most important centers for the whaling industry. Whaling is the hunting of whales in the ocean. Whaling was dangerous work that called for brave men.

Different parts of the whale were used for different things. Whale oil was used for fuel in lamps. In those days there was no electricity, and whale oil was burned to provide light. Whalebones were used in making many things, such as umbrellas, shoehorns, and jewelry. A part of the whale was even used in the making of perfume.

The town of Mystic has been restored to show what an important whaling town was like years ago. The buildings and ships look like those of the whaling days. You can hear the sounds and see the sights of an old seaport.

You can see people doing and making things related to whaling. You can even climb aboard the famous *Charles W. Morgan*, the only wooden whaling ship left from the old whaling days. It set out on its first voyage in 1841 and sailed more miles than any other whaling ship. Today the ship is a whaling museum.

In recent years, people have become aware that whales have nearly disappeared from the Atlantic Ocean. The leaders of our government, as well as the leaders of several other countries, have decided to protect the whales. Now there is a law that prohibits whaling in the waters that surround our country.

This paragraph and the next one provide little information that is useful for understanding whaling, New England, or history. Rather it is a "tour guide" kind of description, and may be read and simply commented on as such.

Now for something completely different! The author switches gears here to tell us how whales are treated nowadays. It might make sense to preface it by saying something on that order. For example, *"Now the author is telling us something very different about whales. What's the message here?"* And then perhaps, *"So, does this connect to what we were learning about here?"* (not exactly).

This section switches gears again to provide a little practice in using a time line. As such, it really breaks the flow of the ideas, which is pretty weak to begin with. This is a time to skip to the next section, possibly returning later.

READING A TIME LINE Because time is often hard to measure, we frequently use time lines to help us keep track of time. A time line is a line that shows facts about events or happenings. Like a map, a time line has a scale. But the scale on a time line measures time, not distance from place to place.

A time line shows events in the order in which they happened. The time line on this page shows seven important events in the story of whaling. To read the time line, begin by looking at the earliest and latest events. What is the first event shown on the time line? What is the last event? What was the name of the first whaler that was built at Mystic, Connecticut?

Immigrants to Our Country

LEAVING HOME You have read that the Pilgrims settled in what is now Massachusetts. Other settlers soon followed, and they, too, started colonies. A colony is a group of people who settle in a distant land. In 1776 the colonies in America created their own nation—the United States of America.

** This paragraph relates to the earlier statement about New England having historic towns. The goal here may be to get students to understand that New England was where the United States started. Such a discussion may begin with a Query such as *"What have we learned about New England here?"* and then going back to the first sentence of this section, which states that New England is famous for historic towns, and asking how that connects. Grappling with the connection can help students appreciate why New England has a special place in our country's history.

In planning how to deal with this text, the teacher first identified the main concept she wanted students to understand. Then, she selected from the text the information that would establish that concept. Since this information was not always explicit and was scattered through the text, she also had to arrange ways to draw attention to significant ideas while downplaying other information.

EXAMPLE 2. This example presents a teacher's first-person commentary as she develops a plan for a chapter about early settlements in the New World. The material is from a textbook on Pennsylvania history. The teacher's initial reaction to the material began as follows:

> I had to read this three times before I could even say what was important to have students know. It starts out telling that the Dutch and Swedish came to Pennsylvania, which implies *one* big idea—that people from different countries started settling here. But the details kind of overwhelm the big idea. I guess the really major idea of the chapter is the one that the chapter ends with—settlements were started by various countries, but England is beginning to dominate the colonies. Now *that* is something that students will need to know in order to develop an understanding of their country's history. So that's the understanding I'll focus on. But how do I deal with all this text up to that point?

The first three sentences in this section are about all we need to know, I think, at this point. The rest of the details are not going to help build an understanding. I think I may have those three sentences read and ask, **"What's the author reminded us of?"** Then I'll read the rest to the class myself and just comment that the author is filling in some details about some of the people who came here.

Here we get another group coming over. Again, all I really want the students to get is that general sense. But instead, we get all kinds of detail about people and places they'll never hear of again! A Dutch man sailing for Sweden, starting a fort in Delaware, named for the queen! How does that help in understanding anything? I mean, I guess that could be interesting to know. But the way it's written, it's like everything is of the same importance. Big ideas aren't treated any differently from little details.

Early Settlers in Pennsylvania

THE DUTCH EXPLORE The Indians were the first people to live in what is now Pennsylvania. Columbus arrived in America in 1492. After this, many countries in Europe sent explorers to America. An explorer is a person who looks for new things and new places. In 1616, an explorer from Holland named Cornelius Hendricksen sailed up the Delaware River. Holland is also called the Netherlands. The people who live in that country are called the Dutch.

Hendricksen found another river that joins the Delaware River where the city of Philadelphia is today. He named this river the Schuylkill. The Dutch sent people to live along the two rivers. These people built forts and began to trade with the Indians for furs.

THE SWEDISH ARRIVE Sometime later, Sweden became interested in sending settlers to the Delaware River area. Settlers are people who move to a new land to live. The place where they live is a settlement. In 1637, a Dutch explorer named Peter Minuit (min' u it) sailed to America for Sweden. He was sent to buy land from the Indians along the Delaware and Schuylkill rivers. This land would be a home for Swedish settlers. With two small ships, Minuit sailed up the Delaware River.

He built a fort at the place on the river that is now Wilmington, Delaware. Minuit named it Fort Christina after the young queen of Sweden. More Swedish settlers arrived 2 years later. But it was not until 1644 that a Swedish settlement was started in what is now Pennsylvania.

NEW SWEDEN A governor for the Swedish settlement, Johan Printz, came to America in 1643. A governor is the most important leader of a settlement or state. One of the first things that Printz did was move the capital of the settlement from Fort Christina to Tinicum Island. A capital is the place where the leaders of a settlement, state, or country work. Tinicum Island is about 20 miles (32 km) south of what is now Philadelphia. Printz called the new capital New Gothenburg. The whole area settled by the Swedes was called New Sweden. It was the first lasting European settlement in what is now Pennsylvania.

The Swedes in New Sweden built log cabins for homes. They were the first to build log cabins in America. This was the kind of house they had in Sweden. The log cabins were warm and cozy. They were good homes for the Swedes during the cold winters in America.

The first paragraph of this section is just little more than a glut of names and places. This governor comes and moves the capital from one place we've never heard of to another place we've never heard of and names it something else we've never heard of! I'm just going to skip this and move to the last sentence of the paragraph, which presents a historical detail of some interest.

That the Swedes had the first lasting settlement in Pennsylvania is interesting, because we tend to think of the state beginning with William Penn. I'll just tell the students, **"Here's something interesting—the very first lasting European settlement in Pennsylvania was founded by the Swedish. I didn't realize that!"**

This information about the log cabins is noteworthy, since log cabins are so stereotypical of pioneer times. It's interesting to know that the Swedish introduced them to America.

I don't know about this paragraph. It doesn't really help in understanding history; it's just a collection of details that aren't very significant. I mean, didn't everybody farm? And what's the big deal with flax? I might just comment after reading this paragraph something like **"Here the author gave us some details about what life was like for these settlers. Let's go on and see what else is happening."** I guess it could be a good idea to ask students if there was anything important, so they begin noticing the difference between the important and the less ideas. But if I did that every time, it would take forever and distract us from anything meaningful.

Now, this is more important information, that the Swedish colony got taken over by the Dutch. But that's it—we don't need to attend to all the specifics. I think I'll have both of the paragraphs read as one segment and then ask, **"So what's the big point here that the author is telling us?"**

The Swedish settlers also began to farm the land. They were the first settlers to bring cattle to America for their farms. The Indians taught the Swedes how to grow corn, beans, and squash. They also planted flax and tobacco. Flax is a plant used to make linen cloth. Tobacco was an important crop because it was worth a lot of money in Europe.

THE DUTCH GAIN CONTROL The Swedish settlers began to have trouble with the Dutch. The Dutch felt that New Sweden really belonged to them, since they had explored the land and built forts there. In 1652 a small Dutch fort on the Delaware River named Fort Casimir was captured by the Swedes. This made the Dutch very angry.

Their governor, Peter Stuyvesant (sti' ve sent), sent an army to recapture the fort and to attack New Sweden. In 1655, the Swedes lost New Sweden to the Dutch. The Dutch let the Swedes stay on their farms if they wanted to. Most of the Swedish settlers stayed. But now they had to obey a Dutch governor.

ENGLAND TAKES OVER England also had settlements in America. The English had settled in what is now New England, Maryland, and Virginia. The Dutch lands, which now included New Sweden, were between these settlements. King Charles II of England wanted to join together the English settlements. In 1664, he sent a large army to attack the Dutch. The Dutch surrendered, or gave up. In this way, the English took control of the Dutch and Swedish settlements. These settlements included the area that is now New York State and the land along the Delaware River. The English capital was moved to Upland, which is now the city of Chester in Pennsylvania.

And now the big finale! All the land is falling into English hands. This really is the most important point of the whole chapter. I think I may say, *"So the author has told us all this information about the Dutch and the Swedish. Now what does it all add up to?"* And if I need to follow up, *"What's happened to all this land in Pennsylvania that we've been reading about?"*

I think I may also probe what students know about the history of their country in general by asking, *"From what you know about history, does this ring any bells—the English taking over the land?"* I want to see if they have the idea that the colonies from which our country grew all belonged to England at one point.

For this text, the teacher had to dig a bit to figure out what was meaningful. To help students build an understanding, she planned to give different portions of text different kinds of attention, according to its significance.

Recapping

Sometimes the information in a text about a topic may seem inadequate. At other times it may be hard to discern what the major idea is supposed to be. When these situations occur, a teacher's first reaction may be that the text is not a good one to use with QtA. But if the topic is important for students to understand, QtA can help a teacher effectively use an imperfect text.

The best approach may be to read the text and "question the author" yourself to identify the big picture. Consider the subject matter being presented and decide what it is that you want students to understand about it. Focus your planning on what the text seems to be trying to get at rather than on what it actually delivers. You may find you want to skip around in the text or tell students that some parts are not important for the discussion.

When It's Hard to Formulate a Query
Is It Time for Modeling?

At times teachers want to draw students' attention to particular text material or a text idea but can't seem to formulate a Query to do so successfully. In these cases, the Discussion Move of modeling can be a very direct way to get to a particular idea.

CLASSROOM SNAPSHOT

Mr. W's class is reading "Don't Think Like a Slave," a story that describes Dr. Martin Luther King, Jr.'s early years. The selection begins with the text segment below, which describes a speech that Dr. King gave when he was a teenager.

Martin gripped the sides of the lectern. "The Negro and the Constitution," he began, and his nervousness started to slip away. His voice grew stronger, more confident. Even though it was still a young voice, it was one that commanded attention. It carried bold new ideas that tugged at listeners' minds and hearts. When Martin finished speaking there was an instant of silence, broken by enthusiastic applause. The crowd had listened, and they liked what they had heard.

Mr. W wants to focus the discussion on the author's use of figurative language to convey the power of Martin's speech, but the students do not pick up this direction.

MR. W: So, the author has said quite a bit here. Can someone tell us what this is all about?

TIM:	That the crowd liked what they heard.
JANET:	And that the crowd listened.
MR. W:	Well, how did the author let us know that?
DANTE:	He says it right here, "The crowd listened."
Mr. W:	Well, wouldn't a crowd listen to any speaker?
PAUL:	They *liked* what they heard.
MR. W:	Why? What was so special about what was going on here? Anybody? No one has an idea?

What Happened and Why?

In response to the Initiating Query, Tim and Janet merely repeated phrases from the text. Mr. W followed up by asking how the author conveyed the idea of the audience's attention in order to focus on the author's description of Martin Luther King's captivating speaking style. But the students persisted in quoting the more literal phrases of the text.

Even though Mr. W's Initiating Query seemed appropriate, it was not effective. The students seemed to avoid the difficult portions of the passage—phrases like "tugged at listeners' minds" and "commanded attention"—and went directly to the parts that they could readily understand.

Dealing with the Problem

When a Query doesn't succeed in drawing attention to ideas that the teacher has targeted, a teacher might use the Discussion Move of modeling, revealing his or her own thinking about the ideas to create a focus for students' attention. For example, Mr. W might have said, "Well, here is a paragraph about Martin Luther King's giving a speech, and the author is saying things like his voice 'commanded attention' and 'tugged at listeners' minds and hearts.' Now I'm thinking, how does what somebody says tug at your mind and heart? What could the author mean by that?"

Two kinds of situations seem to be particularly good candidates for modeling. One involves text passages that may be especially difficult or confusing. Dealing directly with the difficulties through modeling can reduce the risk that students may feel in grappling with them on their own. Modeling is also effective for highlighting an author's expression of ideas or choice of wording. Rather than asking students what they thought of the words an author used, simply express your own response as a reader.

EXAMPLE 1. In this example, a teacher draws attention to a problematic portion of text by revealing her own confusion about what it means. Notice how she then solicits the help of the students in grappling with its meaning.

The students are beginning a new unit in social studies about community and people working together. The author introduces the unit by presenting the musical score and lyrics for a song about flocks of geese flying together. In planning the lesson, the teacher thought that the author's use of flocks of geese—presented through music—as an analogy for the concept of community might go over students' heads or, worse, be distracting. Here is the text and the way the teacher deals with the passage:

> **The song "High and Blue the Sky" that you just read compares people to geese. This is because people, like geese in flocks, depend on one another to help fill their needs. In this chapter you will learn more about the people of the world and about why it is becoming more important for people to work together.**

MS. K: The author shows us a song about geese here; then under the song, the author has a short paragraph saying that we are going to learn about people of the world. I don't get it. What does the paragraph have to do with the song? What does that have to do with geese? I just don't understand what the connection is. Can someone help me out?

JOHN:	I think that, um, it's about people filling their needs, like geese helping each other.
CHARLENE:	I think it's going to be about comparing geese to people.
MS. K:	Well, yeah, that makes sense. You know what I think now? I don't think the geese have anything to do with this chapter. But I think you are right, that he *is* comparing people to geese. Why would the author do that? Just to confuse us?
ANDREW:	'Cause geese help each other, like when they need food or something, they would give it to each other.
CHARLENE:	And they would help each other build nests—like our houses—so it's kinda like people in a neighborhood helping each other out sometimes.

By expressing what she was thinking about it through modeling and then inviting student interpretation, the teacher got the students moving a confusing portion of text in a productive direction.

EXAMPLE 2. The example below shows how modeling can be used to demonstrate the processes of building understanding that go on in the minds of expert readers as they deal with difficult portions of text. In this example, the class has just begun a story that introduces a number of characters without much description. The teacher anticipated that the portion of text would be difficult and that the students would need support in figuring it all out. Here is the text segment and the teacher's comments on it.

> **"Who would have thought that I would be driving to Cooperstown?" Mr. Feldman said the next morning, as they started on their way. What he was really thinking, Ezra imagined, was who would have thought a man like Professor Strauss would care about baseball.**

MS. M: When I read that paragraph, I thought, "Wait a minute! Who *are* these people? And what are they up to?" We have a Mr. Feldman talking, we have someone named Ezra, and we have a Professor Strauss thrown in. So, I went back and read it again and I think I figured out that this Mr. Feldman and Ezra are traveling to Cooperstown together, because it seems that Ezra is reacting in his mind to what Mr. Feldman is really trying to say. And Professor Strauss, I guess, is somebody who's not there with them, but probably somebody who will turn up later in the story. So, I think the best thing we can do here is read on.

In the example above, the teacher modeled how a reader might handle too many details that are not explained. In so doing, she shared both the information and the strategies the students needed to construct meaning from that portion of text.

EXAMPLE 3. Modeling can be a valuable resource for calling students' attention to an author's particularly effective use of language. Here is a simple example based on a line from a story:

He leaped up and gave an angry flash of eyes.

MS. P: Oooh, I love the way the author did that! Just in that one line, he really gave me a strong feeling of how *mad* this guy is!

This kind of modeling can help the students appreciate an author's effective use of language without over analyzing it.

Your Turn

In the example that follows, a class is reading about a contested area of land called the Erie Triangle. The teacher wants students to understand that the state of Pennsylvania gained this territory, but they get off track speculating about the controversy that surrounded claims to the land.

In 1792, Pennsylvania settled an old argument over a piece of land in the northwest, along Lake Erie. This piece of land, which was shaped like a triangle, was called the Erie Triangle. The states of Massachusetts, New York, and Pennsylvania all claimed the Erie Triangle. When New York and Massachusetts gave up their claims to the land, Pennsylvania bought the land from the United States.

MS. P:	What is the author trying to tell us about here?
MIRIAM:	An argument. A really big argument.
MS. P:	You think the author wants us to know about an argument?
MIRIAM:	Well, Massachusetts, New York, and Pennsylvania wanted one piece of land.
CHAD:	See, it's on the map. Maybe if Massachusetts owned that part, maybe it could cut off the way New York got to the lake.
MS. P:	That's possible. But what do we know about the land from this paragraph? Tess?
TESS:	Maybe Massachusetts is closer to New York and it wants to get closer to Pennsylvania, too. To get at both places.

At this point, how could you use modeling to cut off further speculation and guide students to focus on the most important information?

➡️ **Write & Compare** Jot down your ideas for modeling on a sheet of paper. Then, compare your ideas with the one below.

> When I read this first sentence, I thought the author was going to tell me about a fight among three states over some land. But then it didn't say anything more about what the fight was. Or why these three states claimed that land. How did Massachusetts get involved? It's way over to the east of New York! But then I figured out that all the author was trying to tell us was that there had been this piece of land that nobody owned really, because of the different claims, and then Pennsylvania got it. So Pennsylvania got a little bigger in 1792.

By modeling her reaction to the text, the teacher allowed students to see her mind at work, to get a glimpse of her thought processes.

Recapping

Sometimes the most direct way to make a point may be through modeling rather than posing a Query. Modeling provides a way to highlight confusion about text ideas as well as draw attention to particularly well-expressed ideas. As a bonus, it gives students the opportunity to observe the thinking processes of a mature reader.

Building Toward Understanding
Why Should It Take More Than One Step?

Complex ideas call for students to bring together different parts of a text. What kind of guidance can help students access and connect several aspects of text?

Ms. C's class is reading about the characteristics of wetlands. Ms. C's goal is to have students understand two types of wetlands, marshes and swamps, by contrasting them. Although both are labeled wetlands, they differ in that ground plants can grow in marshes but not in swamps because swamps have trees, which block the light. Here is the text segment being discussed:

Different kinds of plants grow in wetlands along the coast. Some wetlands are marshes. These are wetlands where mostly grasses grow. Other kinds of plants such as cattails and reeds also grow there. No trees or shrubs grow in marshes.

Other kinds of wetlands are swamps. Swamps are wetlands where mostly trees grow. Tall trees such as cypress and oak grow well in swamps because the soil is very wet. Few plants, however, grow on the ground because the thick treetops block the sunlight. Poison ivy and other vines climb the tree trunks.

MS. C:	Why do you think grasses grow in marshes but not in the swamps, if they're both wetlands?
NAT:	Different kinds of plants grow in wetlands.
MS. C:	Well, different kinds of plants, but what about marshes and swamps? What did the author tell us?
BECKY:	They're wetlands.

What Happened and Why?

Ms. C's students had difficulty responding meaningfully to her Initiating Query because it encompassed a complex set of ideas. Ms. C wanted to get students to immediately bring together all the ideas they had just read about, that is, to construct the contrast between marshes and swamps. She wanted them to grasp that different kinds of plants grow in different wetlands, and explain why.

Dealing with the Problem

Dealing with complex ideas calls for taking a longer view of the discussion. A teacher needs to stand back a bit and realize that it may take a considerable sequence of exchanges before an understanding of something complex emerges. The key is to recognize such situations and adjust expectations about how readily understanding may be developed. Trying to do it all at once is probably not going to work. A better approach is to build incrementally toward important ideas.

The following examples illustrate how some teachers handled the development of complex ideas. Notice the variety of Discussion Moves they incorporated.

EXAMPLE 1. In this example, the class is reading about the geography of the southeastern United States. The teacher's goal is to have students integrate *Piedmont* into their developing geographical image of the region by focusing on its elevation relative to plains and mountains.

The teacher also wants students to understand that the Piedmont is a plateau. The idea of the Piedmont as a plateau may be difficult to grasp. Although the Piedmont was described as a plateau in the introduction to the chapter, the word *plateau* is not used in the paragraph below. Moreover, the Piedmont is described as "rolling hills" rather than as "flat." Here is the text:

The third major landform of the Southeast region is the Piedmont. Piedmont is a French word that means "foot of the mountain." The Piedmont lies between the Atlantic Coastal Plain and the Appalachian Mountains. If you stood in this belt of rolling hills, you might be able to look down on the coastal plain and up to the Appalachian Mountains.

Below is the teacher's Initiating Query and the response it draws:

Ms. C: Let's stop there. What is the author telling us about what *piedmont* means?

MONICA: When they said *piedmont* is a French word, means "foot of the mountain," they may not have the English word for it, so they try and put it in French, but the top of the Piedmont is flat, so then the foot of the mountain.

Monica has gotten a bit tangled in trying to explain why a French word is used for this landform, rather than focusing on what its translation means in geographical terms. Notice below how the teacher tries to refocus by revoicing Monica's response to mark geographical aspects, and then uses turning-back to text to elicit further comment from Monica.

Ms. C: So you're saying that it has to do with the location then? It said "foot of the mountain," and it's flat.

MONICA: But it still runs on the Appalachian Mountains, so that's why he might be telling us.

Ms. C: Okay, so it has to do with the Appalachian Mountains.

Monica's second comment didn't add much. The teacher clarified Monica's "*it still runs on* the Appalachian Mountains" by revoicing it as "*it has to do with.*" Next, Timmy's comment picks up from there, specifying how the Piedmont "has to do with" both the Appalachian Mountains and the coastal plain.

TIMMY: It has to do with two things. He said also if we go to the foothills, you could look up at the Appalachian Mountains and you can look down at the coastal hills.

The teacher acknowledges Timmy's comment and attempts to clarify the terms he used by turning-back to text. She then poses a Query to have students make explicit the reason for having to look down on the coastal plain.

MS. C: Let's go back to what Timmy said. He kind of quoted from our text, and it was a very good place to quote: "If you stood in this belt of rolling hills, you might be able to look down on the coastal plain and up to the Appalachian Mountains." Why would you have to look down on the coastal plain?

Jeremy's response focuses on the coastal plain rather than the Piedmont's relation to it. The teacher then rephrases her Query, and Jeremy is able to elaborate.

JEREMY: Because it's near the ground. And it's flat.

MS. C: The coastal plain is flat, but how can we stand here and look down on it?

JEREMY: Because the water's right here, the mountains are right here, so all you have to do is look down at the water and look back up. So we're somewhere in between the mountains and the coastal plain.

The teacher then reintroduces the term *piedmont*, which Miriam characterizes as a plateau.

MS. C: And that's called the Piedmont?

MIRIAM: The Piedmont is a plateau.

In the final exchanges, the teacher has Miriam fill out the definition of *plateau* and then recaps the idea of being able to look both up and down from the Piedmont.

MS. C: Okay, and what's a plateau by definition?

MIRIAM: Flat land that is high up.

MS. C: Yes, it's raised up. So we can stand on the Piedmont plateau and look down at some more ground and yet we're not as high as the mountain.

The focus of this example (that a plateau has an intermediate elevation between those of plains and mountains) may not seem a particularly difficult one. Yet understanding it involves several aspects: comparing a plain with a plateau and a plateau with mountains, and understanding that even though the Piedmont is described as "rolling hills," it is a plateau. So the teacher decided to give explicit attention to developing these aspects. Such attention did not bring immediate results, however. The teacher needed to employ a variety of methods to help students consider the text statements about landforms and their relationships and make them meaningful.

EXAMPLE 2. In the next example, the class is reading about the beginnings of the steel industry in Pennsylvania. The portion of text they are working with describes how a new steelmaking process began to replace an older one because it allowed for higher temperatures, which resulted in better steel. Here is the text:

> **Toward the end of the 1800s, the open-hearth process was being used in a large number of steel mills. In the open-hearth process, a bowl-shaped furnace was used to heat iron. The iron could be heated to higher temperatures in this type of furnace. Samples could be taken from the furnace and tested for quality. Although it took longer to make steel this way, a better kind of steel was produced. By 1908 more open-hearth steel was made than Bessemer steel.**

Below is the teacher's Initiating Query, followed by several exchanges in which she poses Follow-Up Queries seeking elaboration about the reasons for the change in the steelmaking process.

MS. C: Alright, what's the author just told us here? Jacob?

JACOB: Um, the open-hearth process was being used more for steel.

MS. C: And does the author tell us why the open-hearth seemed to be more popular? Jamie?

JAMIE: Um, well kind of, but not really. What it says in here is that, like, a new process of how to make steel was developed.

MS. C: A new process—what does the author give us on that?

JAMIE: This process would have to be the open-hearth process. And, um, it was, I think, a little easier than the Bessemer steel.

Jamie's response contains information that contradicts the text—that is, that the open-hearth process is easier. So the teacher revoices Jamie's response, and turns back the responsibility for clarification to students. But notice that Jonathan's response takes a different direction.

MS. C: Alright, Jamie says it was easier to make it open-hearth than Bessemer. What do you think of that, Jonathan?

JONATHAN: Um, it says the iron could be heated to higher temperatures in the open-hearth process than the Bessemer.

Because Jonathan's comment includes information essential to the ideas being developed, the teacher chooses to follow up on it, rather than trying to clear up the misstatement that Jamie introduced.

MS. C: And what does the higher temperatures have to do with the making of steel?

JONATHAN: A stronger steel.

Next, the teacher acknowledges Jonathan's response, finishing up that idea, and then goes back to Jamie's comment.

MS. C: Right. A stronger steel. Now Jamie said that the open-hearth was an easier process than Bessemer. Did she get that from the author, or did she make that up?

Notice in the exchanges below that the teacher draws on a Follow-Up Query and turning-back to text before the issue is resolved.

BART: She made it up.

MS. C: Why do you say she made it up?

BART:	Well, 'cause it really didn't say anything about that in here.
MS. C:	How about the sentence "Although it took longer to make steel this way, a better kind of steel was produced."
JOELLA:	Oh! If it took longer wouldn't that have been kinda like more complicated, not easier?
MS. C:	Ah, yes. But a better steel because of the heat, as Jonathan said.

In this example, the teacher used a variety of ways to probe and follow up students' comments to bring forth the idea that the hotter temperatures of the new steel process led to a better product. Within the discussion, she had to balance following major ideas and addressing a misstatement, but managed successfully by taking it one step at a time.

Your Turn

In the following example, a class is discussing the text segment below, which describes the legislative branch of the federal government:

> **One wing of the Capitol building is where the Senate meets. The other wing is where the House of Representatives meets. The Senate and the House of Representatives are the two houses, or parts, of Congress. Congress is the legislative branch, or part, of the government. It makes the laws for all the people in the United States.**

There are several important ideas embedded in this paragraph, including that one part of the federal government is the legislative branch, and the legislative branch, or Congress, has two parts, the Senate and the House of Representatives. Notice how the teacher attempts to get these ideas on the table with a general Initiating Query.

MR. L: There's a lot of information in this paragraph, but what big idea is the author talking about?

Below are a variety of possible student responses to the above Query. Each represents a potential step on the way to understanding. Based on what each student says, how would you respond initially and then how would you follow up to help students take the next step in building their understanding?

STUDENT RESPONSE 1:

RHONDA: Congress makes the laws for all the people.

➤ Write & Compare Jot down your ideas for following up on a sheet of paper. Then, compare your ideas with the one below.

MR. L: Okay. That's an important idea the author gave us. But why did the author say, "Congress is the... *part* [that] makes the laws?" What does that mean?

The teacher followed up Rhonda's response by focusing on the idea that Congress is one of the parts of the federal government and that Congress itself has two parts.

STUDENT RESPONSE 2:

ROBERT: The Capitol is where the Senate meets.

➤ Write & Compare Jot down your ideas for following up on a sheet of paper. Then, compare your ideas with the one below.

MR. L: Right, the Capitol building—but did the author tell us that that was where only the *Senate* was?

The teacher followed up by directing focus to the idea that both the House and the Senate share the Capitol. From there, the class could pursue the idea that each is part of the legislature, which makes laws, and that the legislature is one branch of the government.

STUDENT RESPONSE 3:

ALICIA: It's like how a bill becomes a law. It has to go through the two houses of government.

➡️ **Write & Compare** Jot down your ideas for following up on a sheet of paper. Then, compare your ideas with the one below.

MR. L: I think you're remembering something you studied in social studies last year about how bills become laws. But what's this about houses of government?

From Alicia's response, the teacher refocused on the legislative branch. And then the class could go on to pursue the idea that two houses of Congress make up the legislature.

STUDENT RESPONSE 4:

TOM: The government has parts and now it's the legislature part.

➡️ **Write & Compare** Jot down your ideas for following up on a sheet of paper. Then, compare your ideas with the one below.

MR. L: Okay. The government has parts and now it's the legislature part. And what do you think the author wants us to know about the legislature?

From Tom's response, the teacher first directed focus on what the legislature does. Then the class could connect that information to its role as one branch of the government.

Recapping

Sometimes text segments encompass a complex set of ideas, and students need help connecting them to one another to make sense of them. To handle such situations, take a long view of the ideas under construction and deal with them in more than one step. A sequence of follow-ups gives students the opportunity to put together ideas in steps rather than all at once.

Assessment and QtA
How Does Assessment Fit in with Questioning the Author?

Teachers have asked about how to assess and grade students who are participating in QtA. They have found it difficult to assess the progress of their QtA students in a way that can be reconciled with report card grades.

In the journal entry that follows, Ms. D describes her concerns about assessing students.

> I love the way my students are responding to QtA. They amaze me at what they can do and how well they are able to think through ideas. But I am concerned about upcoming report cards. I'm not so sure any more about how to assess kids and give them grades. In the QtA discussions, I see students developing understanding that just isn't captured on the kinds of tests I've usually given for reading and social studies. But there are so many things going on in QtA— participating in discussions, figuring out ideas, collaborating together with other students—how does that translate into grades?

What Happened and Why?

Assessing QtA students seems to involve two issues. First, teachers typically see good things happening in class—they see students doing the kind of thinking that seems to indicate deep learning. Yet it's not always reflected in higher scores on traditional tests such as multiple-choice formats. So, one question is, how do you capture the deeper level of learning that QtA promotes?

Second, there isn't an obvious way to grade the things students are doing in QtA—exploring ideas, recognizing their own confusions, and putting together information rather than taking things at face value. In fact, grading the students "doing" QtA may seem contrary to the approach's philosophy and intent.

Dealing with the Problem

Many traditional concepts of grading—emphasis on getting "right" answers and giving back information—don't coincide with the purposes of QtA. However, all the interactions of QtA serve the goal of teaching students comprehension and critical thinking, and these are goals that are typically assessed and translated into grades on almost all types of report cards. So, it is possible to use what students do within QtA discussions as a basis for assessing them. And it is possible to create assessments that go beyond multiple-choice-type tests to capture some of the richer kinds of learning that students are showing in QtA discussions.

Below are some ideas that teachers have found effective for broadening the forms of assessing students' learning and for assessing growth in students' abilities to think, learn, and comprehend.

Testing Format. When testing what students have learned from a unit of study, shift from using multiple-choice to essay tests, which give students opportunities to express understandings they have built rather than merely identify isolated pieces of information.

Journals. Have the students keep a QtA journal, and once or twice a week give them some extra time to write a recap of the content discussed that day. The idea here is to gain some insight about the extent of students' comprehension of the major ideas—not to grade their writing per se. Therefore, the recaps could be in the form of lists, short phrases, and so on.

Student Recalls. Assess both students' learning and their ability to express and integrate ideas from their reading by having them recall major ideas from classroom discussions. You can hold individual conferences with students. Or call on students to recap the lesson of the previous day for the class, instead of doing the recapping yourself.

Assess Participation. Consider participation in discussions as part of students' grade, and tell them that their participation will count toward their grade. Make sure they understand that the point is not to come up with "right" answers, but rather to notice and think about the texts they read. Something like the following may help explain what you are looking for:

> What I want to know is how you're thinking about what you read—not just letting the words on the page pass through your mind, but taking in the words, grappling with them, figuring out what the ideas are that the words are telling you about and why those ideas might be important, if they are. I also want you to tell me what else you might need to know to understand the ideas.

Recapping

Assessing and grading QtA students may at first seem like a challenge. You can take steps to address the challenge. First, you can develop ways to tap into the kind of learning that QtA is fostering. Second, you can use students' participation in discussions as a basis for assessing their comprehension. When students grapple with ideas, make sense of otherwise confusing text, and question content and the intent of an author in QtA discussions, they are practicing the skills of comprehension. Assessing and grading students is really not much different for QtA than it is for other, more traditional comprehension activities.

Excerpted Work

Every effort has been made to find the authors and publishers of the work excerpted in this book. Any errors or ommisions are regretted and will be corrected in reprints.

Anslow, W. F., Elbow, G. S. Greenow, L. L., & Ludwig, G. S. (1993). *People in Time and Place: Comparing Regions.* Morristown, NJ: Silver Burdett Ginn.

Armento, B. J., Garcia, J., & Erickson, R. (1985). *Living in World Regions.* New York, NY: McGraw-Hill Companies.

Babbit, N. (1986). *Tuck Everlasting.* Orlando, FL: Farrar, Straus and Giroux/Harcourt Brace Jovanovich.

Bass, H. J. (1993). *People in Time and Place: Our Country.* Morristown, NJ: Silver Burdett Ginn.

Brenner, Barbara. (1975). *Lizard Tails and Cactus Spines.* New York, NY: HarperCollins.

Byars, B. (1969). *Trouble River.* New York, NY: Viking Penguin.

Cleary, B. (1983). *Ralph S. Mouse.* New York, NY: Dell.

Coutant, H. (1983). *The Gift.* New York, NY: Alfred A. Knopf, Inc.

DiCamillo, K. (2001). *Because of Winn Dixie.* Cambridge, MA: Candlewick Press.

Dineen, J. *Trees and Forests.* Lexington, MA: Schoolhouse Press.

Fleischman, S. (1976). *McBroom Tells a Lie.* (1999). New York, NY: Price, Stern, Sloan.

Fleischman, S. (1986). *The Whipping Boy.* New York, NY: Greenwillow Books.

Follet Social Studies. (1980). *Exploring Our World.* Upper Saddle River, NJ: Prentice Hall.

Forbes, K. (1943). *Mama's Bank Account.* Orlando, FL: Harcourt Brace & Company.

Frost, R. (1916). "The Road Not Taken." In *Mountain Interval.* New York: Henry Holt and Company.

Harcourt Brace & Company. (1984). *Holt Science, Grade 4.* Orlando, FL: Harcourt Brace & Company.

Lawson, R. (1939, republished 1988). *Ben and Me.* Boston, MA: Little, Brown & Company.

Macmillan/McGraw-Hill. (1997). *Regions: Adventures in Time and Place.* New York: Macmillan/McGraw-Hill.

Macmillan/McGraw-Hill. (1997). *World: Adventures in Time and Place.* New York: Macmillan/McGraw-Hill.

Millman, L. (1993). "The Raven and the Whale." Copyright © by Lawrence Millman.

Redding, R. H. (1977). *The Day That Nothing Happened.*

Robe, R. Y. (1979). *Tonweya and the Eagles: And Other Lakota Tales.* New York, NY: Viking Penguin.

San Souci, R. D. (1989). *The Talking Egg.* New York, NY: Dial Books for Young Readers.

Selden, G., & Williams, G. (1960). *The Cricket in Times Square.* New York, NY: Farrar, Straus & Giroux, Inc.

Silver Burdett Ginn. (1993). *Our Country.* Morristown, NJ: Silver Burdett Ginn.

Silver Burdett Ginn. (1989) *Silver Secrets.* Morristown, NJ: Silver Burdett Ginn.

Silver Burdett. (1984). *The United States and Its Neighbors.* Morristown, NJ: Silver Burdett.

Switala, W. (1990). *Pennsylvania Yesterday and Today.* Morristown, NJ: Silver Burdett Ginn.

Van Allsburg, C. (1983). *The Wreck of the Zephyr.* Boston, MA: Houghton Mifflin Company.

Wallower, L. & Wholey, E. J. (1984). Mechanicsburg, PA: Penns Valley Publishers.

Walter, M. P. (1986). *Justin and the Best Biscuits in the World.* New York, NY: Lothrop, Lee & Shepard. (a division of William Morrow & Company, Inc).

Waterton, B. (1991). *Petranella.* New York, NY: Firefly Books.

Wilbur, R. & Moser, B. (1994). *A Game of Catch.* New York, NY: Harcourt Brace & Co.

Yolen, J. (1967). *The Emperor and the Kite.* New York, NY: The World Publishing Company.

References

Anderson, R. C. (1977). "The notion of schemata and the educational enterprise." In R. C. Anderson, R. J. Spiro & W. E. Montague (Eds.), *Schooling and the Acquisition of Knowledge* (pp. 415-431). Hillsdale, NJ: Erlbaum.

Anderson, R. C., Chin, C., Commeyras, M., Stallman, A., Waggoner, M. & Wilkinson, I. (1992, December). "The reflective thinking project." In K. Jongsma (Chair), *Understanding and enhancing literature discussion in elementary classrooms*. Symposium conducted at the meeting of the National Reading Conference, San Antonio, TX.

Applebee, A. N., Langer, J. A., Nystrand, M., & Gamoran, A. (2003). "Discussion-based approaches to developing understanding: Classroom instruction and student performance in middle and high school English." *American Educational Research Journal, 40,* (3), 685-730.

Barrett, T. C. (1967). "Goals of the reading program: The basis for evaluation." In T. C. Barrett (Ed.), *In the Evaluation of Children's Reading Achievement*. Newark, DE: International Reading Association.

Bartolome, P. I. (1968). *A Comparison of Questions and Objectives Listed in Basal Reader Guidebooks with Those Observed in the Reading Lesson.* Doctoral Dissertation, Ohio State University. Dissertation Abstracts International, 1968, vol. 30, p. 138A. (University Microfilms No. 69-11, 606).

Beck, I. L. (1989). Improving practice through understanding reading. In L. B. Resnick & L. E. Klopfer (Eds.), *Toward the Thinking Curriculum: Current Cognitive Research.* (Yearbook of the Association for Supervision and Curriculum Development, pp. 40-58). Washington, D.C.: Association for Supervision and Curriculum Development.

Beck, I. L., & Carpenter, P. A. (1986). "Cognitive approaches to understanding reading: Implications for instructional practice." *American Psychologist, 41* (10), 1098-1105.

Beck, I. L. & McKeown, M. G. (1981). "Developing questions that promote comprehension: The story map." *Language Arts, 58* (8), 913-918.

Beck, I. L., McKeown, M. G., & Gromoll, E. W. (1989). "Learning from social studies texts." *Cognition and Instruction, 6* (2), 99-158.

Beck, I. L., McKeown, M. G., Sandora, C., Kucan, L. & Worthy, J. (1996). "Questioning the Author: A Yearlong Classroom Implementation to Engage Students with Text." *Elementary School Journal,"* 96:4, 385-414.

Beck, I. L., McKeown, M. G., Sinatra, G. M. & Loxterman, J. A. (1991). "Revising social studies text from a text-processing perspective: Evidence of improved comprehensibility." *Reading Research Quarterly,* 26, 251-276.

Beck, I. L., Omanson, R. C. & McKeown, M. G. (1982). "An instructional redesign of reading lessons: Effects on comprehension." *Reading Research Quarterly, 17* (4), 462-481.

Carver, R. P. (1987). "Should reading comprehension skills be taught?" In J. E. Readance & R. S. Baldwin (Eds.), *Research in Literacy: Merging Perspectives* (Thirty-sixth yearbook of the National Reading Conference, pp. 115-126). Rochester, NY: National Reading Conference.

Cazden, C. (1988). *Classroom Discourse: The Language of Teaching and Learning.* Portsmouth, NH: Heinemann Educational Books.

Chi, M. T. H., de Leeuw, N., Chiu, M. & LaVancher, C. (1994). "Eliciting self-explanations improves understanding." *Cognitive Science, 18,* 439-477.

Chi, M. T. H., Bassok, M., Lewis, M., Reimann, P. & Glaser, R. (1989). "Self-explanations: How students study and use examples in learning to solve problems." *Cognitive Science, 13,* 145-182.

Cooke, D. A. (1970). *An Analysis of Reading Comprehension Questions in Basal Reading Series According to the Barrett Taxonomy.* Doctoral Dissertation, Cornell University. Dissertation Abstracts International, 1970, vol. 31, p. 6467A. (University Microfilms No. 71-12, 124).

Denis, R., & Moldof, G. (1983). *A Handbook on Interpretive Reading and Discussion.* Chicago, IL: The Great Books Foundation.

Dillon, J. T. (1988). *Questioning and Teaching: A Manual of Practice.* New York: Teachers College Press.

Dole, J. N., Duffy, G. G., Roehler, L. R. & Pearson, P. D. (1991). "Moving from the old to the new: Research on reading comprehension instruction." *Review of Educational Research, 61,* 239-264.

Duffy, G. G., Roehler, L. R. & Hermann, B. A. (1988). "Modeling mental processes helps poor readers become strategic readers." *The Reading Teacher, 41,* 762-767.

Duffy, G. G., Roehler, L. R., Sivan, E., Rackliffe, G., Book, C., Meloth, M. S., Vavrus, L. G., Wesselman, R., Putnam, J. & Bassiri, D. (1987). "Effects of explaining the reasoning associated with using reading strategies." *Reading Research Quarterly, 22* (3), 347-368.

Fletcher, C. R., van den Broek, P. W. & Arthur, E. (1996). "A model of narrative comprehension and recall." In B. K. Britton & A. C. Graesser (Eds.), *Models of Understanding Text* (pp. 141-163). Mahwah, NJ: Lawrence Erlbaum Associates.

Gaskins, I. W., Anderson, R. C., Pressley, M., Cunicelli, E. A. & Satlow, E. (1993). "Six teachers' dialogue during cognitive process instruction." *The Elementary School Journal*, 93 (3), 277-304.

Goldenberg, C. (1992). "Instructional conversations: Promoting comprehension through discussion." *The Reading Teacher*, 46 (3), 316-326.

Graesser, A. C., Singer, M. & Trabasso, T. (1994). "Constructing inferences during narrative text comprehension." *Psychological Review, 101*, 371-395.

Guszak, F. J. (1967). "Teacher questioning in reading." *The Reading Teacher 21*, 227-234.

J. L., Almasi, J. & Brown, R. (1992). "Beyond direct explanation: Transactional instruction of reading comprehension strategies." *The Elementary School Journal, 92*, 511-553.

Kieras, D. E. (1985). "Thematic processes in the comprehension of technical prose." In B. K. Britton & J. B. Black, (Eds.), *Understanding Expository Text: A Theoretical and Practical Handbook for Analyzing Explanatory Text* (pp. 89-107). Hillsdale, NJ: Erlbaum.

Kintsch, W. & van Dijk, T. A. (1978). "Towards a model of text comprehension and production." *Psychological Review, 85*, 363-394.

Langer, J. A. (1986). *Children Reading and Writing: Structures and Strategies.* Norwood, NJ: Ablex.

Langer, J. A. (1990). "The process of understanding: Reading for literary and informative purposes." *Research in the Teaching of English, 24*, 229-260.

Loxterman, J. A., Beck, I. L. & McKeown, M. G. (1994). "The effects of thinking aloud during reading on students' comprehension of more or less coherent text." *Reading Research Quarterly, 29.4*, 353-368.

McKeown, M. G. & Beck, I. L. (2004). "Transforming knowledge into professional development resources: Six teachers implement a model of teaching for understanding text." *Elementary School Journal, 104:5*, 391-408.

McKeown, M. G. & Beck, I. L. (1998). "Talking to an author: Readers taking charge of the reading process." In R. Calfee & N. Nelson (Eds.), The Reading-Writing Connection. *Ninety-seventh yearbook for the National Society for the Study of Education.* (pp. 112-130). Chicago: National Society for the Study of Education.

McKeown, M. G., Beck, I. L. & Sandora, C. A. (1996). "Questioning the Author: An Approach to Developing Meaningful Classroom Discourse." In: Graves, M. G., Taylor, B. M. & van den Broek, P. *The First R: Every Child's Right to Read*. Teachers College Press. (pp. 97-119).

McKeown, M. G., Beck, I. L., Sinatra, G. M. & Loxterman, J. A., (1992). "The contribution of prior knowledge and coherent text to comprehension." *Reading Research Quarterly, 27*, 79-93.

McMahon, S. I., Raphael, T. E., Goately, V. S., Boyd, F. B. & Pardo, L. S. (1992). The Book Club Project. In K. Jongsma (Chair), *Understanding and enhancing literature discussion in elementary classrooms*. Symposium conducted at the meeting of the National Reading Conference, San Antonio, TX.

Mehan, H. (1979). *Learning Lessons: Social Organization in the Classroom*. Cambridge, MA: Harvard University Press.

Nystrand, M. (1997). *Opening Dialogue. Understanding the Dynamics of Language and Learning in the English Classroom*. New York: Teachers College Press.

O'Flahavan , J. F., & Stein, C. (1992). "The conversational discussion groups project." In K. Jongsma (Chair), *Understanding and enhancing literature discussion in elementary classrooms*. Symposium conducted at the meeting of the National Reading Conference, San Antonio, TX.

Omanson, R. C., Beck, I. L., Voss, J. F. & McKeown, M. G. (1984). "The effects of reading lessons on comprehension: A processing description." *Cognition and Instruction, 1* (1), 45-67.

Palincsar, A. S. & Brown, A. L. (1989). "Instruction for self-regulated reading." In L. Resnick & L. Klopfer (Eds.), *Toward the Thinking Curriculum: Current Cognitive Research* (pp. 19-39). Alexandria, VA: The Association for Curriculum and Supervision Development.

Palincsar, A. S. & Brown, A. L. (1984). "Reciprocal teaching of comprehension-fostering and monitoring activities." *Cognition and Instruction, 1* (2), 117-175.

Palincsar, A., Magnusson, S., Marano, N., Ford, D. & Brown, N. (1998). "Design principles informing and emerging from the GisML Community: A community of practice concerned with guided inquiry science teaching." *Teaching and Teacher Education, 14*(1), 5-19.

Paris, S. G., Cross, D. R. & Lipson, M. Y. (1984). "Informed strategies for learning: A program to improve children's awareness and comprehension." *Journal of Educational Psychology, 76*, 1239-1252.

Pearson, P. D. & Fielding, L. (1991). "Comprehension instruction." In R. Barr, M. Kamil, P. Mosenthal, & P. D. Pearson (Eds.), *Handbook of Reading Research* (Vol. 2, pp. 815-860). New York: Longman.

Pressley, M., El-Dinary, P. B., Gaskins, I., Schuder, T., Bergman, J. L., Almasi, J. & Brown, R. (1992). "Beyond direct explanation: Transactional instruction of reading comprehension strategies." *The Elementary School Journal, 92,* 511-553.Rosecky, M. H. (1976). *An Analysis of Questions and Activities Accompanying Narrative in Selected Basal Guidebooks and Teachers' Use of Guidebooks.* Doctoral Dissertation, University of Pennsylvania, 1976. Dissertation Abstracts International, 1976, vol. 37, p. 6936A. University Microfilms No. 77-10, 731.

Rumelhart, D. E. (1980). "Schemata: The building blocks of cognition." In R. J. Spiro, B. C. Bruce & W. F. Brewer (Eds.), *Theoretical issues in Reading Comprehension* (pp. 35-58). Hillsdale, NJ: Erlbaum.

Sandora, C., Beck, I. & McKeown, M. (1999). "A comparison of two discussion strategies on students' comprehension and interpretation of complex literature." *Reading Psychology, 20* (3), 177-212.

Saunders, W. & Goldenberg, C. (1996). "Four primary teachers define constructivism and teacher-directed learning: Implications for teacher assessment." *Elementary School Journal, 97*(2), 139-161).

Schank, R. C. & Abelson, R. P. (1977). *Scripts, Plans, Goals, and Understanding.* Hillsdale, NJ: Erlbaum.

Sinatra, G. M., Beck, I. L. & McKeown, M. G. (1993). "How knowledge influenced two interventions designed to improve comprehension." *Reading Psychology, 14,* 141-163.

van den Broek, P. , Young, M., Tzeng, Y. & Linderholm, T. (1998). "The landscape model of reading: Inferences and the on-line construction of a memory representation." In H. van Oostendorp & S. R. Goldman (Eds.), *The Construction of Mental Representations During Reading* (pp. 71-98). Mahwah, NJ: Erlbaum.

van den Broek, P. W. (1994). "Comprehension and memory of narrative texts: Inferences and coherence." In M. A. Gernsbacher (Ed.), *Handbook of Psycholinguistics* (pp. 175-191). San Diego, CA: Academic Press.

van Dijk, T. A. & Kintsch, W. (1983). *Strategies of Discourse*

Index